WorkKeys

Secrets
Study Guide

Exam Review and Practice
Test for the ACT's WorkKeys
Assessments

Written and edited by Mometrix Test Prep

Printed in the United States of America

This paper meets the requirements of ANSI/NISO Z39.48-1992 (Permanence of Paper).

Mometrix offers volume discount pricing to institutions. For more information or a price quote, please contact our sales department at sales@mometrix.com or 888-248-1219.

Paperback
ISBN 13: 978-1-5167-4822-8
ISBN

50% OFF
Online WorkKeys Prep Course!

By Mometrix

Dear Customer,

We consider it an honor and a privilege that you chose our WorkKeys Study Guide. As a way of showing our appreciation and to help us better serve you, we are offering **50% off our online WorkKeys Prep Course.** Many WorkKeys courses are needlessly expensive and don't deliver enough value. With our course, you get access to the best WorkKeys prep material, and **you only pay half price**.

We have structured our online course to perfectly complement your printed study guide. The WorkKeys Prep Course contains **in-depth lessons** that cover all the most important topics, **50+ video reviews** that explain difficult concepts, over **500 practice questions** to ensure you feel prepared, and **200+ digital flashcards**, so you can study while you're on the go.

Online WorkKeys Prep Course

Topics Covered:

- Applied Math
    - Fractions and Decimals
    - Order of Operations
    - Statistical Analysis
    - And More
- Graphic Literacy
    - Example Problems
    - Testing Strategies
- Workplace Documents
    - Example Problems
    - Testing Strategies

Course Features:

- WorkKeys Study Guide
    - Get content that complements our best-selling study guide.
- Full-Length Practice Tests
    - With over 500 practice questions, you can test yourself again and again.
- Mobile Friendly
    - If you need to study on the go, the course is easily accessible from your mobile device.
- WorkKeys Flashcards
    - Our course includes a flashcards mode with over 200 content cards for you to study.

To receive this discount, visit our website at mometrix.com/university/workkeys or simply scan this QR code with your smartphone. At the checkout page, enter the discount code: **wk50off**

If you have any questions or concerns, please contact us at support@mometrix.com.

Sincerely,

FREE Study Skills Videos/DVD Offer

Dear Customer,

Thank you for your purchase from Mometrix! We consider it an honor and a privilege that you have purchased our product and we want to ensure your satisfaction.

As part of our ongoing effort to meet the needs of test takers, we have developed a set of Study Skills Videos that we would like to give you for FREE. These videos cover our *best practices* for getting ready for your exam, from how to use our study materials to how to best prepare for the day of the test.

All that we ask is that you email us with feedback that would describe your experience so far with our product. Good, bad, or indifferent, we want to know what you think!

To get your FREE Study Skills Videos, you can use the **QR code** below, or send us an **email** at studyvideos@mometrix.com with *FREE VIDEOS* in the subject line and the following information in the body of the email:

- The name of the product you purchased.
- Your product rating on a scale of 1-5, with 5 being the highest rating.
- Your feedback. It can be long, short, or anything in between. We just want to know your impressions and experience so far with our product. (Good feedback might include how our study material met your needs and ways we might be able to make it even better. You could highlight features that you found helpful or features that you think we should add.)

If you have any questions or concerns, please don't hesitate to contact me directly.

Thanks again!

Sincerely,

Jay Willis
Vice President
jay.willis@mometrix.com
1-800-673-8175

DEAR FUTURE EXAM SUCCESS STORY

First of all, **THANK YOU** for purchasing Mometrix study materials!

Second, congratulations! You are one of the few determined test-takers who are committed to doing whatever it takes to excel on your exam. **You have come to the right place.** We developed these study materials with one goal in mind: to deliver you the information you need in a format that's concise and easy to use.

In addition to optimizing your guide for the content of the test, we've outlined our recommended steps for breaking down the preparation process into small, attainable goals so you can make sure you stay on track.

We've also analyzed the entire test-taking process, identifying the most common pitfalls and showing how you can overcome them and be ready for any curveball the test throws you.

Standardized testing is one of the biggest obstacles on your road to success, which only increases the importance of doing well in the high-pressure, high-stakes environment of test day. Your results on this test could have a significant impact on your future, and this guide provides the information and practical advice to help you achieve your full potential on test day.

Your success is our success

We would love to hear from you! If you would like to share the story of your exam success or if you have any questions or comments in regard to our products, please contact us at **800-673-8175** or **support@mometrix.com**.

Thanks again for your business and we wish you continued success!

Sincerely,
The Mometrix Test Preparation Team

TABLE OF CONTENTS

Introduction

Thank you for purchasing this resource! You have made the choice to prepare yourself for a test that could have a huge impact on your future, and this guide is designed to help you be fully ready for test day. Obviously, it's important to have a solid understanding of the test material, but you also need to be prepared for the unique environment and stressors of the test, so that you can perform to the best of your abilities.

For this purpose, the first section that appears in this guide is the **Secret Keys**. We've devoted countless hours to meticulously researching what works and what doesn't, and we've boiled down our findings to the five most impactful steps you can take to improve your performance on the test. We start at the beginning with study planning and move through the preparation process, all the way to the testing strategies that will help you get the most out of what you know when you're finally sitting in front of the test.

We recommend that you start preparing for your test as far in advance as possible. However, if you've bought this guide as a last-minute study resource and only have a few days before your test, we recommend that you skip over the first two Secret Keys since they address a long-term study plan.

If you struggle with **test anxiety**, we strongly encourage you to check out our recommendations for how you can overcome it. Test anxiety is a formidable foe, but it can be beaten, and we want to make sure you have the tools you need to defeat it.

1

Secret Key #1 – Plan Big, Study Small

There's a lot riding on your performance. If you want to ace this test, you're going to need to keep your skills sharp and the material fresh in your mind. You need a plan that lets you review everything you need to know while still fitting in your schedule. We'll break this strategy down into three categories.

Information Organization

Start with the information you already have: the official test outline. From this, you can make a complete list of all the concepts you need to cover before the test. Organize these concepts into groups that can be studied together, and create a list of any related vocabulary you need to learn so you can brush up on any difficult terms. You'll want to keep this vocabulary list handy once you actually start studying since you may need to add to it along the way.

Time Management

Once you have your set of study concepts, decide how to spread them out over the time you have left before the test. Break your study plan into small, clear goals so you have a manageable task for each day and know exactly what you're doing. Then just focus on one small step at a time. When you manage your time this way, you don't need to spend hours at a time studying. Studying a small block of content for a short period each day helps you retain information better and avoid stressing over how much you have left to do. You can relax knowing that you have a plan to cover everything in time. In order for this strategy to be effective though, you have to start studying early and stick to your schedule. Avoid the exhaustion and futility that comes from last-minute cramming!

Study Environment

The environment you study in has a big impact on your learning. Studying in a coffee shop, while probably more enjoyable, is not likely to be as fruitful as studying in a quiet room. It's important to keep distractions to a minimum. You're only planning to study for a short block of time, so make the most of it. Don't pause to check your phone or get up to find a snack. It's also important to **avoid multitasking**. Research has consistently shown that multitasking will make your studying dramatically less effective. Your study area should also be comfortable and well-lit so you don't have the distraction of straining your eyes or sitting on an uncomfortable chair.

 The time of day you study is also important. You want to be rested and alert. Don't wait until just before bedtime. Study when you'll be most likely to comprehend and remember. Even better, if you know what time of day your test will be, set that time aside for study. That way your brain will be used to working on that subject at that specific time and you'll have a better chance of recalling information.

Finally, it can be helpful to team up with others who are studying for the same test. Your actual studying should be done in as isolated an environment as possible, but the work of organizing the information and setting up the study plan can be divided up. In between study sessions, you can discuss with your teammates the concepts that you're all studying and quiz each other on the details. Just be sure that your teammates are as serious about the test as you are. If you find that your study time is being replaced with social time, you might need to find a new team.

2

Secret Key #2 – Make Your Studying Count

You're devoting a lot of time and effort to preparing for this test, so you want to be absolutely certain it will pay off. This means doing more than just reading the content and hoping you can remember it on test day. It's important to make every minute of study count. There are two main areas you can focus on to make your studying count.

Retention

It doesn't matter how much time you study if you can't remember the material. You need to make sure you are retaining the concepts. To check your retention of the information you're learning, try recalling it at later times with minimal prompting. Try carrying around flashcards and glance at one or two from time to time or ask a friend who's also studying for the test to quiz you.

To enhance your retention, look for ways to put the information into practice so that you can apply it rather than simply recalling it. If you're using the information in practical ways, it will be much easier to remember. Similarly, it helps to solidify a concept in your mind if you're not only reading it to yourself but also explaining it to someone else. Ask a friend to let you teach them about a concept you're a little shaky on (or speak aloud to an imaginary audience if necessary). As you try to summarize, define, give examples, and answer your friend's questions, you'll understand the concepts better and they will stay with you longer. Finally, step back for a big picture view and ask yourself how each piece of information fits with the whole subject. When you link the different concepts together and see them working together as a whole, it's easier to remember the individual components.

Finally, practice showing your work on any multi-step problems, even if you're just studying. Writing out each step you take to solve a problem will help solidify the process in your mind, and you'll be more likely to remember it during the test.

Modality

Modality simply refers to the means or method by which you study. Choosing a study modality that fits your own individual learning style is crucial. No two people learn best in exactly the same way, so it's important to know your strengths and use them to your advantage.

For example, if you learn best by visualization, focus on visualizing a concept in your mind and draw an image or a diagram. Try color-coding your notes, illustrating them, or creating symbols that will trigger your mind to recall a learned concept. If you learn best by hearing or discussing information, find a study partner who learns the same way or read aloud to yourself. Think about how to put the information in your own words. Imagine that you are giving a lecture on the topic and record yourself so you can listen to it later.

For any learning style, flashcards can be helpful. Organize the information so you can take advantage of spare moments to review. Underline key words or phrases. Use different colors for different categories. Mnemonic devices (such as creating a short list in which every item starts with the same letter) can also help with retention. Find what works best for you and use it to store the information in your mind most effectively and easily.

3

Secret Key #3 – Practice the Right Way

Your success on test day depends not only on how many hours you put into preparing, but also on whether you prepared the right way. It's good to check along the way to see if your studying is paying off. One of the most effective ways to do this is by taking practice tests to evaluate your progress. Practice tests are useful because they show exactly where you need to improve. Every time you take a practice test, pay special attention to these three groups of questions:

- The questions you got wrong
- The questions you had to guess on, even if you guessed right
- The questions you found difficult or slow to work through

This will show you exactly what your weak areas are, and where you need to devote more study time. Ask yourself why each of these questions gave you trouble. Was it because you didn't understand the material? Was it because you didn't remember the vocabulary? Do you need more repetitions on this type of question to build speed and confidence? Dig into those questions and figure out how you can strengthen your weak areas as you go back to review the material.

 Additionally, many practice tests have a section explaining the answer choices. It can be tempting to read the explanation and think that you now have a good understanding of the concept. However, an explanation likely only covers part of the question's broader context. Even if the explanation makes perfect sense, **go back and investigate** every concept related to the question until you're positive you have a thorough understanding.

As you go along, keep in mind that the practice test is just that: practice. Memorizing these questions and answers will not be very helpful on the actual test because it is unlikely to have any of the same exact questions. If you only know the right answers to the sample questions, you won't be prepared for the real thing. **Study the concepts** until you understand them fully, and then you'll be able to answer any question that shows up on the test.

It's important to wait on the practice tests until you're ready. If you take a test on your first day of study, you may be overwhelmed by the amount of material covered and how much you need to learn. Work up to it gradually.

On test day, you'll need to be prepared for answering questions, managing your time, and using the test-taking strategies you've learned. It's a lot to balance, like a mental marathon that will have a big impact on your future. Like training for a marathon, you'll need to start slowly and work your way up. When test day arrives, you'll be ready.

Start with the strategies you've read in the first two Secret Keys—plan your course and study in the way that works best for you. If you have time, consider using multiple study resources to get different approaches to the same concepts. It can be helpful to see difficult concepts from more than one angle. Then find a good source for practice tests. Many times, the test website will suggest potential study resources or provide sample tests.

4

Practice Test Strategy

If you're able to find at least three practice tests, we recommend this strategy:

UNTIMED AND OPEN-BOOK PRACTICE

Take the first test with no time constraints and with your notes and study guide handy. Take your time and focus on applying the strategies you've learned.

TIMED AND OPEN-BOOK PRACTICE

Take the second practice test open-book as well, but set a timer and practice pacing yourself to finish in time.

TIMED AND CLOSED-BOOK PRACTICE

Take any other practice tests as if it were test day. Set a timer and put away your study materials. Sit at a table or desk in a quiet room, imagine yourself at the testing center, and answer questions as quickly and accurately as possible.

Keep repeating timed and closed-book tests on a regular basis until you run out of practice tests or it's time for the actual test. Your mind will be ready for the schedule and stress of test day, and you'll be able to focus on recalling the material you've learned.

Secret Key #4 – Pace Yourself

Once you're fully prepared for the material on the test, your biggest challenge on test day will be managing your time. Just knowing that the clock is ticking can make you panic even if you have plenty of time left. Work on pacing yourself so you can build confidence against the time constraints of the exam. Pacing is a difficult skill to master, especially in a high-pressure environment, so **practice is vital**.

Set time expectations for your pace based on how much time is available. For example, if a section has 60 questions and the time limit is 30 minutes, you know you have to average 30 seconds or less per question in order to answer them all. Although 30 seconds is the hard limit, set 25 seconds per question as your goal, so you reserve extra time to spend on harder questions. When you budget extra time for the harder questions, you no longer have any reason to stress when those questions take longer to answer.

Don't let this time expectation distract you from working through the test at a calm, steady pace, but keep it in mind so you don't spend too much time on any one question. Recognize that taking extra time on one question you don't understand may keep you from answering two that you do understand later in the test. If your time limit for a question is up and you're still not sure of the answer, mark it and move on, and come back to it later if the time and the test format allow. If the testing format doesn't allow you to return to earlier questions, just make an educated guess; then put it out of your mind and move on.

On the easier questions, be careful not to rush. It may seem wise to hurry through them so you have more time for the challenging ones, but it's not worth missing one if you know the concept and just didn't take the time to read the question fully. Work efficiently but make sure you understand the question and have looked at all of the answer choices, since more than one may seem right at first.

Even if you're paying attention to the time, you may find yourself a little behind at some point. You should speed up to get back on track, but do so wisely. Don't panic; just take a few seconds less on each question until you're caught up. Don't guess without thinking, but do look through the answer choices and eliminate any you know are wrong. If you can get down to two choices, it is often worthwhile to guess from those. Once you've chosen an answer, move on and don't dwell on any that you skipped or had to hurry through. If a question was taking too long, chances are it was one of the harder ones, so you weren't as likely to get it right anyway.

On the other hand, if you find yourself getting ahead of schedule, it may be beneficial to slow down a little. The more quickly you work, the more likely you are to make a careless mistake that will affect your score. You've budgeted time for each question, so don't be afraid to spend that time. Practice an efficient but careful pace to get the most out of the time you have.

Secret Key #5 – Have a Plan for Guessing

When you're taking the test, you may find yourself stuck on a question. Some of the answer choices seem better than others, but you don't see the one answer choice that is obviously correct. What do you do?

The scenario described above is very common, yet most test takers have not effectively prepared for it. Developing and practicing a plan for guessing may be one of the single most effective uses of your time as you get ready for the exam.

In developing your plan for guessing, there are three questions to address:

- When should you start the guessing process?
- How should you narrow down the choices?
- Which answer should you choose?

When to Start the Guessing Process

Unless your plan for guessing is to select C every time (which, despite its merits, is not what we recommend), you need to leave yourself enough time to apply your answer elimination strategies. Since you have a limited amount of time for each question, that means that if you're going to give yourself the best shot at guessing correctly, you have to decide quickly whether or not you will guess.

Of course, the best-case scenario is that you don't have to guess at all, so first, see if you can answer the question based on your knowledge of the subject and basic reasoning skills. Focus on the key words in the question and try to jog your memory of related topics. Give yourself a chance to bring the knowledge to mind, but once you realize that you don't have (or you can't access) the knowledge you need to answer the question, it's time to start the guessing process.

It's almost always better to start the guessing process too early than too late. It only takes a few seconds to remember something and answer the question from knowledge. Carefully eliminating wrong answer choices takes longer. Plus, going through the process of eliminating answer choices can actually help jog your memory.

Summary: Start the guessing process as soon as you decide that you can't answer the question based on your knowledge.

7

How to Narrow Down the Choices

The next chapter in this book (**Test-Taking Strategies**) includes a wide range of strategies for how to approach questions and how to look for answer choices to eliminate. You will definitely want to read those carefully, practice them, and figure out which ones work best for you. Here though, we're going to address a mindset rather than a particular strategy.

Your odds of guessing an answer correctly depend on how many options you are choosing from.

Number of options left	5	4	3	2	1
Odds of guessing correctly	20%	25%	33%	50%	100%

You can see from this chart just how valuable it is to be able to eliminate incorrect answers and make an educated guess, but there are two things that many test takers do that cause them to miss out on the benefits of guessing:

- Accidentally eliminating the correct answer
- Selecting an answer based on an impression

We'll look at the first one here, and the second one in the next section.

To avoid accidentally eliminating the correct answer, we recommend a thought exercise called **the $5 challenge**. In this challenge, you only eliminate an answer choice from contention if you are willing to bet $5 on it being wrong. Why $5? Five dollars is a small but not insignificant amount of money. It's an amount you could afford to lose but wouldn't want to throw away. And while losing

$5 once might not hurt too much, doing it twenty times will set you back $100. In the same way, each small decision you make—eliminating a choice here, guessing on a question there—won't by itself impact your score very much, but when you put them all together, they can make a big difference. By holding each answer choice elimination decision to a higher standard, you can reduce the risk of accidentally eliminating the correct answer.

The $5 challenge can also be applied in a positive sense: If you are willing to bet $5 that an answer choice *is* correct, go ahead and mark it as correct.

Summary: Only eliminate an answer choice if you are willing to bet $5 that it is wrong.

8

Which Answer to Choose

You're taking the test. You've run into a hard question and decided you'll have to guess. You've eliminated all the answer choices you're willing to bet $5 on. Now you have to pick an answer. Why do we even need to talk about this? Why can't you just pick whichever one you feel like when the time comes?

The answer to these questions is that if you don't come into the test with a plan, you'll rely on your impression to select an answer choice, and if you do that, you risk falling into a trap. The test writers know that everyone who takes their test will be guessing on some of the questions, so they intentionally write wrong answer choices to seem plausible. You still have to pick an answer though, and if the wrong answer choices are designed to look right, how can you ever be sure that you're not falling for their trap? The best solution we've found to this dilemma is to take the decision out of your hands entirely. Here is the process we recommend:

Once you've eliminated any choices that you are confident (willing to bet $5) are wrong, select the first remaining choice as your answer.

Whether you choose to select the first remaining choice, the second, or the last, the important thing is that you use some preselected standard. Using this approach guarantees that you will not be enticed into selecting an answer choice that looks right, because you are not basing your decision on how the answer choices look.

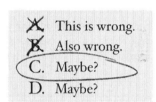

This is not meant to make you question your knowledge. Instead, it is to help you recognize the difference between your knowledge and your impressions. There's a huge difference between thinking an answer is right because of what you know, and thinking an answer is right because it looks or sounds like it should be right.

Summary: To ensure that your selection is appropriately random, make a predetermined selection from among all answer choices you have not eliminated.

Test-Taking Strategies

This section contains a list of test-taking strategies that you may find helpful as you work through the test. By taking what you know and applying logical thought, you can maximize your chances of answering any question correctly!

It is very important to realize that every question is different and every person is different: no single strategy will work on every question, and no single strategy will work for every person. That's why we've included all of them here, so you can try them out and determine which ones work best for different types of questions and which ones work best for you.

Question Strategies

⊘ READ CAREFULLY

Read the question and the answer choices carefully. Don't miss the question because you misread the terms. You have plenty of time to read each question thoroughly and make sure you understand what is being asked. Yet a happy medium must be attained, so don't waste too much time. You must read carefully and efficiently.

⊘ CONTEXTUAL CLUES

Look for contextual clues. If the question includes a word you are not familiar with, look at the immediate context for some indication of what the word might mean. Contextual clues can often give you all the information you need to decipher the meaning of an unfamiliar word. Even if you can't determine the meaning, you may be able to narrow down the possibilities enough to make a solid guess at the answer to the question.

⊘ PREFIXES

If you're having trouble with a word in the question or answer choices, try dissecting it. Take advantage of every clue that the word might include. Prefixes can be a huge help. Usually, they allow you to determine a basic meaning. *Pre-* means before, *post-* means after, *pro-* is positive, *de-* is negative. From prefixes, you can get an idea of the general meaning of the word and try to put it into context.

⊘ HEDGE WORDS

Watch out for critical hedge words, such as *likely, may, can, sometimes, often, almost, mostly, usually, generally, rarely,* and *sometimes*. Question writers insert these hedge phrases to cover every possibility. Often an answer choice will be wrong simply because it leaves no room for exception. Be on guard for answer choices that have definitive words such as *exactly* and *always*.

⊘ SWITCHBACK WORDS

Stay alert for *switchbacks*. These are the words and phrases frequently used to alert you to shifts in thought. The most common switchback words are *but, although,* and *however*. Others include *nevertheless, on the other hand, even though, while, in spite of, despite,* and *regardless of*. Switchback words are important to catch because they can change the direction of the question or an answer choice.

10

⊘ FACE VALUE

When in doubt, use common sense. Accept the situation in the problem at face value. Don't read too much into it. These problems will not require you to make wild assumptions. If you have to go beyond creativity and warp time or space in order to have an answer choice fit the question, then you should move on and consider the other answer choices. These are normal problems rooted in reality. The applicable relationship or explanation may not be readily apparent, but it is there for you to figure out. Use your common sense to interpret anything that isn't clear.

Answer Choice Strategies

⊘ ANSWER SELECTION

The most thorough way to pick an answer choice is to identify and eliminate wrong answers until only one is left, then confirm it is the correct answer. Sometimes an answer choice may immediately seem right, but be careful. The test writers will usually put more than one reasonable answer choice on each question, so take a second to read all of them and make sure that the other choices are not equally obvious. As long as you have time left, it is better to read every answer choice than to pick the first one that looks right without checking the others.

⊘ ANSWER CHOICE FAMILIES

An answer choice family consists of two (in rare cases, three) answer choices that are very similar in construction and cannot all be true at the same time. If you see two answer choices that are direct opposites or parallels, one of them is usually the correct answer. For instance, if one answer choice says that quantity x increases and another either says that quantity x decreases (opposite) or says that quantity y increases (parallel), then those answer choices would fall into the same family. An answer choice that doesn't match the construction of the answer choice family is more likely to be incorrect. Most questions will not have answer choice families, but when they do appear, you should be prepared to recognize them.

⊘ ELIMINATE ANSWERS

Eliminate answer choices as soon as you realize they are wrong, but make sure you consider all possibilities. If you are eliminating answer choices and realize that the last one you are left with is also wrong, don't panic. Start over and consider each choice again. There may be something you missed the first time that you will realize on the second pass.

⊘ AVOID FACT TRAPS

Don't be distracted by an answer choice that is factually true but doesn't answer the question. You are looking for the choice that answers the question. Stay focused on what the question is asking for so you don't accidentally pick an answer that is true but incorrect. Always go back to the question and make sure the answer choice you've selected actually answers the question and is not merely a true statement.

⊘ EXTREME STATEMENTS

In general, you should avoid answers that put forth extreme actions as standard practice or proclaim controversial ideas as established fact. An answer choice that states the "process should be used in certain situations, if..." is much more likely to be correct than one that states the "process should be discontinued completely." The first is a calm rational statement and doesn't even make a definitive, uncompromising stance, using a hedge word *if* to provide wiggle room, whereas the second choice is far more extreme.

⊘ Benchmark

As you read through the answer choices and you come across one that seems to answer the question well, mentally select that answer choice. This is not your final answer, but it's the one that will help you evaluate the other answer choices. The one that you selected is your benchmark or standard for judging each of the other answer choices. Every other answer choice must be compared to your benchmark. That choice is correct until proven otherwise by another answer choice beating it. If you find a better answer, then that one becomes your new benchmark. Once you've decided that no other choice answers the question as well as your benchmark, you have your final answer.

⊘ Predict the Answer

Before you even start looking at the answer choices, it is often best to try to predict the answer. When you come up with the answer on your own, it is easier to avoid distractions and traps because you will know exactly what to look for. The right answer choice is unlikely to be word-for-word what you came up with, but it should be a close match. Even if you are confident that you have the right answer, you should still take the time to read each option before moving on.

General Strategies

⊘ Tough Questions

If you are stumped on a problem or it appears too hard or too difficult, don't waste time. Move on! Remember though, if you can quickly check for obviously incorrect answer choices, your chances of guessing correctly are greatly improved. Before you completely give up, at least try to knock out a couple of possible answers. Eliminate what you can and then guess at the remaining answer choices before moving on.

⊘ Check Your Work

Since you will probably not know every term listed and the answer to every question, it is important that you get credit for the ones that you do know. Don't miss any questions through careless mistakes. If at all possible, try to take a second to look back over your answer selection and make sure you've selected the correct answer choice and haven't made a costly careless mistake (such as marking an answer choice that you didn't mean to mark). This quick double check should more than pay for itself in caught mistakes for the time it costs.

⊘ Pace Yourself

It's easy to be overwhelmed when you're looking at a page full of questions; your mind is confused and full of random thoughts, and the clock is ticking down faster than you would like. Calm down and maintain the pace that you have set for yourself. Especially as you get down to the last few minutes of the test, don't let the small numbers on the clock make you panic. As long as you are on track by monitoring your pace, you are guaranteed to have time for each question.

⊘ Don't Rush

It is very easy to make errors when you are in a hurry. Maintaining a fast pace in answering questions is pointless if it makes you miss questions that you would have gotten right otherwise. Test writers like to include distracting information and wrong answers that seem right. Taking a little extra time to avoid careless mistakes can make all the difference in your test score. Find a pace that allows you to be confident in the answers that you select.

⊘ Keep Moving

Panicking will not help you pass the test, so do your best to stay calm and keep moving. Taking deep breaths and going through the answer elimination steps you practiced can help to break through a stress barrier and keep your pace.

Final Notes

The combination of a solid foundation of content knowledge and the confidence that comes from practicing your plan for applying that knowledge is the key to maximizing your performance on test day. As your foundation of content knowledge is built up and strengthened, you'll find that the strategies included in this chapter become more and more effective in helping you quickly sift through the distractions and traps of the test to isolate the correct answer.

Now that you're preparing to move forward into the test content chapters of this book, be sure to keep your goal in mind. As you read, think about how you will be able to apply this information on the test. If you've already seen sample questions for the test and you have an idea of the question format and style, try to come up with questions of your own that you can answer based on what you're reading. This will give you valuable practice applying your knowledge in the same ways you can expect to on test day.

Good luck and good studying!

Three-Week WorkKeys Study Plan

On the next few pages, we've provided an optional study plan to help you use this study guide to its fullest potential over the course of three weeks. If you have six weeks available and want to spread it out more, spend two weeks on each section of the plan.

Below is a quick summary of the subjects covered in each week of the plan.

- Week 1: Applied Math
- Week 2: Graphic Literacy
- Week 3: Workplace Documents

Please note that not all subjects will take the same amount of time to work through.

Three full-length practice tests are included in this study guide. We recommend saving the third practice test and any additional tests for after you've completed the study plan. Take these practice tests timed and without any reference materials a day or two before the real thing as one last practice run to get you in the mode of answering questions at a good pace.

Week 1: Applied Math

INSTRUCTIONAL CONTENT

First, read carefully through the Applied Math chapter in this book, checking off your progress as you go:

- ❏ Formula Sheet
- ❏ Units of Measurement
- ❏ Numbers
- ❏ Operations
- ❏ Factoring
- ❏ Rational Numbers

- ❏ Proportions and Ratios
- ❏ Two-Dimensional Shapes
- ❏ Three-Dimensional Shapes
- ❏ Statistical Analysis
- ❏ Additional Math Concepts
- ❏ Example Applied Math Problems

As you read, do the following:

- Highlight any areas you think are important
- Draw an asterisk (*) next to any areas you are struggling with
- Work through the practice problems at the end of each section
- Watch the review videos to gain more understanding of a particular topic
- Take notes in your notebook or in the margins of this book

After you've read through everything, go back and review any sections that you highlighted or that you drew an asterisk next to, referencing your notes along the way.

PRACTICE TEST #1

Now that you've read over the instructional content, it's time to take a practice test. Complete the Applied Math section of Practice Test #1. Take this test with **no time constraints**, and feel free to reference the applicable sections of this guide as you go. Once you've finished, check your answers against the provided answer key. For any questions you answered incorrectly, review the answer rationale, and then **go back and review** the applicable sections of the book. The goal in this stage is to understand why you answered the question incorrectly, and make sure that the next time you see a similar question, you will get it right.

PRACTICE TEST #2

Next, take the Applied Math section of Practice Test #2. This time, give yourself **45 minutes** (the amount of time you will have on the real WorkKeys) to complete all of the questions. You should again feel free to reference the guide and your notes, but be mindful of the clock. If you run out of time before you finish all of the questions, mark where you were when time expired, but go ahead and finish taking the practice test—note that both the Computer and Spanish versions will have **55 minutes**. Once you've finished, check your answers against the provided answer key and as before, review the answer rationale for any that you answered incorrectly and go back and review the associated instructional content. Your goal is still to increase understanding of the content but also to get used to the time constraints you will face on the test.

Week 2: Graphic Literacy

INSTRUCTIONAL CONTENT

First, read carefully through the Graphic Literacy chapter in this book, checking off your progress as you go:

- ❏ What is This Section Testing?
- ❏ What Do the Questions Look Like, and How Difficult Are They?
- ❏ What Strategies Can I Use to Do Well on This Section?
- ❏ Level 3 Sample Question
- ❏ Level 5 Sample Question
- ❏ Level 7 Sample Question

As you read, do the following:

- Highlight any areas you think are important
- Draw an asterisk (*) next to any areas you are struggling with
- Work through the practice problems at the end of each section
- Watch the review videos to gain more understanding of a particular topic
- Take notes in your notebook or in the margins of this book

After you've read through everything, go back and review any sections that you highlighted or that you drew an asterisk next to, referencing your notes along the way.

PRACTICE TEST #1

Now that you've read over the instructional content, it's time to take a practice test. Complete the Graphic Literacy section of Practice Test #1. Take this test with **no time constraints**, and feel free to reference the applicable sections of this guide as you go. Once you've finished, check your answers against the provided answer key. For any questions you answered incorrectly, review the answer rationale, and then **go back and review** the applicable sections of the book. The goal in this stage is to understand why you answered the question incorrectly, and make sure that the next time you see a similar question, you will get it right.

PRACTICE TEST #2

Next, take the Graphic Literacy section of Practice Test #2. This time, give yourself **45 minutes** (the amount of time you will have on the real WorkKeys) to complete all of the questions. You should again feel free to reference the guide and your notes, but be mindful of the clock. If you run out of time before you finish all of the questions, mark where you were when time expired, but go ahead and finish taking the practice test—note that both the Computer and Spanish versions will have **55 minutes**. Once you've finished, check your answers against the provided answer key and as before, review the answer rationale for any that you answered incorrectly and go back and review the associated instructional content. Your goal is still to increase understanding of the content but also to get used to the time constraints you will face on the test.

16

Week 3: Workplace Documents

INSTRUCTIONAL CONTENT

First, read carefully through the Workplace Documents chapter in this book, checking off your progress as you go:

❏ What is This Section Testing?
❏ What Do the Questions Look Like, and How Difficult Are They?
❏ What Strategies Can I Use to Do Well on This Section?
❏ Level 3 Sample Question
❏ Level 5 Sample Question
❏ Level 7 Sample Question

As you read, do the following:

- Highlight any areas you think are important
- Draw an asterisk (*) next to any areas you are struggling with
- Work through the practice problems at the end of each section
- Watch the review videos to gain more understanding of a particular topic
- Take notes in your notebook or in the margins of this book

After you've read through everything, go back and review any sections that you highlighted or that you drew an asterisk next to, referencing your notes along the way.

PRACTICE TEST #1

Now that you've read over the instructional content, it's time to take a practice test. Complete the Workplace Documents section of Practice Test #1. Take this test with **no time constraints**, and feel free to reference the applicable sections of this guide as you go. Once you've finished, check your answers against the provided answer key. For any questions you answered incorrectly, review the answer rationale, and then **go back and review** the applicable sections of the book. The goal in this stage is to understand why you answered the question incorrectly, and make sure that the next time you see a similar question, you will get it right.

PRACTICE TEST #2

Next, take the Workplace Documents section of Practice Test #2. This time, give yourself **45 minutes** (the amount of time you will have on the real WorkKeys) to complete all of the questions. You should again feel free to reference the guide and your notes, but be mindful of the clock. If you run out of time before you finish all of the questions, mark where you were when time expired, but go ahead and finish taking the practice test—note that both the Computer and Spanish versions will have **55 minutes**. Once you've finished, check your answers against the provided answer key and as before, review the answer rationale for any that you answered incorrectly and go back and review the associated instructional content. Your goal is still to increase understanding of the content but also to get used to the time constraints you will face on the test.

17

About the WorkKeys Assessments

The WorkKeys assessments are a battery of workplace readiness tests produced by ACT. There are currently eight different WorkKeys assessments in all, but three of them are given special emphasis. As part of their WorkKeys program, ACT awards a credential called the **National Career Readiness Certificate (NCRC)** to applicants who successfully complete the three core WorkKeys assessments: **Applied Math**, **Graphic Literacy**, and **Workplace Documents**. This study guide contains the tools and knowledge you need to ace all three of these assessments and earn your NCRC!

If you will be taking the WorkKeys as part of an employment application process, please note that each employer gets to choose which of the WorkKeys assessments they require their applicants to take. Some employers may not require you to take all three of the core assessments, while other employers may require you to take one of the less common WorkKeys assessments not covered here. We **strongly recommend** that you ask your contact at your prospective employer for information on exactly which of the WorkKeys assessments you will be required to take.

Applied Math

WHAT IS THIS SECTION TESTING?

This section tests your ability to apply mathematical principles and critical reasoning to real-world situations you might encounter in a workplace. To succeed, you will have to recognize different types of problems and convert word problems into one or more mathematical equations.

Many of the questions on the test will involve doing calculations with money, taking averages or totals, and working with geometric quantities like volume or area. Doing well on this section of the test is more about your ability to recognize the basic math principles that apply to a given situation than it is about your ability to do complicated math.

WHAT DO THE QUESTIONS LOOK LIKE, AND HOW DIFFICULT ARE THEY?

The difficulty of the questions varies considerably from the easiest to the hardest levels. The most basic questions will require you to convert a straightforward scenario into a simple equation and solve it using just one or two of the basic operations. For the more advanced questions, you will have to decipher what a question is looking for and perform a multistep calculation to arrive at the answer.

The questions in this section are assigned a difficulty level between 3 and 7, with 3 being the easiest and 7 being the hardest. The questions will all be presented as word problems describing a scenario that you must solve using math. Questions at all levels may involve concepts such as money or time and may include operations with negative numbers.

- **Level 3:** Level 3 questions are very straightforward. All the information needed to answer the question will be presented in a logical order and there won't be any extra information in the question that you don't need.
- **Level 4:** Level 4 questions are slightly more difficult. The information needed to answer the question may not be presented in the simplest order. There may be information given that you do not need to answer the question. The computations may include finding averages, ratios, rates, etc.
- **Level 5:** Level 5 questions require more logical steps than the previous levels. You may be asked to perform operations on numbers given to you in different forms, such as decimals, fractions, and percentages such that you must convert all numbers to the same form. Level 5 also introduces basic geometry, including perimeter and area of circles and rectangles.
- **Level 6:** Level 6 questions require more work than in previous levels to convert the word problem to an equation or set of equations. The calculations are more complicated as well, potentially involving multiple unit conversions. The geometry at this level can include more complicated calculations with rectangles, circles, and simple rectangular solids.
- **Level 7:** Level 7 questions are the most difficult you will encounter on this section. The questions may be presented in an unusual or complicated format. Some information may not be given explicitly and will have to be inferred from other information given. The geometry needed at this level may include everything used to this point, with the addition of spheres, cylinders, and cones. Questions may require some basic statistical concepts.

19

WHAT STRATEGIES CAN I USE TO DO WELL ON THIS SECTION?

- **Read the questions carefully.** The most important thing to do on the lower level questions is make sure you don't make a mistake when you are translating the word problem to an equation. It should be obvious what the question is asking, and the actual math will be relatively simple, so as long as you don't mistranslate something, you should be fine. On the higher-level questions, you may have to spend some time deciphering what information the question is asking for. Do not rush through this part of the process unless you are very confident in your understanding of the problem. Setting up the right equation is just as important as solving the equation correctly.
- **Systematically eliminate answers that are obviously wrong.** If you know intuitively that the answer should be a number between 10 and 20, and two of the answer choices are above 20, you can eliminate them right away. This way, even if you have to guess, you will have narrowed down your options to give you the best shot at getting lucky.
- **Know the basics.** This WorkKeys assessment doesn't include anything more advanced than basic high school geometry. Make sure you are familiar with all the concepts that are fair game on the test. There is no reason you should lose points on the test because of an unfamiliar concept.

WHAT FORMULAS WILL I NEED TO KNOW FOR THIS SECTION?

There will be a formula sheet provided with the Applied Math Assessment. The conversion factors on the sheet **MUST** be the ones used to get the correct answer. Since the formulas are provided, they do not need to be memorized. However, it would be helpful to be familiar with what will be on the sheet as well as how to use the formulas. The following section will go over the provided formulas and how to use them.

Formula Sheet

MEASUREMENT CONVERSIONS

DISTANCE

1 foot = 12 inches
1 yard = 3 feet
1 mile = 5,280 feet
1 mile ≈ 1.61 kilometers
1 inch = 2.54 centimeters
1 foot = 0.3048 meters
1 meter = 1,000 millimeters
1 meter = 100 centimeters
1 kilometer = 1,000 meters

AREA

1 square foot = 144 square inches
1 square yard = 9 square feet
1 acre = 43,560 square feet

VOLUME

1 cup = 8 fluid ounces
1 quart = 4 cups
1 gallon = 4 quarts
1 gallon = 231 cubic inches
1 liter ≈ 0.264 gallons
1 cubic foot = 1,728 cubic inches
1 cubic yard = 27 cubic feet
1 board foot = 1 in. by 12 in. by 12 in.

WEIGHT/MASS

1 ounce ≈ 28.350 grams
1 pound = 16 ounces
1 pound ≈ 453.592 grams
1 milligram = 0.001 grams
1 kilogram = 1,000 grams
1 kilogram ≈ 2.2 pounds
1 ton = 2,000 pounds

2-DIMENSIONAL SHAPES

RECTANGLE

perimeter = 2(length + width)
area = length × width

TRIANGLE

sum of angles = 180°
$$\text{area} = \frac{\text{base} \times \text{height}}{2}$$

CIRCLE

number of degrees in a circle = 360°
circumference ≈ π × diameter
π ≈ 3.14

3-DIMENSIONAL SHAPES

RECTANGULAR SOLID (BOX)

volume = length × width × height

CUBE

volume = (length of side)^3

CYLINDER

volume ≈ π × (radius)^2 × height

CONE

volume ≈ π × (radius)^2 × height ÷ 3

SPHERE (BALL)

$$\text{volume} \approx \frac{4}{3} \times \pi(\text{radius})^3$$

ELECTRICITY

1 kilowatt − hour = 1,000 watt − hours
$$\text{amps} = \frac{\text{watts}}{\text{volts}}$$

TEMPERATURE

$$°C = \frac{5}{9}(°F \quad 32)$$
$$°F = \frac{9}{5}(°C) + 32$$

21

Units of Measurement

Converting from one set of units to another is a critical skill in the WorkKeys Applied Math Assessment. Often it can be necessary to chain together conversions to get the desired units. Each conversion factor is a ratio that has a value of 1 and can be rearranged from the conversion equation.

$$1 = \frac{60 \text{ sec}}{1 \text{ min}} \quad \leftarrow \quad 1 \text{ min} = 60 \text{ sec} \quad \rightarrow \quad \frac{1 \text{ min}}{60 \text{ sec}} = 1$$

That is why we can multiply by a conversion factor and not change the true value, so that the end result is the same value with different units. For example, if you are given a time of 279457 seconds and want to know how many days that is, you can use a chain of conversion factors to go from seconds to minutes to hours to days.

$$\frac{279{,}457 \text{ sec}}{1} \times \frac{1 \text{ min}}{60 \text{ sec}} \times \frac{1 \text{ hr}}{60 \text{ min}} \times \frac{1 \text{ day}}{24 \text{ hr}}$$

The factors are arranged so that everything except the units we want will cancel out.

$$\frac{279{,}457 \cancel{\text{ sec}}}{1} \times \frac{1 \cancel{\text{ min}}}{60 \cancel{\text{ sec}}} \times \frac{1 \cancel{\text{ hr}}}{60 \cancel{\text{ min}}} \times \frac{1 \text{ day}}{24 \cancel{\text{ hr}}}$$

$$\frac{279{,}457}{60 \times 60 \times 24} \text{ days} = \frac{279{,}457}{86{,}400} \text{ days} \approx 3.234 \text{ days}$$

The correct answer choice would then be whichever option is closest to 3.234 days.

CONVERTING BETWEEN RELATED UNITS

It can be challenging to keep track of all the different ways of communicating the same information about money, time, and other units. Much like how synonyms express the same idea using different words, the same value can be expressed using related units. Often, the simplest way to see the relationship between similar units is in a table like this one for American currency:

Unit	Dollar	Quarter	Dime	Nickel	Penny
Dollar Value	$1 One dollar	$0.25 One quarter of a dollar	$0.10 One tenth of a dollar	$0.05 One twentieth of a dollar	$0.01 One hundredth of a dollar
Cent Value	100¢ One hundred cents	25¢ Twenty-five cents	10¢ Ten cents	5¢ Five cents	1¢ One cent

From this table it is clear that there are many ways to communicate a value. For instance, the value $0.50 can be thought of as half of a dollar, two quarters, fifty cents, or several other possibilities. In this case, there are two relationships to understand: First, there are one hundred cents in a dollar. Second, the different increments of quarters, dimes, nickels, and pennies can be thought of as groups of cents or as fractions of a dollar.

A common example of expressing the same amount of something in different ways is in the measurement of time. There are many different units for time, including seconds, minutes, hours, days, weeks, months, and years. The key is to understand what units are being used and how each relates to the others, a day consists of 24 hours, an hour consists of 60 minutes, and so on. The table below lists the relationships between the various units, and also explains some commonly used phrases referring to time:

60 seconds in 1 minute
60 minutes in 1 hour
24 hours in 1 day
7 days in 1 week
365 days in 1 year
52 weeks in 1 year
12 months in 1 year
13 weeks in 1 quarter
3 months in 1 quarter
4 quarters in 1 year

- A quarter hour is 15 minutes
- "Quarter 'til three" means 2:45
- A half hour is 30 minutes
- "Half past six" means 6:30
- A fortnight is 2 weeks
- A year is often separated into four quarters (Q), specifically:
- Q1 - January to March
- Q2 - April to June
- Q3 - July to September
- Q4 - October to December

Suppose you just got a new job that pays ten dollars and 55 cents per hour. You get paid every two weeks. If you are assured that you will work at least 6 hours per shift and have 4 shifts per week, then what is the minimum you should expect (before taxes) in your first paycheck?

To begin, let's determine the minimum number of hours you will work in the pay period:

$$\frac{6 \text{ hours}}{\text{shift}} \times \frac{4 \text{ shifts}}{\text{week}} \times \frac{2 \text{ weeks}}{\text{pay period}} = \frac{48 \text{ hours}}{\text{pay period}}$$

Now, multiply the number of hours by the pay rate to find your expected minimum pay:

$$\frac{48 \text{ hours}}{\text{pay period}} \times \frac{\$10.55}{\text{hour}} = \frac{\$506.40}{\text{pay period}}$$

WORKING WITH MIXED UNITS

Mixed units occur when an amount is communicated in two or more parts with different units on each part. Common examples include measurements in feet and inches as well as times in minutes and seconds or hours and minutes. When solving problems with mixed units, it is very important to check that everything is compatible with the operations required. It is often best to convert the amounts given in the initial problem before beginning any work. Depending on the problem, it may be best to leave the converted units as fractions or as decimals. In some cases, it may even be best to perform the operation on the units separately. Regardless, it is essential to know how units are related to simplify the process of converting.≈

23

Suppose you want to find the total height of a two-story house. You determined that each story is 9 ft 9 in tall and the peak of the roof is 6 ft 1 3/4 in above the second story. To begin, combine all the like units and then simplify:

$$\text{Total height} = (9 \text{ ft } 9 \text{ in}) \times 2 + 6 \text{ ft } 1\frac{3}{4} \text{ in}$$
$$= 18 \text{ ft } 18 \text{ in} + 6 \text{ ft } 1\frac{3}{4} \text{ in}$$
$$= 24 \text{ ft } 19\frac{3}{4} \text{ in}$$
$$= 24 \text{ ft } \left(12 + 7\frac{3}{4}\right) \text{ in}$$
$$= (24 + 1)\text{ft } 7\frac{3}{4} \text{ in}$$
$$= 25 \text{ ft } 7\frac{3}{4} \text{ in}$$

On the other hand, suppose you wanted to find the total square footage (rounded to the nearest square foot) of the same house and the first story is 27 ft 4 in by 64 ft 3 in and the second story is 27 ft 4 in by 57 ft 8 in. In this case, since finding the area requires multiplication, it would be best to convert the measurements to just feet and then multiply:

$$27 \text{ ft } 4 \text{ in} = 27\frac{4}{12} \text{ ft} = 27\frac{1}{3} \text{ ft} = 27.333 \text{ ft}$$
$$64 \text{ ft } 3 \text{ in} = 64\frac{3}{12} \text{ ft} = 64.25 \text{ ft}$$
$$21 \text{ ft } 8 \text{ in} = 21\frac{8}{12} \text{ ft} = 21\frac{2}{3} \text{ ft} = 21.666 \text{ f}$$

$$\text{Total square footage} = (\text{Area of the first story}) + (\text{Area of the second story})$$
$$= (27.333 \text{ ft} \times 64.25 \text{ ft}) + (27.333 \text{ ft} \times 57.666 \text{ ft})$$
$$= 1756.165 \text{ ft}^2 + 1576.218 \text{ ft}^2$$
$$= 3332.383 \text{ ft}^2$$
$$\cong 3332 \text{ ft}^2$$

PRACTICE

P1. Perform the following conversions:

(a) 1.4 meters to centimeters

(b) 218 centimeters to meters

(c) 42 inches to feet

(d) 15 kilograms to pounds

(e) 80 ounces to pounds

(f) 2 miles to kilometers

(g) 5 feet to centimeters

(h) 15.14 liters to gallons

(i) 8 quarts to liters

(j) 13.2 pounds to grams

P2. How many seconds are there in one week and a day?

P3. Determine the total value of the following amount of money in cents: three nickels, seven dimes, a quarter, twelve pennies and a dollar.

PRACTICE SOLUTIONS

P1. (a) $\frac{100 \text{ cm}}{1 \text{ m}} = \frac{x \text{ cm}}{1.4 \text{ m}}$ Cross multiply to get $x = 140$

(b) $\frac{100 \text{ cm}}{1 \text{ m}} = \frac{218 \text{ cm}}{x \text{ m}}$ Cross multiply to get $100x = 218$, or $x = 2.18$

(c) $\frac{12 \text{ in}}{1 \text{ ft}} = \frac{42 \text{ in}}{x \text{ ft}}$ Cross multiply to get $12x = 42$, or $x = 3.5$

(d) 15 kilograms $\times \frac{2.2 \text{ pounds}}{1 \text{ kilogram}} = 33$ pounds

(e) 80 ounces $\times \frac{1 \text{ pound}}{16 \text{ ounces}} = 5$ pounds

(f) 2 miles $\times \frac{1.609 \text{ kilometers}}{1 \text{ mile}} = 3.218$ kilometers

(g) 5 feet $\times \frac{12 \text{ inches}}{1 \text{ foot}} \times \frac{2.54 \text{ centimeters}}{1 \text{ inch}} = 152.4$ centimeters

(h) 15.14 liters $\times \frac{1 \text{ gallon}}{3.785 \text{ liters}} = 4$ gallons

(i) 8 quarts $\times \frac{1 \text{ gallon}}{4 \text{ quarts}} \times \frac{3.785 \text{ liters}}{1 \text{ gallon}} = 7.57$ liters

(j) 13.2 pounds $\times \frac{1 \text{ kilogram}}{2.2 \text{ pounds}} \times \frac{1000 \text{ grams}}{1 \text{ kilogram}} = 6000$ grams

P2. 1 week and 1 day is the same as 8 days. Using that, multiply each of the conversion factors:

$$1 \text{ week} + 1 \text{ day} = (8 \text{ days}) \times \frac{24 \text{ hours}}{\text{day}} \times \frac{60 \text{ minutes}}{\text{hour}} \times \frac{60 \text{ seconds}}{\text{minute}}$$
$$1 \text{ week} + 1 \text{ day} = 8 \times 24 \times 60 \times 60 \text{ seconds}$$
$$1 \text{ week} + 1 \text{ day} = 691{,}200 \text{ seconds}$$

P3. To find the total value, multiply the amount of each coin by the corresponding value and then add the result:

$$Total = (3 \times \$0.05) + (7 \times \$0.10) + (1 \times \$0.25) + (12 \times \$0.01) + (1 \times \$1.00)$$
$$Total = \$0.15 + \$0.70 + \$0.25 + \$0.12 + \$1.00$$
$$Total = \$2.22 = 222¢$$

Numbers

CLASSIFICATIONS OF NUMBERS

Numbers are the basic building blocks of mathematics. Specific features of numbers are identified by the following terms:

Integer – any positive or negative whole number, including zero. Integers do not include fractions $\left(\frac{1}{3}\right)$, decimals (0.56), or mixed numbers $\left(7\frac{3}{4}\right)$.

Prime number – any whole number greater than 1 that has only two factors, itself and 1; that is, a number that can be divided evenly only by 1 and itself.

Composite number – any whole number greater than 1 that has more than two different factors; in other words, any whole number that is not a prime number. For example: The composite number 8 has the factors of 1, 2, 4, and 8.

Even number – any integer that can be divided by 2 without leaving a remainder. For example: 2, 4, 6, 8, and so on.

Odd number – any integer that cannot be divided evenly by 2. For example: 3, 5, 7, 9, and so on.

Decimal number – any number that uses a decimal point to show the part of the number that is less than one. Example: 1.234.

Decimal point – a symbol used to separate the ones place from the tenths place in decimals or dollars from cents in currency.

Decimal place – the position of a number to the right of the decimal point. In the decimal 0.123, the 1 is in the first place to the right of the decimal point, indicating tenths; the 2 is in the second place, indicating hundredths; and the 3 is in the third place, indicating thousandths.

The **decimal**, or base 10, system is a number system that uses ten different digits (0, 1, 2, 3, 4, 5, 6, 7, 8, 9). An example of a number system that uses something other than ten digits is the **binary**, or base 2, number system, used by computers, which uses only the numbers 0 and 1. It is thought that the decimal system originated because people had only their 10 fingers for counting.

Rational numbers include all integers, decimals, and fractions. Any terminating or repeating decimal number is a rational number.

Irrational numbers cannot be written as fractions or decimals because the number of decimal places is infinite and there is no recurring pattern of digits within the number. For example, pi (π) begins with 3.141592 and continues without terminating or repeating, so pi is an irrational number.

Real numbers are the set of all rational and irrational numbers.

> **Review Video: Classification of Numbers**
> Visit mometrix.com/academy and enter code: 461071
>
> **Review Video: Rational and Irrational Numbers**
> Visit mometrix.com/academy and enter code: 280645
>
> **Review Video: Prime and Composite Numbers**
> Visit mometrix.com/academy and enter code: 565581

THE NUMBER LINE

A number line is a graph to see the distance between numbers. Basically, this graph shows the relationship between numbers. So a number line may have a point for zero and may show negative numbers on the left side of the line. Also, any positive numbers are placed on the right side of the line. For example, consider the points labeled on the following number line:

We can use the dashed lines on the number line to identify each point. Each dashed line between two whole numbers is $\frac{1}{4}$. The line halfway between two numbers is $\frac{1}{2}$.

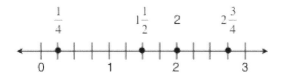

> **Review Video: Negative and Positive Number Line**
> Visit mometrix.com/academy and enter code: 816439

NUMBERS IN WORD FORM AND PLACE VALUE

When writing numbers out in word form or translating word form to numbers, it is essential to understand how a place value system works. In the decimal or base-10 system, each digit of a number represents how many of the corresponding place value – a specific factor of 10 – are contained in the number being represented. To make reading numbers easier, every three digits to the left of the decimal place is preceded by a comma. The following table demonstrates some of the place values:

Power of 10	10^3	10^2	10^1	10^0	10^{-1}	10^{-2}	10^{-3}
Value	1,000	100	10	1	0.1	0.01	0.001
Place	thousands	hundreds	tens	ones	tenths	hundredths	thousandths

For example, consider the number 4,546.09, which can be separated into each place value like this:

4: thousands
5: hundreds
4: tens
6: ones
0: tenths
9: hundredths

This number in word form would be *four thousand five hundred forty-six and nine hundredths.*

ABSOLUTE VALUE

A precursor to working with negative numbers is understanding what **absolute values** are. A number's absolute value is simply the distance away from zero a number is on the number line. The absolute value of a number is always positive and is written $|x|$. For example, the absolute value of 3, written as $|3|$, is 3 because the distance between 0 and 3 on a number line is three units. Likewise, the absolute value of –3, written as $|-3|$, is 3 because the distance between 0 and –3 on a number line is three units. So $|3| = |-3|$.

PRACTICE

P1. Write the place value of each digit in 14,059.826

P2. Write out each of the following in words:

   (a) 29
   (b) 478
   (c) 98,542
   (d) 0.06
   (e) 13.113

P3. Write each of the following in numbers:

   (a) nine thousand four hundred thirty-five
   (b) three hundred two thousand eight hundred seventy-six
   (c) nine hundred one thousandths
   (d) nineteen thousandths
   (e) seven thousand one hundred forty-two and eighty-five hundredths

28

PRACTICE SOLUTIONS

P1. The place value for each digit would be as follows:

Digit	Place Value
1	ten-thousands
4	thousands
0	hundreds
5	tens
9	ones
8	tenths
2	hundredths
6	thousandths

P2. Each written out in words would be:

(a) twenty-nine
(b) four hundred seventy-eight
(c) ninety-eight thousand five hundred forty-two
(d) six hundredths
(e) thirteen and one hundred thirteen thousandths

P3. Each in numeric form would be:

(a) 9,435
(b) 302876
(c) 0.901
(d) 0.019
(e) 7,142.85

Operations

OPERATIONS

An **operation** is simply a mathematical process that takes some value(s) as input(s) and produces an output. Elementary operations are often written in the following form: *value operation value*. For instance, in the expression $1 + 2$ the values are 1 and 2 and the operation is addition. Performing the operation gives the output of 3. In this way we can say that $1 + 2$ and 3 are equal, or $1 + 2 = 3$.

ADDITION

Addition increases the value of one quantity by the value of another quantity (both called **addends**). For example, $2 + 4 = 6$; $8 + 9 = 17$. The result is called the **sum**. With addition, the order does not matter, $4 + 2 = 2 + 4$.

When adding signed numbers, if the signs are the same simply add the absolute values of the addends and apply the original sign to the sum. For example, $(+4) + (+8) = +12$ and $(-4) + (-8) = -12$. When the original signs are different, take the absolute values of the addends and subtract the smaller value from the larger value, then apply the original sign of the larger value to the difference. For instance, $(+4) + (-8) = -4$ and $(-4) + (+8) = +4$.

SUBTRACTION

Subtraction is the opposite operation to addition; it decreases the value of one quantity (the **minuend**) by the value of another quantity (the **subtrahend**). For example, $6 - 4 = 2$; $17 - 8 = 9$. The result is called the **difference**. Note that with subtraction, the order does matter, $6 - 4 \neq 4 - 6$.

For subtracting signed numbers, change the sign of the subtrahend and then follow the same rules used for addition. For example, $(+4) - (+8) = (+4) + (-8) = -4$.

MULTIPLICATION

Multiplication can be thought of as repeated addition. One number (the **multiplier**) indicates how many times to add the other number (the **multiplicand**) to itself. For example, 3×2 (three times two) $= 2 + 2 + 2 = 6$. With multiplication, the order does not matter: $2 \times 3 = 3 \times 2$ or $3 + 3 = 2 + 2 + 2$, either way the result (the **product**) is the same.

If the signs are the same the product is positive when multiplying signed numbers. For example, $(+4) \times (+8) = +32$ and $(-4) \times (-8) = +32$. If the signs are opposite, the product is negative. For example, $(+4) \times (-8) = -32$ and $(-4) \times (+8) = -32$. When more than two factors are multiplied together, the sign of the product is determined by how many negative factors are present. If there are an odd number of negative factors then the product is negative, whereas an even number of negative factors indicates a positive product. For instance, $(+4) \times (-8) \times (-2) = +64$ and $(-4) \times (-8) \times (-2) = -64$.

DIVISION

Division is the opposite operation to multiplication; one number (the **divisor**) tells us how many parts to divide the other number (the **dividend**) into. The result of division is called the **quotient**. For example, $20 \div 4 = 5$; if 20 is split into 4 equal parts, each part is 5. With division, the order of the numbers does matter, $20 \div 4 \neq 4 \div 20$.

The rules for dividing signed numbers are similar to multiplying signed numbers. If the dividend and divisor have the same sign, the quotient is positive. If the dividend and divisor have opposite signs, the quotient is negative. For example, $(-4) \div (+8) = -0.5$.

> **Review Video: Mathematical Operations**
> Visit mometrix.com/academy and enter code: 208095

PARENTHESES

Parentheses are used to designate which operations should be done first when there are multiple operations. Example: $4 - (2 + 1) = 1$; the parentheses tell us that we must add 2 and 1, and then subtract the sum from 4, rather than subtracting 2 from 4 and then adding 1 (this would give us an answer of 3).

> **Review Video: Mathematical Parentheses**
> Visit mometrix.com/academy and enter code: 978600

EXPONENTS

An **exponent** is a superscript number placed next to another number at the top right. It indicates how many times the base number is to be multiplied by itself. Exponents provide a shorthand way to write what would be a longer mathematical expression, for example: $2^4 = 2 \times 2 \times 2 \times 2$. A number with an exponent of 2 is said to be "squared," while a number with an exponent of 3 is said to be "cubed." The value of a number raised to an exponent is called its power. So 8^4 is read as "8 to the 4th power," or "8 raised to the power of 4."

The properties of exponents are as follows:

Property	Description
$a^1 = a$	Any number to the power of 1 is equal to itself
$1^n = 1$	The number 1 raised to any power is equal to 1
$a^0 = 1$	Any number raised to the power of 0 is equal to 1
$a^n \times a^m = a^{n+m}$	Add exponents to multiply powers of the same base number
$a^n \div a^m = a^{n-m}$	Subtract exponents to divide powers of the same base number
$(a^n)^m = a^{n \times m}$	When a power is raised to a power, the exponents are multiplied
$(a \times b)^n = a^n \times b^n$ $(a \div b)^n = a^n \div b^n$	Multiplication and division operations inside parentheses can be raised to a power. This is the same as each term being raised to that power.
$a^{-n} = \dfrac{1}{a^n}$	A negative exponent is the same as the reciprocal of a positive exponent

Note that exponents do not have to be integers. Fractional or decimal exponents follow all the rules above as well. Example: $5^{\frac{1}{4}} \times 5^{\frac{3}{4}} = 5^{\frac{1}{4}+\frac{3}{4}} = 5^1 = 5$.

> **Review Video: What is an Exponent?**
> Visit mometrix.com/academy and enter code: 600998
>
> **Review Video: Laws of Exponents**
> Visit mometrix.com/academy and enter code: 532558

ROOTS

A **root**, such as a square root, is another way of writing a fractional exponent. Instead of using a superscript, roots use the radical symbol ($\sqrt{}$) to indicate the operation. A radical will have a number underneath the bar, and may sometimes have a number in the upper left: $\sqrt[n]{a}$, read as "the nth root of a." The relationship between radical notation and exponent notation can be described by this equation: $\sqrt[n]{a} = a^{\frac{1}{n}}$. The two special cases of $n = 2$ and $n = 3$ are called square roots and cube roots. If there is no number to the upper left, it is understood to be a square root ($n = 2$). Nearly all of the roots you encounter will be square roots. A square root is the same as a number raised to the one-half power. When we say that a is the square root of b ($a = \sqrt{b}$), we mean that a multiplied by itself equals b: ($a \times a = b$).

A **perfect square** is a number that has an integer for its square root. There are 10 perfect squares from 1 to 100: 1, 4, 9, 16, 25, 36, 49, 64, 81, 100 (the squares of integers 1 through 10).

> **Review Video: Roots**
> Visit mometrix.com/academy and enter code: 795655

ORDER OF OPERATIONS

Order of operations is a set of rules that dictates the order in which we must perform each operation in an expression so that we will evaluate it accurately. If we have an expression that includes multiple different operations, order of operations tells us which operations to do first. The most common mnemonic for order of operations is **PEMDAS**, or "Please Excuse My Dear Aunt Sally." PEMDAS stands for parentheses, exponents, multiplication, division, addition, and subtraction. It is important to understand that multiplication and division have equal precedence,

31

as do addition and subtraction, so those pairs of operations are simply worked from left to right in order.

For example, evaluating the expression $5 + 20 \div 4 \times (2 + 3) - 6$ using the correct order of operations would be done like this:

- **P:** Perform the operations inside the parentheses: $(2 + 3) = 5$
- **E:** Simplify the exponents.
  - The equation now looks like this: $5 + 20 \div 4 \times 5 - 6$
- **MD:** Perform multiplication and division from left to right: $20 \div 4 = 5$; then $5 \times 5 = 25$
  - The equation now looks like this: $5 + 25 - 6$
- **AS:** Perform addition and subtraction from left to right: $5 + 25 = 30$; then $30 - 6 = 24$

> **Review Video: <u>Order of Operations</u>**
> Visit mometrix.com/academy and enter code: 259675

SUBTRACTION WITH REGROUPING

A great way to make use of some of the features built into the decimal system would be regrouping when attempting longform subtraction operations. When subtracting within a place value, sometimes the minuend is smaller than the subtrahend. **Regrouping** enables you to 'borrow' a unit from a place value to the left in order to get a positive difference. For example, consider subtracting 189 from 525 with regrouping.

First, set up the subtraction problem in vertical form:

$$
\begin{array}{r}
525 \\
-\ 189 \\
\hline
\end{array}
$$

Notice that the numbers in the ones and tens columns of 525 are smaller than the numbers in the ones and tens columns of 189. This means you will need to use regrouping to perform subtraction:

$$
\begin{array}{cccc}
  & 5 & 2 & 5 \\
- & 1 & 8 & 9 \\
\hline
\end{array}
$$

To subtract 9 from 5 in the ones column you will need to borrow from the 2 in the tens columns:

$$
\begin{array}{cccc}
  & 5 & 1 & 15 \\
- & 1 & 8 & 9 \\
\hline
  &   &   & 6 \\
\end{array}
$$

Next, to subtract 8 from 1 in the tens column you will need to borrow from the 5 in the hundreds column:

$$
\begin{array}{cccc}
  & 4 & 11 & 15 \\
- & 1 & 8 & 9 \\
\hline
  &   & 3 & 6 \\
\end{array}
$$

Last, subtract the 1 from the 4 in the hundreds column:

```
   4  11  15
-  1   8   9
   3   3   6
```

PRACTICE

P1. Demonstrate how to subtract 477 from 620 using regrouping.

P2. Simplify the following expressions with exponents:

(a) 37^0
(b) 1^{30}
(c) $2^3 \times 2^4 \times 2^x$
(d) $(3^x)^3$
(e) $(12 \div 3)^2$

PRACTICE SOLUTIONS

P1. First, set up the subtraction problem in vertical form:

```
   6  2  0
-  4  7  7
```

To subtract 7 from 0 in the ones column you will need to borrow from the 2 in the tens column:

```
   6  1  10
-  4  7   7
          3
```

Next, to subtract 7 from the 1 that's still in the tens column you will need to borrow from the 6 in the hundreds column:

```
   5  11  10
-  4   7   7
       4   3
```

Lastly, subtract 4 from the 5 remaining in the hundreds column:

```
   5  11  10
-  4   7   7
   1   4   3
```

P2. Using the properties of exponents and the proper order of operations:

(a) Any number raised to the power of 0 is equal to 1: $37^0 = 1$
(b) The number 1 raised to any power is equal to 1: $1^{30} = 1$
(c) Add exponents to multiply powers of the same base: $2^3 \times 2^4 \times 2^x = 2^{(3+4+x)} = 2^{(7+x)}$
(d) When a power is raised to a power, the exponents are multiplied: $(3^x)^3 = 3^{3x}$
(e) Perform the operation inside the parentheses first: $(12 \div 3)^2 = 4^2 = 16$

Factoring

FACTORS AND GREATEST COMMON FACTOR

Factors are numbers that are multiplied together to obtain a **product**. For example, in the equation $2 \times 3 = 6$, the numbers 2 and 3 are factors. A **prime number** has only two factors (1 and itself), but other numbers can have many factors.

A **common factor** is a number that divides exactly into two or more other numbers. For example, the factors of 12 are 1, 2, 3, 4, 6, and 12, while the factors of 15 are 1, 3, 5, and 15. The common factors of 12 and 15 are 1 and 3.

A **prime factor** is also a prime number. Therefore, the prime factors of 12 are 2 and 3. For 15, the prime factors are 3 and 5.

The **greatest common factor (GCF)** is the largest number that is a factor of two or more numbers. For example, the factors of 15 are 1, 3, 5, and 15; the factors of 35 are 1, 5, 7, and 35. Therefore, the greatest common factor of 15 and 35 is 5.

> **Review Video: Factors**
> Visit mometrix.com/academy and enter code: 920086
>
> **Review Video: Greatest Common Factor and Least Common Multiple**
> Visit mometrix.com/academy and enter code: 838699

MULTIPLES AND LEAST COMMON MULTIPLE

Often listed out in multiplication tables, **multiples** are integer increments of a given factor. In other words, dividing a multiple by the factor number will result in an integer. For example, the multiples of 7 include: $1 \times 7 = 7$, $2 \times 7 = 14$, $3 \times 7 = 21$, $4 \times 7 = 28$, $5 \times 7 = 35$. Dividing 7, 14, 21, 28, or 35 by 7 will result in the integers 1, 2, 3, 4, and 5, respectively.

The **least common multiple (LCM)** is the smallest number that is a multiple of two or more numbers. For example, the multiples of 3 include 3, 6, 9, 12, 15, etc.; the multiples of 5 include 5, 10, 15, 20, etc. Therefore, the least common multiple of 3 and 5 is 15.

> **Review Video: Multiples**
> Visit mometrix.com/academy and enter code: 626738

Rational Numbers

FRACTIONS

A **fraction** is a number that is expressed as one integer written above another integer, with a dividing line between them $\left(\frac{x}{y}\right)$. It represents the **quotient** of the two numbers: "x divided by y." It can also be thought of as x out of y equal parts.

The top number of a fraction is called the **numerator**, and it represents the number of parts under consideration. The 1 in $\frac{1}{4}$ means that 1 part out of the whole is being considered in the calculation. The bottom number of a fraction is called the **denominator**, and it represents the total number of equal parts. The 4 in $\frac{1}{4}$ means that the whole consists of 4 equal parts. A fraction cannot have a denominator of zero; this is referred to as "*undefined.*"

Fractions can be manipulated, without changing the value of the fraction, by multiplying or dividing (but not adding or subtracting) both the numerator and denominator by the same number. If you divide both numbers by a common factor, you are **reducing** or simplifying the fraction. Two fractions that have the same value but are expressed differently are known as **equivalent fractions**. For example, $\frac{2}{10}, \frac{3}{15}, \frac{4}{20}$, and $\frac{5}{25}$ are all equivalent fractions. They can also all be reduced or simplified to $\frac{1}{5}$.

When two fractions are manipulated so that they have the same denominator, this is known as finding a **common denominator**. The number chosen to be that common denominator should be the least common multiple of the two original denominators. Example: $\frac{3}{4}$ and $\frac{5}{6}$; the least common multiple of 4 and 6 is 12. Manipulating to achieve the common denominator: $\frac{3}{4} = \frac{9}{12}; \frac{5}{6} = \frac{10}{12}$.

PROPER FRACTIONS AND MIXED NUMBERS

A fraction whose denominator is greater than its numerator is known as a **proper fraction**, while a fraction whose numerator is greater than its denominator is known as an **improper fraction**. Proper fractions have values *less than one* and improper fractions have values *greater than one.*

A **mixed number** is a number that contains both an integer and a fraction. Any improper fraction can be rewritten as a mixed number. Example: $\frac{8}{3} = \frac{6}{3} + \frac{2}{3} = 2 + \frac{2}{3} = 2\frac{2}{3}$. Similarly, any mixed number can be rewritten as an improper fraction. Example: $1\frac{3}{5} = 1 + \frac{3}{5} = \frac{5}{5} + \frac{3}{5} = \frac{8}{5}$.

> **Review Video: Proper and Improper Fractions and Mixed Numbers**
> Visit mometrix.com/academy and enter code: 211077
>
> **Review Video: Overview of Fractions**
> Visit mometrix.com/academy and enter code: 262335

ADDING AND SUBTRACTING FRACTIONS

If two fractions have a common denominator, they can be added or subtracted simply by adding or subtracting the two numerators and retaining the same denominator. If the two fractions do not already have the same denominator, one or both of them must be manipulated to achieve a common denominator before they can be added or subtracted. Example: $\frac{1}{2} + \frac{1}{4} = \frac{2}{4} + \frac{1}{4} = \frac{3}{4}$.

> **Review Video: Adding and Subtracting Fractions**
> Visit mometrix.com/academy and enter code: 378080

MULTIPLYING FRACTIONS

Two fractions can be multiplied by multiplying the two numerators to find the new numerator and the two denominators to find the new denominator. Example: $\frac{1}{3} \times \frac{2}{3} = \frac{1\times2}{3\times3} = \frac{2}{9}$.

DIVIDING FRACTIONS

Two fractions can be divided by flipping the numerator and denominator of the second fraction and then proceeding as though it were a multiplication. Example: $\frac{2}{3} \div \frac{3}{4} = \frac{2}{3} \times \frac{4}{3} = \frac{8}{9}$.

> **Review Video: Multiplying and Dividing Fractions**
> Visit mometrix.com/academy and enter code: 473632

MULTIPLYING A MIXED NUMBER BY A WHOLE NUMBER OR A DECIMAL

When multiplying a mixed number by something, it is usually best to convert it to an improper fraction first. Additionally, if the multiplicand is a decimal, it is most often simplest to convert it to a fraction. For instance, to multiply $4\frac{3}{8}$ by 3.5, begin by rewriting each quantity as a whole number plus a proper fraction. Remember, a mixed number is a fraction added to a whole number and a decimal is a representation of the sum of fractions, specifically tenths, hundredths, thousandths, and so on:

$$4\frac{3}{8} \times 3.5 = \left(4 + \frac{3}{8}\right) \times \left(3 + \frac{1}{2}\right)$$

Next, the quantities being added need to be expressed with the same denominator. This is achieved by multiplying and dividing the whole number by the denominator of the fraction. Recall that a whole number is equivalent to that number divided by 1:

$$= \left(\frac{4}{1} \times \frac{8}{8} + \frac{3}{8}\right) \times \left(\frac{3}{1} \times \frac{2}{2} + \frac{1}{2}\right)$$

When multiplying fractions, remember to multiply the numerators and denominators separately:

$$= \left(\frac{4 \times 8}{1 \times 8} + \frac{3}{8}\right) \times \left(\frac{3 \times 2}{1 \times 2} + \frac{1}{2}\right)$$
$$= \left(\frac{32}{8} + \frac{3}{8}\right) \times \left(\frac{6}{2} + \frac{1}{2}\right)$$

Now that the fractions have the same denominators, they can be added:

$$= \frac{35}{8} \times \frac{7}{2}$$

Finally, perform the last multiplication and then simplify:

$$= \frac{35 \times 7}{8 \times 2} = \frac{245}{16} = \frac{240}{16} + \frac{5}{16} = 15\frac{5}{16}$$

DECIMALS

Decimals are one way to represent parts of a whole. Using the place value system, each digit to the right of a decimal point denotes the number of units of a corresponding *negative* power of ten. For example, consider the decimal 0.24. We can use a model to represent the decimal. Since a dime is worth one-tenth of a dollar and a penny is worth one-hundredth of a dollar, one possible model to represent this fraction is to have 2 dimes representing the 2 in the tenths place and 4 pennies representing the 4 in the hundredths place:

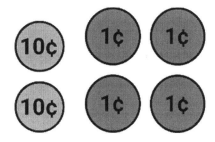

To write the decimal as a fraction, put the decimal in the numerator with 1 in the denominator. Multiply the numerator and denominator by tens until there are no more decimal places. Then simplify the fraction to lowest terms. For example, converting 0.24 to a fraction:

$$0.24 = \frac{0.24}{1} = \frac{0.24 \times 100}{1 \times 100} = \frac{24}{100} = \frac{6}{25}$$

> **Review Video: Decimals**
> Visit mometrix.com/academy and enter code: 837268

OPERATIONS WITH DECIMALS
ADDING AND SUBTRACTING DECIMALS

When adding and subtracting decimals, the decimal points must always be aligned. Adding decimals is just like adding regular whole numbers. Example: $4.5 + 2.0 = 6.5$.

If the problem-solver does not properly align the decimal points, an incorrect answer of 4.7 may result. An easy way to add decimals is to align all of the decimal points in a vertical column visually. This will allow one to see exactly where the decimal should be placed in the final answer. Begin adding from right to left. Add each column in turn, making sure to carry the number to the left if a column adds up to more than 9. The same rules apply to the subtraction of decimals.

> **Review Video: Adding and Subtracting Decimals**
> Visit mometrix.com/academy and enter code: 381101

MULTIPLYING DECIMALS

A simple multiplication problem has two components: a **multiplicand** and a **multiplier**. When multiplying decimals, work as though the numbers were whole rather than decimals. Once the final product is calculated, count the number of places to the right of the decimal in both the multiplicand and the multiplier. Then, count that number of places from the right of the product and place the decimal in that position.

For example, 12.3×2.56 has a total of three places to the right of the respective decimals. Multiply 123×256 to get 31488. Now, beginning on the right, count three places to the left and insert the decimal. The final product will be 31.488.

> **Review Video: Multiplying Decimals**
> Visit mometrix.com/academy and enter code: 731574

DIVIDING DECIMALS

Every division problem has a **divisor** and a **dividend**. The dividend is the number that is being divided. In the problem 14 ÷ 7, 14 is the dividend and 7 is the divisor. In a division problem with decimals, the divisor must be converted into a whole number. Begin by moving the decimal in the divisor to the right until a whole number is created. Next, move the decimal in the dividend the same number of spaces to the right. For example, 4.9 into 24.5 would become 49 into 245. The decimal was moved one space to the right to create a whole number in the divisor, and then the same was done for the dividend. Once the whole numbers are created, the problem is carried out normally: 245 ÷ 49 = 5.

> **Review Video: Dividing Decimals**
> Visit mometrix.com/academy and enter code: 560690

RETURNING CORRECT CHANGE TO A CUSTOMER

Determining the correct change to return to a customer is an exercise in mental math. As such, it can be helpful to learn shortcuts, but most often, such skills are developed through repeated practice. To be clear, the term 'correct change' is usually used to mean two things: the correct value and the fewest number of coins or bills necessary. Obviously, the most important part is giving the right amount in change, but it would be considered poor service, for instance, to give someone 110 pennies rather than a dollar bill and a dime.

However, there are situations where your options may be limited and you must be creative in the way you put the change together. For example, if you are working at a register and run out of dollar bills, you could substitute 4 quarters for each dollar in change you give out until you get some more dollar bills.

The process for finding the correct change begins with a purchase total and the amount of cash given. In other words, **change amount = cash paid − purchase total**. Once you determine the change amount, you can then divide by each monetary unit starting with the largest one that is less than the change amount, then divide the remainder by the next largest, and so on. For instance, if the purchase total is $7.69 and the customer gives you a ten-dollar bill, the change amount is $10.00 − $7.69 = $2.31. To determine the correct change, divide by $1 to get 2 with a remainder of $0.31. This means that you will need two dollar bills. The remainder is what is left after dividing; in this case that is $0.31. Now, divide the remainder by $0.25 to get 1 with a remainder of $0.06. This means that you will need one quarter. Next, divide $0.06 by $0.05 to get 1 with a remainder of $0.01. This means that you will need one nickel. Finally, a remainder of $0.01 means you will need one penny.

Another way to think about this is to break the change amount into parts based on the coin or bill:

Change Amount	$1	$0.25	$0.10	$0.05	$0.01
$2.31	2	1	0	1	1

Check that this selection actually equals the desired amount:

$$2 \times (\$1) + 1 \times (\$0.25) + 1 \times (\$0.05) + 1 \times (\$0.01) = \$2.31$$

PERCENTAGES

Percentages can be thought of as fractions that are based on a whole of 100; that is, one whole is equal to 100%. The word **percent** means "per hundred." Percentage problems are often presented in three main ways:

- Find what percentage of some number another number is.
  - Example: What percentage of 40 is 8?
- Find what number is some percentage of a given number.
  - Example: What number is 20% of 40?
- Find what number another number is a given percentage of.
  - Example: What number is 8 20% of?

There are three components in each of these cases: a **whole** (W), a **part** (P), and a **percentage** (%). These are related by the equation: $P = W \times \%$. This can easily be rearranged into other forms that may suit different questions better: $\% = \frac{P}{W}$ and $W = \frac{P}{\%}$. Percentage problems are often also word problems. As such, a large part of solving them is figuring out which quantities are what. For example, consider the following word problem:

In a school cafeteria, 7 students choose pizza, 9 choose hamburgers, and 4 choose tacos. What percentage of student choose tacos?

To find the whole, you must first add all of the parts: $7 + 9 + 4 = 20$. The percentage can then be found by dividing the part by the whole ($\% = \frac{P}{W}$): $\frac{4}{20} = \frac{20}{100} = 20\%$.

CONVERTING BETWEEN PERCENTAGES, FRACTIONS, AND DECIMALS

Converting decimals to percentages and percentages to decimals is as simple as moving the decimal point. To *convert from a decimal to a percentage*, move the decimal point **two places to the right**. To *convert from a percentage to a decimal*, move it **two places to the left**. It may be helpful to remember that the percentage number will always be larger than the equivalent decimal number. For example:

$$0.23 = 23\% \quad 5.34 = 534\% \quad 0.007 = 0.7\%$$
$$700\% = 7.00 \quad 86\% = 0.86 \quad 0.15\% = 0.0015$$

To convert a fraction to a decimal, simply divide the numerator by the denominator in the fraction. To convert a decimal to a fraction, put the decimal in the numerator with 1 in the denominator. Multiply the numerator and denominator by tens until there are no more decimal places. Then simplify the fraction to lowest terms. For example, converting 0.24 to a fraction:

$$0.24 = \frac{0.24}{1} = \frac{0.24 \times 100}{1 \times 100} = \frac{24}{100} = \frac{6}{25}$$

Fractions can be converted to a percentage by finding equivalent fractions with a denominator of 100. For example,

$$\frac{7}{10} = \frac{70}{100} = 70\% \qquad \frac{1}{4} = \frac{25}{100} = 25\%$$

To convert a percentage to a fraction, divide the percentage number by 100 and reduce the fraction to its simplest possible terms. For example,

$$60\% = \frac{60}{100} = \frac{3}{5} \qquad 96\% = \frac{96}{100} = \frac{24}{25}$$

> **Review Video: <u>Converting Fractions to Percentages and Decimals</u>**
> Visit mometrix.com/academy and enter code: 306233
>
> **Review Video: <u>Converting Percentages to Decimals and Fractions</u>**
> Visit mometrix.com/academy and enter code: 287297

RATIONAL NUMBERS

The term **rational** means that the number can be expressed as a ratio or fraction. That is, a number, r, is rational if and only if it can be represented by a fraction $\frac{a}{b}$ where a and b are integers and b does not equal 0. The set of rational numbers includes integers and decimals. If there is no finite way to represent a value with a fraction of integers, then the number is **irrational**. Common examples of irrational numbers include: $\sqrt{5}$, $\left(1 + \sqrt{2}\right)$, and π.

PRACTICE

P1. What is 30% of 120?

P2. What is 150% of 20?

P3. What is 14.5% of 96?

P4. Simplify the following expressions:

    (a) $\left(\frac{2}{5}\right)/\left(\frac{4}{7}\right)$
    (b) $\frac{7}{8} - \frac{8}{16}$
    (c) $\frac{1}{2} + \left(3\left(\frac{3}{4}\right) - 2\right) + 4$
    (d) $0.22 + 0.5 - (5.5 + 3.3 \div 3)$
    (e) $\frac{3}{2} + (4(0.5) - 0.75) + 2$

P5. Convert the following to a fraction and to a decimal: **(a)** 15%; **(b)** 24.36%

P6. Convert the following to a decimal and to a percentage. **(a)** 4/5; **(b)** $3\frac{2}{5}$

P7. A woman's age is thirteen more than half of 60. How old is the woman?

P8. A patient was given pain medicine at a dosage of 0.22 grams. The patient's dosage was then increased to 0.80 grams. By how much was the patient's dosage increased?

P9. At a hotel, $\frac{3}{4}$ of the 100 rooms are occupied today. Yesterday, $\frac{4}{5}$ of the 100 rooms were occupied. On which day were more of the rooms occupied and by how much more?

P10. At a school, 40% of the teachers teach English. If 20 teachers teach English, how many teachers work at the school?

P11. A patient was given blood pressure medicine at a dosage of 2 grams. The patient's dosage was then decreased to 0.45 grams. By how much was the patient's dosage decreased?

P12. Two weeks ago, $\frac{2}{3}$ of the 60 customers at a skate shop were male. Last week, $\frac{3}{6}$ of the 80 customers were male. During which week were there more male customers?

P13. Jane ate lunch at a local restaurant. She ordered a $4.99 appetizer, a $12.50 entrée, and a $1.25 soda. If she wants to tip her server 20%, how much money will she spend in all?

P14. According to a survey, about 82% of engineers were highly satisfied with their job. If 145 engineers were surveyed, how many reported that they were highly satisfied?

P15. A patient was given 40 mg of a certain medicine. Later, the patient's dosage was increased to 45 mg. What was the percent increase in his medication?

P16. Order the following rational numbers from least to greatest: $0.55, 17\%, \sqrt{25}, \frac{64}{4}, \frac{25}{50}, 3$.

P17. Order the following rational numbers from greatest to least: $0.3, 27\%, \sqrt{100}, \frac{72}{9}, \frac{1}{9}, 4.5$

P18. Perform the following multiplication. Write each answer as a mixed number.

(a) $\left(1\frac{11}{16}\right) \times 4$

(b) $\left(12\frac{1}{3}\right) \times 1.1$

(c) $3.71 \times \left(6\frac{1}{5}\right)$

P19. Suppose you are making doughnuts and you want to triple the recipe you have. If the following list is the original amounts for the ingredients, what would be the amounts for the tripled recipe?

$1\,^3/_4$	cup	Flour
$1\,^1/_4$	tsp	Baking powder
$^3/_4$	tsp	Salt
$^3/_8$	cup	Sugar
$1\,^1/_2$	Tbsp	Butter
2	large	Eggs
$^3/_4$	tsp	Vanilla extract
$^3/_8$	cup	Sour cream

PRACTICE SOLUTIONS

P1. The word *of* indicates multiplication, so 30% of 120 is found by multiplying 120 by 30%. Change 30% to a decimal, then multiply: $120 \times 0.3 = 36$

P2. The word *of* indicates multiplication, so 150% of 20 is found by multiplying 20 by 150%. Change 150% to a decimal, then multiply: $20 \times 1.5 = 30$

P3. Change 14.5% to a decimal before multiplying. $0.145 \times 96 = 13.92$.

P4. Follow the order of operations and utilize properties of fractions to solve each:

(a) Rewrite the problem as a multiplication problem: $\frac{2}{5} \times \frac{7}{4} = \frac{2\times7}{5\times4} = \frac{14}{20}$. Make sure the fraction is reduced to lowest terms. Both 14 and 20 can be divided by 2.

$$\frac{14}{20} = \frac{14 \div 2}{20 \div 2} = \frac{7}{10}$$

(b) The denominators of $\frac{7}{8}$ and $\frac{8}{16}$ are 8 and 16, respectively. The lowest common denominator of 8 and 16 is 16 because 16 is the least common multiple of 8 and 16. Convert the first fraction to its equivalent with the newly found common denominator of 16: $\frac{7\times2}{8\times2} = \frac{14}{16}$. Now that the fractions have the same denominator, you can subtract them.

$$\frac{14}{16} - \frac{8}{16} = \frac{6}{16} = \frac{3}{8}$$

(c) When simplifying expressions, first perform operations within groups. Within the set of parentheses are multiplication and subtraction operations. Perform the multiplication first to get $\frac{1}{2} + \left(\frac{9}{4} - 2\right) + 4$. Then, subtract two to obtain $\frac{1}{2} + \frac{1}{4} + 4$. Finally, perform addition from left to right:

$$\frac{1}{2} + \frac{1}{4} + 4 = \frac{2}{4} + \frac{1}{4} + \frac{16}{4} = \frac{19}{4} = 4\frac{3}{4}$$

(d) First, evaluate the terms in the parentheses $(5.5 + 3.3 \div 3)$ using order of operations. $3.3 \div 3 = 1.1$, and $5.5 + 1.1 = 6.6$. Next, rewrite the problem: $0.22 + 0.5 - 6.6$. Finally, add and subtract from left to right: $0.22 + 0.5 = 0.72$; $0.72 - 6.6 = -5.88$. The answer is -5.88.

(e) First, simplify within the parentheses, then change the fraction to a decimal and perform addition from left to right:

$$\frac{3}{2} + (2 - 0.75) + 2 =$$
$$\frac{3}{2} + 1.25 + 2 =$$
$$1.5 + 1.25 + 2 = 4.75$$

P5. (a) 15% can be written as $\frac{15}{100}$. Both 15 and 100 can be divided by 5: $\frac{15\div5}{100\div5} = \frac{3}{20}$

When converting from a percentage to a decimal, drop the percent sign and move the decimal point two places to the left: $15\% = 0.15$.

(b) 24.36% written as a fraction is $\frac{24.36}{100}$, or $\frac{2436}{10,000}$, which reduces to $\frac{609}{2500}$. 24.36% written as a decimal is 0.2436. Recall that dividing by 100 moves the decimal two places to the left.

P6. (a) Recall that in the decimal system the first decimal place is one tenth: $\frac{4 \times 2}{5 \times 2} = \frac{8}{10} = 0.8$

Percent means "per hundred." $\frac{4 \times 20}{5 \times 20} = \frac{80}{100} = 80\%$

(b) The mixed number $3\frac{2}{5}$ has a whole number and a fractional part. The fractional part $\frac{2}{5}$ can be written as a decimal by dividing 5 into 2, which gives 0.4. Adding the whole to the part gives 3.4.

To find the equivalent percentage, multiply the decimal by 100. $3.4(100) = 340\%$. Notice that this percentage is greater than 100%. This makes sense because the original mixed number $3\frac{2}{5}$ is greater than 1.

P7. "More than" indicates addition, and "of" indicates multiplication. The expression can be written as $\frac{1}{2}(60) + 13$. So the woman's age is equal to $\frac{1}{2}(60) + 13 = 30 + 13 = 43$. The woman is 43 years old.

P8. The first step is to determine what operation (addition, subtraction, multiplication, or division) the problem requires. Notice the keywords and phrases "by how much" and "increased." "Increased" means that you go from a smaller amount to a larger amount. This change can be found by subtracting the smaller amount from the larger amount: 0.80 grams– 0.22 grams = 0.58 grams.

Remember to line up the decimal when subtracting:

$$\begin{array}{r} 0.80 \\ - 0.22 \\ \hline 0.58 \end{array}$$

P9. First, find the number of rooms occupied each day. To do so, multiply the fraction of rooms occupied by the number of rooms available:

$$\text{Number occupied} = \text{Fraction occupied} \times \text{Total number}$$
$$\text{Number of rooms occupied today} = \frac{3}{4} \times 100 = 75$$
$$\text{Number of rooms occupied} = \frac{4}{5} \times 100 = 80$$

The difference in the number of rooms occupied is: $80 - 75 = 5$ rooms

P10. To answer this problem, first think about the number of teachers that work at the school. Will it be more or less than the number of teachers who work in a specific department such as English? More teachers work at the school, so the number you find to answer this question will be greater than 20.

40% of the teachers are English teachers. "Of" indicates multiplication, and words like "is" and "are" indicate equivalence. Translating the problem into a mathematical sentence gives $40\% \times t = 20$, where t represents the total number of teachers. Solving for t gives $t = \frac{20}{40\%} = \frac{20}{0.40} = 50$. Fifty teachers work at the school.

P11. The decrease is represented by the difference between the two amounts:

$$2 \text{ grams} - 0.45 \text{ grams} = 1.55 \text{ grams.}$$

43

Remember to line up the decimal point before subtracting.

$$\begin{array}{r} 2.00 \\ -\ 0.45 \\ \hline 1.55 \end{array}$$

P12. First, you need to find the number of male customers that were in the skate shop each week. You are given this amount in terms of fractions. To find the actual number of male customers, multiply the fraction of male customers by the number of customers in the store.

Actual number of male customers = fraction of male customers × total customers

Number of male customers two weeks ago $= \dfrac{2}{3} \times 60 = \dfrac{120}{3} = 40$

Number of male customers last week $= \dfrac{3}{6} \times 80 = \dfrac{1}{2} \times 80 = \dfrac{80}{2} = 40$

The number of male customers was the same both weeks.

P13. To find total amount, first find the sum of the items she ordered from the menu and then add 20% of this sum to the total.

$$\$4.99 + \$12.50 + \$1.25 = \$18.74$$

$$\$18.74 \times 20\% = (0.20)(\$18.74) = \$3.748 \approx \$3.75$$

$$\text{Total} = \$18.74 + \$3.75 = \$22.49$$

P14. 82% of 145 is 0.82 × 145 = 118.9. Because you can't have 0.9 of a person, we must round up to say that 119 engineers reported that they were highly satisfied with their jobs.

P15. To find the percent increase, first compare the original and increased amounts. The original amount was 40 mg, and the increased amount is 45 mg, so the dosage of medication was increased by 5 mg (45– 40 = 5). Note, however, that the question asks not by how much the dosage increased but by what percentage it increased.

$$\text{Percent increase} = \frac{\text{new amount} - \text{original amount}}{\text{original amount}} \times 100\%$$

$$= \frac{45 \text{ mg} - 40 \text{ mg}}{40 \text{ mg}} \times 100\% = \frac{5}{40} \times 100\% = 0.125 \times 100\% = 12.5\%$$

P16. Recall that the term rational simply means that the number can be expressed as a ratio or fraction. Notice that each of the numbers in the problem can be written as a decimal or an integer:

$$17\% = 0.1717$$
$$\sqrt{25} = 5$$
$$\frac{64}{4} = 16$$
$$\frac{25}{50} = \frac{1}{2} = 0.5$$

So, the answer is 17%, $\frac{25}{50}$, 0.55, 3, $\sqrt{25}$, $\frac{64}{4}$.

P17. Converting all the numbers to integers and decimals makes it easier to compare the values:

$$27\% = 0.27$$
$$\sqrt{100} = 10$$
$$\frac{72}{9} = 8$$
$$\frac{1}{9} \approx 0.11$$

So, the answer is $\sqrt{100}, \frac{72}{9}, 4.5, 0.3, 27\%, \frac{1}{9}$.

> **Review Video: <u>Ordering Rational Numbers</u>**
> Visit mometrix.com/academy and enter code: 419578

P18. For each, convert improper fractions, adjust to a common denominator, perform the operations, and then simplify:

(a) Sometimes, you can skip converting the denominator and just distribute the multiplication.

$$\left(1\frac{11}{16}\right) \times 4 = \left(1 + \frac{11}{16}\right) \times 4$$
$$= 1 \times 4 + \frac{11}{16} \times 4$$
$$= 4 + \frac{11}{16} \times \frac{4}{1}$$
$$= 4 + \frac{44}{16} = 4 + \frac{11}{4} = 4 + 2\frac{3}{4} = 6\frac{3}{4}$$

(b)

$$\left(12\frac{1}{3}\right) \times 1.1 = \left(12 + \frac{1}{3}\right) \times \left(1 + \frac{1}{10}\right)$$
$$= \left(\frac{12}{1} \times \frac{3}{3} + \frac{1}{3}\right) \times \left(\frac{10}{10} + \frac{1}{10}\right)$$
$$= \left(\frac{36}{3} + \frac{1}{3}\right) \times \frac{11}{10}$$
$$= \frac{37}{3} \times \frac{11}{10}$$
$$= \frac{407}{30} = \frac{390}{30} + \frac{17}{30} = 13\frac{17}{30}$$

(c)

$$3.71 \times \left(6\frac{1}{5}\right) = \left(3 + \frac{71}{100}\right) \times \left(6 + \frac{1}{5}\right)$$
$$= \left(\frac{300}{100} + \frac{71}{100}\right) \times \left(\frac{6}{1} \times \frac{5}{5} + \frac{1}{5}\right)$$
$$= \frac{371}{100} \times \left(\frac{30}{5} + \frac{1}{5}\right)$$
$$= \frac{371}{100} \times \frac{31}{5}$$
$$= \frac{11501}{500} = \frac{11500}{500} + \frac{1}{500} = 23\frac{1}{500}$$

P19. Fortunately, some of the amounts are duplicated, so we do not need to figure out every amount.

$$1\frac{3}{4} \times 3 = (1 \times 3) + \left(\frac{3}{4} \times 3\right)$$
$$= 3 + \frac{9}{4}$$
$$= 3 + 2\frac{1}{4}$$
$$= 5\frac{1}{4}$$

$$1\frac{1}{4} \times 3 = (1 \times 3) + \left(\frac{1}{4} \times 3\right)$$
$$= 3 + \frac{3}{4}$$
$$= 3\frac{3}{4}$$

$$\frac{3}{4} \times 3 = \frac{3}{4} \times 3$$
$$= \frac{9}{4}$$
$$= 2\frac{1}{4}$$

$$\frac{3}{8} \times 3 = \frac{3}{8} \times 3$$
$$= \frac{9}{8}$$
$$= 1\frac{1}{8}$$

$$1\frac{1}{2} \times 3 = 1 \times 3 + \frac{1}{2} \times 3$$
$$= 3 + \frac{3}{2}$$
$$= 3 + 1\frac{1}{2}$$
$$= 4\frac{1}{2}$$

$$2 \times 3 = 6$$

So, the result for the triple recipe is:

5 1/4	cup	Flour
3 3/4	tsp	Baking powder
2 1/4	tsp .	Salt
1 1/8	cup	Sugar
4 1/2	Tbsp	Butter
6	large	Eggs
2 1/4	tsp	Vanilla extract
1 1/8	cup	Sour cream

46

Proportions and Ratios

PROPORTIONS

A proportion is a relationship between two quantities that dictates how one changes when the other changes. A **direct proportion** describes a relationship in which a quantity increases by a set amount for every increase in the other quantity, or decreases by that same amount for every decrease in the other quantity. Example: Assuming a constant driving speed, the time required for a car trip increases as the distance of the trip increases. The distance to be traveled and the time required to travel are directly proportional.

Inverse proportion is a relationship in which an increase in one quantity is accompanied by a decrease in the other, or vice versa. Example: the time required for a car trip decreases as the speed increases, and increases as the speed decreases, so the time required is inversely proportional to the speed of the car.

> **Review Video: Proportions**
> Visit mometrix.com/academy and enter code: 505355

RATIOS

A **ratio** is a comparison of two quantities in a particular order. Example: If there are 14 computers in a lab, and the class has 20 students, there is a student to computer ratio of 20 to 14, commonly written as 20:14. Ratios are normally reduced to their smallest whole number representation, so 20:14 would be reduced to 10:7 by dividing both sides by 2.

> **Review Video: Ratios**
> Visit mometrix.com/academy and enter code: 996914

CONSTANT OF PROPORTIONALITY

When two quantities have a proportional relationship, there exists a **constant of proportionality** between the quantities; the product of this constant and one of the quantities is equal to the other quantity. For example, if one lemon costs $0.25, two lemons cost $0.50, and three lemons cost $0.75, there is a proportional relationship between the total cost of lemons and the number of lemons purchased. The constant of proportionality is the **unit price**, namely $0.25/lemon. Notice that the total price of lemons, t, can be found by multiplying the unit price of lemons, p, and the number of lemons, n: $t = pn$.

WORK/UNIT RATE

Unit rate expresses a quantity of one thing in terms of one unit of another. For example, if you travel 30 miles every two hours, a unit rate expresses this comparison in terms of one hour: in one hour you travel 15 miles, so your unit rate is 15 miles per hour. Other examples are how much one ounce of food costs (price per ounce) or figuring out how much one egg costs out of the dozen (price per 1 egg, instead of price per 12 eggs). The denominator of a unit rate is always 1. Unit rates are used to compare different situations to solve problems. For example, to make sure you get the best deal when deciding which kind of soda to buy, you can find the unit rate of each. If soda #1 costs $1.50 for a 1-liter bottle, and soda #2 costs $2.75 for a 2-liter bottle, it would be a better deal to buy soda #2, because its unit rate is only $1.375 per 1-liter, which is cheaper than soda #1. Unit rates can also help determine the length of time a given event will take. For example, if you can paint 2 rooms in 4.5 hours, you can determine how long it will take you to paint 5 rooms by solving for the unit rate per room and then multiplying that by 5.

SLOPE

On a graph with two points, (x_1, y_1) and (x_2, y_2), the **slope** is found with the formula $m = \frac{y_2 - y_1}{x_2 - x_1}$; where $x_1 \neq x_2$ and m stands for slope. If the value of the slope is **positive**, the line has an *upward direction* from left to right. If the value of the slope is **negative**, the line has a *downward direction* from left to right. Consider the following example:

A new book goes on sale in bookstores and online stores. In the first month, 5,000 copies of the book are sold. Over time, the book continues to grow in popularity. The data for the number of copies sold is in the table below.

# of Months on Sale	1	2	3	4	5
# of Copies Sold (In Thousands)	5	10	15	20	25

So, the number of copies that are sold and the time that the book is on sale is a proportional relationship. In this example, an equation can be used to show the data: $y = 5x$, where x is the number of months that the book is on sale. Also, y is the number of copies sold. So the slope of the corresponding line is $\frac{\text{rise}}{\text{run}} = \frac{5}{1} = 5$.

FINDING AN UNKNOWN IN EQUIVALENT EXPRESSIONS

It is often necessary to apply information given about a rate or proportion to a new scenario. For example, if you know that Jedha can run a marathon (26 miles) in 3 hours, how long would it take her to run 10 miles at the same pace? Start by setting up equivalent expressions:

$$\frac{26 \text{ mi}}{3 \text{ hr}} = \frac{10 \text{ mi}}{x \text{ hr}}$$

Now, cross multiply and solve for x:

$$26x = 30$$
$$x = \frac{30}{26} = \frac{15}{13}$$
$$x \cong 1.15 \text{ hrs } or \text{ 1 hr 9 min}$$

So, at this pace, Jedha could run 10 miles in about 1.15 hours or about 1 hour and 9 minutes.

PRACTICE

P1. Solve the following for x.

(a) $\frac{45}{12} = \frac{15}{x}$

(b) $\frac{0.50}{2} = \frac{1.50}{x}$

(c) $\frac{40}{8} = \frac{x}{24}$

P2. At a school, for every 20 female students there are 15 male students. This same student ratio happens to exist at another school. If there are 100 female students at the second school, how many male students are there?

P3. In a hospital emergency room, there are 4 nurses for every 12 patients. What is the ratio of nurses to patients? If the nurse-to-patient ratio remains constant, how many nurses must be present to care for 24 patients?

P4. In a bank, the banker-to-customer ratio is 1:2. If seven bankers are on duty, how many customers are currently in the bank?

P5. Janice made $40 during the first 5 hours she spent babysitting. She will continue to earn money at this rate until she finishes babysitting in 3 more hours. Find how much money Janice earns per hour and the total she earned babysitting.

P6. The McDonalds are taking a family road trip, driving 300 miles to their cabin. It took them 2 hours to drive the first 120 miles. They will drive at the same speed all the way to their cabin. Find the speed at which the McDonalds are driving and how much longer it will take them to get to their cabin.

P7. It takes Andy 10 minutes to read 6 pages of his book. He has already read 150 pages in his book that is 210 pages long. Find how long it takes Andy to read 1 page and also find how long it will take him to finish his book if he continues to read at the same speed.

PRACTICE SOLUTIONS

P1. First, cross multiply then solve for x:

(a) $45x = 12 \times 15$
$45x = 180$
$x = \frac{180}{45} = 4$

(b) $0.5x = 1.5 \times 2$
$0.5x = 3$
$x = \frac{3}{0.5} = 6$

(c) $8x = 40 \times 24$
$8x = 960$
$x = \frac{960}{8} = 120$

P2. One way to find the number of male students is to set up and solve a proportion.

$$\frac{\text{number of female students}}{\text{number of male students}} = \frac{20}{15} = \frac{100}{\text{number of male students}}$$

Represent the unknown number of male students as the variable x: $\frac{20}{15} = \frac{100}{x}$

Cross multiply and then solve for x:

$$20x = 15 \times 100$$
$$x = \frac{1500}{20}$$
$$x = 75$$

P3. The ratio of nurses to patients can be written as 4 to 12, 4:12, or $\frac{4}{12}$. Because four and twelve have a common factor of four, the ratio should be reduced to 1:3, which means that there is one nurse present for every three patients. If this ratio remains constant, there must be eight nurses present to care for 24 patients.

P4. Use proportional reasoning or set up a proportion to solve. Because there are twice as many customers as bankers, there must be fourteen customers when seven bankers are on duty. Setting up and solving a proportion gives the same result:

$$\frac{\text{number of bankers}}{\text{number of customers}} = \frac{1}{2} = \frac{7}{\text{number of customers}}$$

Represent the unknown number of patients as the variable x: $\frac{1}{2} = \frac{7}{x}$.

To solve for x, cross multiply: $1 \times x = 7 \times 2$, so $x = 14$.

P5. Janice earns $8 per hour. This can be found by taking her initial amount earned, $40, and dividing it by the number of hours worked, 5. Since $\frac{40}{5} = 8$, Janice makes $8 in one hour. This can also be found by finding the unit rate, money earned per hour: $\frac{40}{5} = \frac{x}{1}$. Since cross multiplying yields $5x = 40$, and division by 5 shows that $x = 8$, Janice earns $8 per hour.

Janice will earn $64 babysitting in her 8 total hours (adding the first 5 hours to the remaining 3 gives the 8-hour total). Since Janice earns $8 per hour and she worked 8 hours, $\frac{\$8}{\text{hr}} \times 8 \text{ hrs} = \$64$. This can also be found by setting up a proportion comparing money earned to babysitting hours. Since she earns $40 for 5 hours and since the rate is constant, she will earn a proportional amount in 8 hours: $\frac{40}{5} = \frac{x}{8}$. Cross multiplying will yield $5x = 320$, and division by 5 shows that $x = 64$.

P6. The McDonalds are driving 60 miles per hour. This can be found by setting up a proportion to find the unit rate, the number of miles they drive per one hour: $\frac{120}{2} = \frac{x}{1}$. Cross multiplying yields $2x = 120$ and division by 2 shows that $x = 60$.

Since the McDonalds will drive this same speed, it will take them another 3 hours to get to their cabin. This can be found by first finding how many miles the McDonalds have left to drive, which is $300 - 120 = 180$. The McDonalds are driving at 60 miles per hour, so a proportion can be set up to determine how many hours it will take them to drive 180 miles: $\frac{180}{x} = \frac{60}{1}$. Cross multiplying yields

$60x = 180$, and division by 60 shows that $x = 3$. This can also be found by using the formula $D = r \times t$ (or distance = rate × time), where $180 = 60 \times t$, and division by 60 shows that $t = 3$.

P7. It takes Andy 10 minutes to read 6 pages, $\frac{10}{6} = 1\frac{2}{3}$ minutes, which is 1 minute and 40 seconds.

Next, determine how many pages Andy has left to read, $210 - 150 = 60$. Since it is now known that it takes him $1\frac{2}{3}$ minutes to read each page, then that rate must be multiplied by however many pages he has left to read (60) to find the time he'll need: $60 \times 1\frac{2}{3} = 100$, so it will take him 100 minutes, or 1 hour and 40 minutes, to read the rest of his book.

Two-Dimensional Shapes

TRIANGLES

A triangle is a three-sided figure with the sum of its interior angles being 180° The **perimeter of any triangle** is found by summing the three side lengths; $P = a + b + c$. For an equilateral triangle, this is the same as $P = 3a$, where a is any side length, since all three sides are the same length.

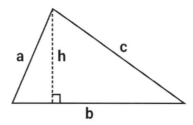

The **area of any triangle** can be found by taking half the product of one side length, referred to as the base and often given the variable b, and the perpendicular distance from that side to the opposite vertex called the altitude or height and given the variable h. In equation form that is $A = \frac{1}{2}bh$. Another formula that works for any triangle is $A = \sqrt{s(s-a)(s-b)(s-c)}$, where s is the semiperimeter: $\frac{a+b+c}{2}$, and a, b, and c are the lengths of the three sides. Special cases include isosceles triangles: $A = \frac{1}{2}b\sqrt{a^2 - \frac{b^2}{4}}$, where b is the unique side and a is the length of one of the two congruent sides, and equilateral triangles: $A = \frac{\sqrt{3}}{4}a^2$, where a is the length of a side.

> **Review Video: <u>Area and Perimeter of a Triangle</u>**
> Visit mometrix.com/academy and enter code: 853779

Rectangle: A quadrilateral with four right angles. All rectangles are parallelograms and trapezoids, but not all parallelograms or trapezoids are rectangles. The diagonals of a rectangle are congruent.

Rectangles have 2 lines of symmetry (through each pair of opposing midpoints) and 180-degree rotational symmetry about the midpoint.

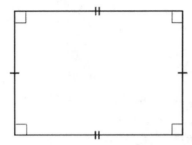

The **area of a rectangle** is found by the formula $A = lw$, where A is the area of the rectangle, l is the length (usually considered to be the longer side) and w is the width (usually considered to be the shorter side). The numbers for l and w are interchangeable.

The **perimeter of a rectangle** is found by the formula $P = 2l + 2w$ or $P = 2(l + w)$, where l is the length, and w is the width. It may be easier to add the length and width first and then double the result, as in the second formula.

Square: A quadrilateral with four right angles and four congruent sides. Squares satisfy the criteria of all other types of quadrilaterals. The diagonals of a square are congruent and perpendicular to each other. Squares have 4 lines of symmetry (through each pair of opposing midpoints and along each of the diagonals) as well as 90-degree rotational symmetry about the midpoint.

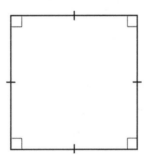

The **area of a square** is found by using the formula $A = s^2$, where s is the length of one side. The **perimeter of a square** is found by using the formula $P = 4s$, where s is the length of one side. Because all four sides are equal in a square, it is faster to multiply the length of one side by 4 than to add the same number four times. You could use the formulas for rectangles and get the same answer.

CIRCLES

The **center** of a circle is the single point from which every point on the circle is **equidistant**. The **radius** is a line segment that joins the center of the circle and any one point on the circle. All radii of a circle are equal. Circles that have the same center, but not the same length of radii are **concentric**. The **diameter** is a line segment that passes through the center of the circle and has both endpoints on the circle. The length of the diameter is exactly twice the length of the radius. Point O in the

52

diagram below is the center of the circle, segments $\overline{OX}$, $\overline{OY}$, and $\overline{OZ}$ are radii, and segment $\overline{XZ}$ is a diameter.

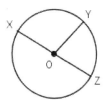

The **area of a circle** is found by the formula $A = \pi r^2$, where r is the length of the radius. If the diameter of the circle is given, remember to divide it in half to get the length of the radius before proceeding.

The **circumference** of a circle is found by the formula $C = 2\pi r$, where r is the radius. Again, remember to convert the diameter if you are given that measure rather than the radius.

PRACTICE

P1. Find the area and perimeter of a square with side length 2.5 cm.

P2. Calculate the area of a triangle with side lengths of 7 ft, 8 ft, and 9 ft.

PRACTICE SOLUTIONS

P1. (a) $A = s^2 = (2.5 \text{ cm})^2 = 6.25 \text{ cm}^2$; $P = 4s = 4 \times 2.5 \text{ cm} = 10 \text{ cm}$

P2. Given only side lengths, we can use the semi perimeter to the find the area based on the formula, $A = \sqrt{s(s-a)(s-b)(s-c)}$, where s is the semiperimeter, $\frac{a+b+c}{2} = \frac{7+8+9}{2} = 12$ ft:

$$A = \sqrt{12(12-7)(12-8)(12-9)}$$
$$= \sqrt{(12)(5)(4)(3)}$$
$$= 12\sqrt{5} \text{ ft}^2$$

Three-Dimensional Shapes

SOLIDS

The **surface area of a solid object** is the area of all sides or exterior surfaces. For objects such as prisms and pyramids, a further distinction is made between base surface area (B) and lateral surface area (LA). For a prism, the total surface area (SA) is $SA = LA + 2B$. For a pyramid or cone, the total surface area is $SA = LA + B$.

The **surface area of a sphere** can be found by the formula $A = 4\pi r^2$, where r is the radius. The volume is given by the formula $V = \frac{4}{3}\pi r^3$, where r is the radius. Both quantities are generally given in terms of π.

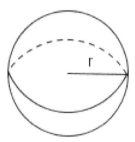

The **volume of any prism** is found by the formula $V = Bh$, where B is the area of the base, and h is the height (perpendicular distance between the bases). The surface area of any prism is the sum of the areas of both bases and all sides. It can be calculated as $SA = 2B + Ph$, where P is the perimeter of the base.

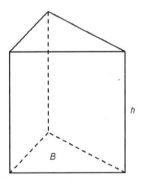

For a **rectangular prism**, the volume can be found by the formula $V = lwh$, where V is the volume, l is the length, w is the width, and h is the height. The surface area can be calculated as $SA = 2lw + 2hl + 2wh$ or $SA = 2(lw + hl + wh)$.

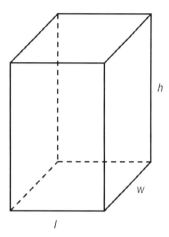

The **volume of a cube** can be found by the formula $V = s^3$, where s is the length of a side. The surface area of a cube is calculated as $SA = 6s^2$, where SA is the total surface area and s is the length of a side. These formulas are the same as the ones used for the volume and surface area of a rectangular prism, but simplified since all three quantities (length, width, and height) are the same.

> **Review Video: <u>Volume and Surface Area of a Cube</u>**
> Visit mometrix.com/academy and enter code: 664455

The **volume of a cylinder** can be calculated by the formula $V = \pi r^2 h$, where r is the radius, and h is the height. The surface area of a cylinder can be found by the formula $SA = 2\pi r^2 + 2\pi rh$. The first term is the base area multiplied by two, and the second term is the perimeter of the base multiplied by the height.

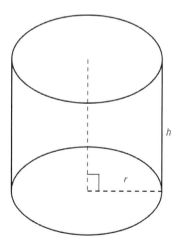

The **volume of a cone** is found by the formula $V = \frac{1}{3}\pi r^2 h$, where r is the radius, and h is the height. Notice this is the same as $\frac{1}{3}$ times the volume of a cylinder. The surface area can be calculated as $SA = \pi r^2 + \pi rs$, where s is the slant height. The slant height can be calculated using the

Pythagorean theorem to be $\sqrt{r^2 + h^2}$, so the surface area formula can also be written as $SA = \pi r^2 + \pi r\sqrt{r^2 + h^2}$.

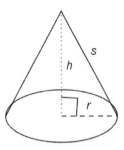

PRACTICE

P1. Find the surface area and volume of the following solids:

(a) A cylinder with radius 5 m and height 0.5 m.

(b) A half sphere (radius 5 yds) on the base of an inverted cone with the same radius and a height of 7 yds.

PRACTICE SOLUTIONS

P1. (a) $SA = 2\pi r^2 + 2\pi rh = 2\pi(5\text{ m})^2 + 2\pi(5\text{ m})(0.5\text{ m}) = 55\pi\text{ m}^2 \cong 172.79\text{ m}^2$;

$V = \pi r^2 h = \pi(5\text{ m})^2(0.5\text{ m}) = 12.5\pi\text{ m}^3 \cong 39.27\text{ m}^3$

(b) We can find s, the slant height using the Pythagorean theorem, and since this solid is made of parts of simple solids, we can combine the formulas to find surface area and volume:

$$s = \sqrt{r^2 + h^2} = \sqrt{(5\text{ yd})^2 + (7\text{ yd})^2} = \sqrt{74}\text{ yd}$$

$SA_{Total} = (SA_{sphere})/2 + SA_{cone} - SA_{base}$
$= \dfrac{4\pi r^2}{2} + (\pi rs + \pi r^2) - \pi r^2$
$= 2\pi(5\text{ yd})^2 + \pi(5\text{ yd})(\sqrt{74}\text{ yd})$
$= 5\pi(10 + \sqrt{74})\text{ yd}^2$
$\cong 292.20\text{ yd}^2$

$V_{Total} = (V_{sphere})/2 + V_{cone}$
$= \dfrac{\frac{4}{3}\pi r^3}{2} + \dfrac{1}{3}\pi r^2 h$
$= \dfrac{2}{3}\pi(5\text{ yd})^3 + \dfrac{1}{3}\pi(5\text{ yd})^2(7\text{ yd})$
$= \dfrac{5^2 \times \pi}{3}(10 + 7)\text{ yd}^3$
$\cong 445.06\text{ yd}^3$

Statistical Analysis

MEASURES OF CENTRAL TENDENCY

A **measure of central tendency** is a statistical value that gives a reasonable estimate for the center of a group of data. There are several different ways of describing the measure of central tendency. Each one has a unique way it is calculated, and each one gives a slightly different perspective on the data set. Whenever you give a measure of central tendency, always make sure the units are the same. If the data has different units, such as hours, minutes, and seconds, convert all the data to the same unit, and use the same unit in the measure of central tendency. If no units are given in the data, do not give units for the measure of central tendency.

MEAN

The **statistical mean** of a group of data is the same as the arithmetic average of that group. To find the mean of a set of data, first convert each value to the same units, if necessary. Then find the sum of all the values, and count the total number of data values, making sure you take into consideration each individual value. If a value appears more than once, count it more than once. Divide the sum of the values by the total number of values and apply the units, if any. Note that the mean does not have to be one of the data values in the set, and may not divide evenly.

$$\text{mean} = \frac{\text{sum of the data values}}{\text{quantity of data values}}$$

For instance, the mean of the data set {88, 72, 61, 90, 97, 68, 88, 79, 86, 93, 97, 71, 80, 84, 89} would be the sum of the fifteen numbers divided by 15:

$$\frac{88 + 72 + 61 + 90 + 97 + 68 + 88 + 79 + 86 + 93 + 97 + 71 + 80 + 84 + 89}{15} = \frac{1242}{15}$$
$$= 82.8$$

While the mean is relatively easy to calculate and averages are understood by most people, the mean can be very misleading if it is used as the sole measure of central tendency. If the data set has outliers (data values that are unusually high or unusually low compared to the rest of the data values), the mean can be very distorted, especially if the data set has a small number of values. If unusually high values are countered with unusually low values, the mean is not affected as much. For example, if five of twenty students in a class get a 100 on a test, but the other 15 students have an average of 60 on the same test, the class average would appear as 70. Whenever the mean is skewed by outliers, it is always a good idea to include the median as an alternate measure of central tendency.

A **weighted mean**, or weighted average, is a mean that uses "weighted" values. The formula is weighted mean $= \frac{w_1 x_1 + w_2 x_2 + w_3 x_3 \ldots + w_n x_n}{w_1 + w_2 + w_3 + \cdots + w_n}$. Weighted values, such as $w_1, w_2, w_3, \ldots w_n$ are assigned to each member of the set $x_1, x_2, x_3, \ldots x_n$. If calculating weighted mean, make sure to use a weight value for each member of the set.

MEDIAN

The **statistical median** is the value in the middle of the set of data. To find the median, list all data values in order from smallest to largest or from largest to smallest. Any value that is repeated in the set must be listed the number of times it appears. If there are an odd number of data values, the median is the value in the middle of the list. If there is an even number of data values, the median is the arithmetic mean of the two middle values.

For example, the median of the data set {88, 72, 61, 90, 97, 68, 88, 79, 86, 93, 97, 71, 80, 84, 88} is 86 since the ordered set is {61, 68, 71, 72, 79, 80, 84, **86**, 88, 88, 88, 90, 93, 97, 97}.

The big disadvantage of using the median as a measure of central tendency is that it relies solely on a value's relative size as compared to the other values in the set. When the individual values in a set of data are evenly dispersed, the median can be an accurate tool. However, if there is a group of rather large values or a group of rather small values that are not offset by a different group of values, the information that can be inferred from the median may not be accurate because the distribution of values is skewed.

MODE

The **statistical mode** is the data value that occurs the greatest number of times in the data set. It is possible to have exactly one mode, more than one mode, or no mode. To find the mode of a set of data, arrange the data like you do to find the median (all values in order, listing all multiples of data values). Count the number of times each value appears in the data set. If all values appear an equal number of times, there is no mode. If one value appears more than any other value, that value is the mode. If two or more values appear the same number of times, but there are other values that appear fewer times and no values that appear more times, all of those values are the modes.

For example, the mode of the data set {**88**, 72, 61, 90, 97, 68, **88**, 79, 86, 93, 97, 71, 80, 84, **88**} is 88.

The main disadvantage of the mode is that the values of the other data in the set have no bearing on the mode. The mode may be the largest value, the smallest value, or a value anywhere in between in the set. The mode only tells which value or values, if any, occurred the greatest number of times. It does not give any suggestions about the remaining values in the set.

> **Review Video: Mean, Median, and Mode**
> Visit mometrix.com/academy and enter code: 286207

DISPERSION

The **measure of dispersion** is a single value that helps to "interpret" the measure of central tendency by providing more information about how the data values in the set are distributed about the measure of central tendency. The measure of dispersion helps to eliminate or reduce the disadvantages of using the mean, median, or mode as a single measure of central tendency, and gives a more accurate picture of the dataset as a whole.

RANGE

The **range** of a set of data is the difference between the greatest and lowest values of the data in the set. To calculate the range, you must first make sure the units for all data values are the same, and then identify the greatest and lowest values. If there are multiple data values that are equal for the highest or lowest, just use one of the values in the formula. Write the answer with the same units as the data values you used to do the calculations.

STANDARD DEVIATION

Standard deviation is a measure of dispersion that compares all the data values in the set to the mean of the set to give a more accurate picture. To find the standard deviation of a sample, use the formula

$$s = \sqrt{\frac{\sum_{i=1}^{n}(x_i - \bar{x})^2}{n-1}}$$

Note that s is the standard deviation of a sample, x represents the individual values in the data set, $\bar{x}$ is the mean of the data values in the set, and n is the number of data values in the set. The higher the value of the standard deviation is, the greater the variance of the data values from the mean. The units associated with the standard deviation are the same as the units of the data values.

> **Review Video: Standard Deviation**
> Visit mometrix.com/academy and enter code: 419469

VARIANCE

The **variance** of a sample, or just variance, is the square of the standard deviation of that sample. While the mean of a set of data gives the average of the set and gives information about where a specific data value lies in relation to the average, the variance of the sample gives information about the degree to which the data values are spread out and tell you how close an individual value is to the average compared to the other values. The units associated with variance are the same as the units of the data values squared.

PERCENTILE

Percentiles and quartiles are other methods of describing data within a set. **Percentiles** tell what percentage of the data in a set fall below a specific point. For example, achievement test scores are often given in percentiles. A score at the 80th percentile is one which is equal to or higher than 80 percent of the scores in the set. In other words, 80 percent of the scores were lower than that score.

Quartiles are percentile groups that make up quarter sections of the data set. The first quartile, Q_1, is the 25th percentile. The second quartile, Q_2, is the 50th percentile; this is also the median of the dataset. The third quartile, Q_3, is the 75th percentile. The interquartile range (IQR) is the difference between the third quartile and the first quartile, $Q_3 - Q_1$.

OUTLIER

An outlier is an extremely high or extremely low value in the data set. It may be the result of a measurement error, in which case, the outlier is not a valid member of the data set. However, it may also be a valid member of the distribution. Unless a measurement error is identified, the experimenter cannot know for certain if an outlier is or is not a member of the distribution. There are arbitrary methods that can be employed to designate an extreme value as an outlier. One method designates an outlier (or possible outlier) to be any value less than $Q_1 - 1.5(IQR)$ or any value greater than $Q_3 + 1.5(IQR)$.

PRACTICE

P1. Given the following graph, determine the range of patient ages:

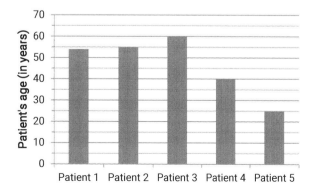

59

P2. Calculate the sample variance for the dataset $\{10, 13, 12, 5, 8, 18\}$

Practice Solutions

P1. Patient 1 is 54 years old; Patient 2 is 55 years old; Patient 3 is 60 years old; Patient 4 is 40 years old; and Patient 5 is 25 years old. The range of patient ages is the age of the oldest patient minus the age of the youngest patient. In other words, $60 - 25 = 35$. The range of ages is 35 years.

P2. To find the variance, first find the mean:

$$\frac{10 + 13 + 12 + 5 + 8 + 18}{6} = \frac{66}{6} = 11$$

Now, apply the formula for sample variance:

$$
\begin{aligned}
s^2 &= \frac{\sum_{i=1}^{n}(x_i - \bar{x})^2}{n-1} = \frac{\sum_{i=1}^{6}(x_i - 11)^2}{6-1} \\
&= \frac{(10-11)^2 + (13-11)^2 + (12-11)^2 + (5-11)^2 + (8-11)^2 + (18-11)^2}{5} \\
&= \frac{(-1)^2 + 2^2 + 1^2 + (-6)^2 + (-3)^2 + 7^2}{5} \\
&= \frac{1 + 4 + 1 + 36 + 9 + 49}{5} \\
&= \frac{100}{5} = 20
\end{aligned}
$$

Additional Math Concepts

IDENTIFYING THE BEST DEAL

It can be difficult to compare the final price of something at competing retailers when each states a different price and also has a sale or promotion that changes the price. Consider a situation where you want to buy a specific new tablet. Buy-Tech-Here has the tablet listed for $399, but they currently have a 25%-off sale on electronics. Meanwhile, at Gadgets-B-We, the tablet is listed for $359 with a 10%-off sale on items storewide and you have a Gadgets-B-We coupon for $25 off any purchase over $100. Which is the better deal?

To determine the final price of each, apply the discounts. 25% of $399 is $0.25 \times \$399 = \$99.75$, so, the final price at Buy-Tech-Here would be $\$399 - \$99.75 = \$299.25$. For Gadgets-B-We, 10% of $359 is $0.1 \times \$359 = \$35.90$. In addition to this discount, you have $25 coupon, so the final price at Gadgets-B-We is $\$359 - \$35.90 - \$25 = \$298.10$. Since $298.10 is less than $299.25, that means the best deal is at Gadgets-B-We.

DETERMINING RELATIVE ECONOMIC VALUE

GRAPHICALLY

When comparing the value of various alternatives, it can be helpful to plot a graph of each to more easily see how they compare. The options could result in a variety of functions that, once graphed, clearly show which offers the best value. For instance, Company T is comparing deals offered from four different manufacturers on the cost of producing mechanical pencils. The summary of the offers is listed in the table below:

Manufacturer	Base Order Cost	Price Per Pencil	Quantity Discounts
A	$10,000	$0.19	If more than 500,000 in an order, then $0.15 per pencil. If more than 1 million in an order, then $0.10 per pencil
B	$20,000	$0.09	None
C	$15,000	$0.25	Price decreases by $0.02 for every 100,000 pencils in the order up to 1 million pencils
D	$50,000	$0.03	None

It is not clear from the table which of the manufacturers would be best for a given order size without calculating the total cost of a certain order size for each. However, looking at the graph depicting each of the offers over a range of order sizes, it is much more obvious which manufacturer offers the best deal for any given order size:

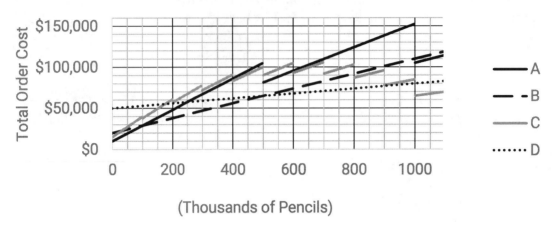

For instance, if the company wants to order 50,000 pencils, then Manufacturer A is the cheapest. On the other hand, if they want 700,000 pencils, then Manufacturer D has the best price. It is worth noting that you could order 1 million pencils for about the same price as 500,000, but that would mean that you need to store all of those pencils, which may not be feasible.

PERCENTAGE CHANGE

Percentage change is calculated by dividing the absolute value of the difference between two values by one of those values as a reference and then multiplying the result by 100. In equation form:

$$\text{Percentage change} = \frac{|\text{Compared Value} - \text{Reference Value}|}{\text{Reference Value}} \times 100$$

This is a method for gauging the relative size difference between the values in terms of the magnitude of those values. For example, it may seem obvious that the difference between $8 and $10 is more significant than between $998 and $1000, but in order to quantify the comparison, you can use the percentage change of each:

$$\begin{aligned} \text{Percentage change from \$10 to \$8} &= \frac{|8 - 10|}{10} \times 100 \\ &= \frac{2}{10} \times 100 \\ &= 20\% \\ \text{Percentage change from \$1000 to \$998} &= \frac{|998 - 1000|}{1000} \times 100 \\ &= \frac{2}{1000} \times 100 \\ &= 0.20\% \end{aligned}$$

Even though the difference between each pair is the same, the percentage changes are very different! So, saving $2 dollars on a $10 purchase is much more significant than saving $2 on a $1000 purchase. Again, that may seem obvious, but it is useful to be able to compare them and verify your intuition with clear data.

Unit Cost

Often when shopping, it is best to compare the unit costs of items to be certain which has the best value. The unit cost is the total price of an item divided by the units contained within that item.

$$\text{Unit cost} = \frac{\text{Total price}}{\text{Total units}}$$

Consider going to a store to buy bar soap. You see three brands that you like equally—Young Herb, Vulture, and Crank. The Young Herb soap is available in single 255-gram bars at $1.29 each, the Vulture soap comes in a 3-pack of 210-gram bars at $3.19 per pack, and the Crank soap comes in a 10-pack of 300-gram bars at $14.99 per pack.

To determine the best value, we can compare the unit cost, in this case the cost per gram.

$$\text{Unit cost of Young Herb soap} = \frac{\$1.29}{255 \text{ g}} = \$0.00506 \text{ per gram}$$

$$\text{Unit cost of Vulture soap} = \frac{\$3.19}{3 \times (215 \text{ g})} = \frac{\$3.19}{645 \text{ g}} = \$0.00495 \text{ per gram}$$

$$\text{Unit cost of Crank soap} = \frac{\$14.99}{10 \times (275 \text{ g})} = \frac{\$14.99}{2750 \text{ g}} = \$0.00545 \text{ per gram}$$

Now we can see that the Vulture soap is the best value.

Example Applied Math Problems

LEVEL 3 SAMPLE QUESTION

Question: At the grocery store, Steve bought $33.81 of food. He paid in cash, handing the cashier $40. How much change should he receive?

   A. $3.81
   B. $6.19
   C. $16.19
   D. $13.81
   E. $40.00

This is a level 3 problem because it is straightforward in what it asks and it presents only the information you need to answer the question.

Explanation: To figure out how much change Steve should receive you must subtract the cost of the food from the amount of money he handed the cashier. The following demonstrates that **the correct answer is choice B:**

$40.00
$33.81
$ 6.19

LEVEL 5 SAMPLE QUESTION

Question: A warehouse club member purchased flooring for $27.18 per box. The warehouse club reported that the member had saved over $250 by purchasing the flooring from them rather than from the local retailer who was selling it for $61.04 per box. What is the minimum number of boxes of flooring the member would have had to purchase to save over $250?

   A. 7
   B. 8
   C. 27
   D. 33
   E. 34

This is a level 5 problem because the way in which the information is presented is more complicated and because it requires higher reasoning and more varied operations to solve.

Explanation: The amount saved per box of flooring is $61.04 − $27.18 = $33.86. To find the number of boxes of flooring the member would have to purchase to save $250, divide $250 by the amount saved per box, or $33.86, and you get $250 ÷ $33.86 = 7.38 rounded to the nearest hundredth. Although this number rounds to 7 when you round to the nearest whole number, if the member purchased 7 boxes of flooring, the total savings would be 7 × $33.86 = 237.02, which is not over $250. The member would have to purchase at least 8 boxes of flooring to save over $250. 8 × $33.86 = $270.88, which clearly meets the requirements of the given conditions. **Answer choice B is correct.**

LEVEL 7 SAMPLE QUESTION

Question: A manufacturer uses an aluminum can 4 inches in diameter and 8 inches tall to sell soup. The manufacturer wants to switch to a cylindrical glass jar with a base only 3 inches in diameter. Which of the following best represents the required height of the glass jar, if the jar is to hold exactly the same amount of soup?

A. $12\frac{4}{9}$ inches

B. $10\frac{1}{4}$ inches

C. $11\frac{2}{9}$ inches

D. $9\frac{4}{9}$ inches

E. $14\frac{1}{4}$ inches

This is a level 7 question because it required you to use the volume formula for a cylinder to calculate multiple volumes and fill in missing information.

Explanation: The volume of a cylinder can be determined by using the formula $V = \pi r^2 h$, where r is the radius of the cylinder and h is the height. In both cylinders in the problem, the diameter is given rather than the radius, so it must be divided by 2. The volume of the aluminum can is equal to $\pi(2)^2 8$, or 32π inches. In order to find the necessary height of the glass jar, the radius of 1.5 inches and prior volume of the aluminum can need to be substituted into the volume formula as follows: $32\pi = \pi(1.5)^2 h$. Simplifying this gives us $32\pi = 2.25\pi h$. Rearranging to solve for h gives us $h = \frac{32\pi}{2.25\pi}$. Dividing this out, the two pi's cancel and h is approximately 14.22 inches. The height of $14\frac{1}{4}$ inches **given by answer choice E** is the choice that best represents the required height.

Graphic Literacy

WHAT IS THIS SECTION TESTING?

This section tests your ability to interpret typical graphics you might encounter in the workplace. Such graphics might include various types of graphs, charts, tables, diagrams, schematics, and measurement instruments, among other things.

Thus, there is a significant variety of graphics that might appear on the test. Although some of the graphics might be more commonly encountered in certain occupations, the questions are intended to test your general ability to analyze and draw conclusions from graphics; you will not need any specialized knowledge to answer the questions.

WHAT DO THE QUESTIONS LOOK LIKE, AND HOW DIFFICULT ARE THEY?

The complexity of both the graphics themselves and the questions varies considerably. The Graphic Complexity Categories table is the set of criteria used in the definitions of difficulty levels from the ACT organization.

GRAPHIC COMPLEXITY CATEGORIES

Stimulus Characteristics	Simple	Low Moderate	High Moderate	Difficult
Number of Axes	One or two axes	One or two axes	One or two axes	One, two, or more axes
Levels of Data	One level of data	More than one level of data; no nesting	More than one level of data; nesting allowed	More than one level of data; nesting allowed
Number of Variables	Few variables (1 to 2)	Several variables (3 to 5)	Many variables	Many variables
Number of Representations of Data	No more than 20 data points/fields	Moderate number of data points/fields	Moderate number of data points/fields	Densely presented data
Familiarity of Graphic Type	Common graphic types	Common graphic types	Less common graphic types	Less common graphic types (Composite graphics)
Total Number of Graphics	One	May be two	May be multiple	May be multiple

The graphics and test questions are assigned a difficulty level between 3 and 7, depending on the following criteria:

- **Level 3:** The graphics are simple to low moderate in complexity. The questions are straightforward, requiring you to only locate information or identify the next step in a process.
- **Level 4:** The graphics are either low moderate or high moderate in complexity. For high moderate graphics, you must locate information or identify the next step in a process. For low moderate graphics, you must compare, infer, or assess data representation.

66

- **Level 5:** The graphics are low moderate, high moderate, or difficult in complexity. For difficult graphics, you must locate information or identify the next step in a process. For high moderate graphics, you must compare, infer, or assess data representation. For low moderate graphics, you must compare and identify trends, draw conclusions, justify an inference, or select a graphic to suit a need.
- **Level 6:** The graphics are high moderate or difficult in complexity. For difficult graphics, you must compare, infer, or assess data representation. For high moderate graphics, you must compare and identify trends, draw conclusions, justify an inference, or select a graphic to suit a need.
- **Level 7:** The graphics are difficult in complexity. The questions require you to compare and identify trends, draw conclusions, justify an inference, or select a graphic to suit a need.

WHAT STRATEGIES CAN I USE TO DO WELL ON THIS SECTION?

- **Read the questions before examining the graphic.** Reading the questions first can give you a good idea of what to look for in the graphics, and help you complete the questions more efficiently.
- **Systematically eliminate obviously wrong answer choices.** If you can reduce the number of answer choices by one or two, you can drastically improve your chances of answering the question correctly, even if you randomly guess. In addition, eliminating wrong answer choices may help you better focus on the remaining ones, removing some of the "clutter" from the problem.
- **For difficult questions, look for the *best* answer rather than the *right* answer.** Most of the easy questions are black and white: they require you to simply locate a particular item of information. Such questions usually have questions that are clearly right or wrong. However, some of the more difficult questions require you to make generalizations or explanations. These types of questions don't always have clearly right or wrong answers, but better and worse answers. For these questions, some of the answer choices might seem reasonable, but another answer choice might be better. Therefore, for more difficult questions, you should focus on finding the *best* answer, not necessarily the *right* answer.

Example Graphic Literacy Problems

LEVEL 3 SAMPLE QUESTION

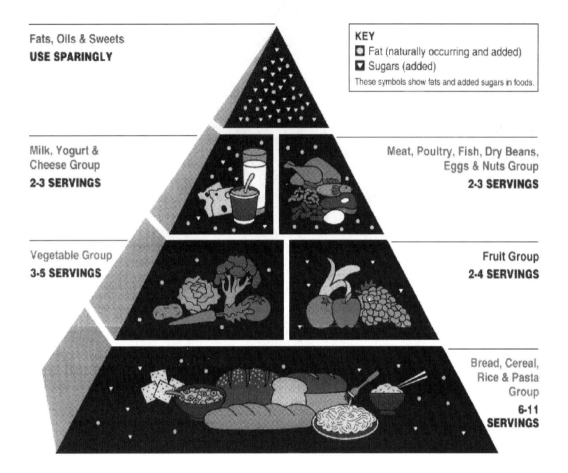

Question: Based on the picture above, the greatest number of servings should come from which food group?

A. Fats, oils, and sweets
B. Vegetable group
C. Fruit group
D. Bread, cereal, rice, and pasta group

Explanation: Begin by reading the question. The question is asking which food group should provide the *greatest* number of servings per day. Knowing what you are looking for will help you find the answer more quickly.

Once you know this, you can easily determine that the bread, cereal, rice, and pasta group should provide the greatest number of servings. The picture explicitly states that a person should eat 6-11 servings daily, more than any other group. **Thus, the correct answer is D.**

You could also answer this question by eliminating incorrect answers. The larger a group appears on the pyramid, the more of that group a person should eat. You can see that fats, oils, and sweets should be "used sparingly," so you can eliminate that answer. In addition, you can see that the vegetable and fruit groups are relatively small, while the grains group is relatively large. Thus, you can also eliminate the vegetable and fruit groups as possible answers, leaving only the bread, cereal, rice and pasta group.

LEVEL 5 SAMPLE QUESTION

Education Pays

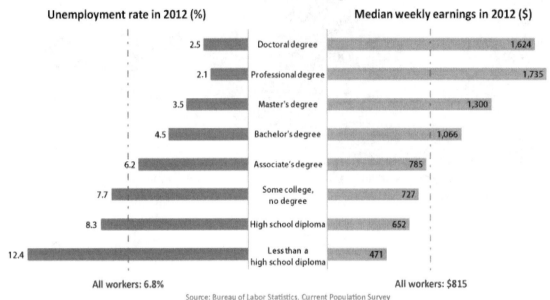

Unemployment rate in 2012 (%)   Median weekly earnings in 2012 ($)

	Unemployment rate	Degree	Median weekly earnings
	2.5	Doctoral degree	1,624
	2.1	Professional degree	1,735
	3.5	Master's degree	1,300
	4.5	Bachelor's degree	1,066
	6.2	Associate's degree	785
	7.7	Some college, no degree	727
	8.3	High school diploma	652
	12.4	Less than a high school diploma	471

All workers: 6.8%   All workers: $815

Source: Bureau of Labor Statistics, Current Population Survey

Question: According to the above chart, which of the following is the *least* accurate:

A. In general, people with professional degrees have the lowest unemployment rates and the highest median salaries.
B. In general, people with bachelor's degrees or a greater level of education have lower unemployment rates and higher salary rates than workers as a whole.
C. People with a high school diploma, but no college, have the highest unemployment rate of all the groups listed.
D. People with an associate's degree, or a lesser level of education, have lower median salaries than workers as a whole.

Explanation: The question requires you to evaluate each of the answer choices, so it's not as easy to apply the technique of reading the question first and find the answer.

It's easiest to start by evaluating answer choice A. According to the chart, people with professional degrees have lower unemployment rates than any other group listed above, with 2.1%. In addition, they also have the highest median salaries of any group, so choice A is true. You can eliminate answer choice A.

Continuing to choice B, you can see that people with bachelor's degrees have unemployment rates of 4.5%, compared to 6.8% for all workers. In addition, they earn a median salary of $1,066 per week, compared to a median of $815 for all workers. Thus, choice B is accurate, so you can eliminate it.

Regarding choice C, people with a high school diploma and no college have relatively high rates of unemployment (8.3%), but not as high as people with less than a high school diploma (12.4%). Thus, choice C is *not* accurate, so you can mark it down as a possible answer. Even so, it's a good idea to evaluate answer choice D unless you happen to have very little time left.

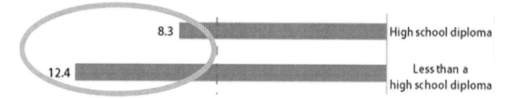

According to the chart, people with associate's degrees earn $785 per week, which is lower than $815, the median for all workers. Therefore, answer choice D is accurate, so you can eliminate it.

Eliminating A, B, and D leaves only choice C as a possible answer.

LEVEL 7 SAMPLE QUESTION

The following is a graph, based on fictional data, of the price vs. weight of new car models in the United States. Each circle or diamond represents a different model of car or truck, respectively.

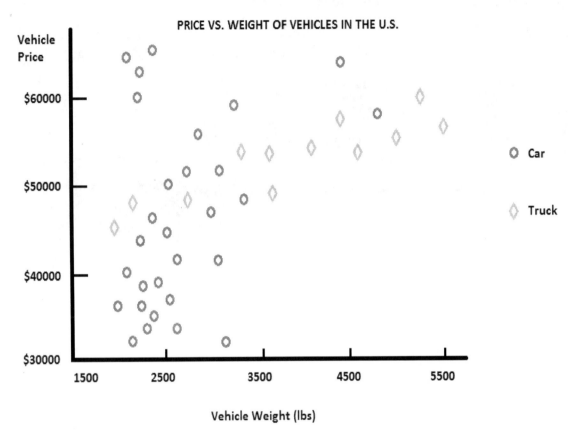

Question: Which of the following is the most plausible explanation for the cluster of four circles in the upper left portion of the graph?

A. To meet the needs of modest-income families, a number of large, inexpensive sedans were recently released.

B. There are four models of large, high-end luxury sedans, which are targeted to affluent professionals with children.

C. In order to appeal to younger buyers, several manufacturers released new models of small, inexpensive economy cars.

D. Several manufacturers sell premium sports cars, which feature advanced materials that are very expensive but greatly reduce the weight of the cars.

72

Copyright © Mometrix Media. You have been licensed one copy of this document for personal use only. Any other reproduction or redistribution is strictly prohibited. All rights reserved.
This content is provided for test preparation purposes only and does not imply an endorsement by Mometrix of any particular political, scientific, or religious point of view.

Explanation: Like the preceding question, this type of question will require you to evaluate each of the answer choices individually. But first, read the question: the question is asking you to find a plausible explanation for the four circles in the upper left.

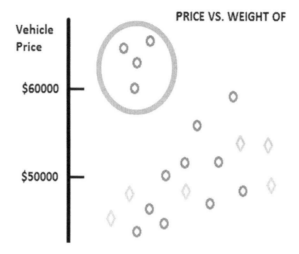

What can you tell about these four cars? They are all located on the left side of the graph, which means they are relatively light compared to most of the other automobiles; they only weigh between 2000 and 2500 pounds. In addition, they all cost $60,000 or more, making them much more expensive than most of the other autos shown on the graph. Thus, you need to find an answer choice that explains why these four cars would be so lightweight, yet so expensive.

Start by evaluating answer choice A, which explains that several large, inexpensive family sedans were recently released. You could reasonably expect a large sedan to be heavy. So, answer choice A would explain the existence of heavy but cheap sedans, which would be located in the lower right of the graph. However, this would not explain the cluster of light, expensive cars in the upper left. Therefore, you can eliminate A as a possible answer choice.

Answer choice B explains the existence of large, high-end luxury sedans. You could expect such a car to be both heavy and expensive, so these cars would be located in the upper right portion of the graph. This does not explain the phenomenon of light, expensive cars, so you can eliminate B as a choice.

Answer choice C explains the existence of "small, inexpensive" cars. Such cars would be located in the lower left part of the graph, not the upper left, so you can eliminate answer choice C as a plausible explanation.

Finally, answer choice D explains that some high-end sports cars incorporate lightweight materials that greatly increase the price of the cars. You could expect such cars to have relatively low weights and relatively high prices, and such cars would be located in the upper left portion of the graph. Of all the answer choices, D provides the best explanation for this cluster of circles in the upper left, so **D is the best answer choice**.

Note that on some of the more difficult questions, you will have to pick the "best" answer, rather than an answer that is clearly right or wrong. For questions that require you to draw a conclusion or explain something about the graph, you should carefully read every answer choice. Sometimes an answer may seem reasonable even though there is a better answer further down the list.

Workplace Documents

WHAT IS THIS SECTION TESTING?

This section tests your ability to read and understand typical documents you might encounter in the workplace. Such documents might include but are by no means limited to: contracts or other legal documents, safety warnings or instructions, checklists, lists of instructions or procedures, OSHA (Occupational Safety and Health Administration) guidelines, or employee memorandums.

Thus, there is a huge variety of literature that might appear on this section. Many of the more difficult passages, particularly those derived from legal documents, will feature technical or legal jargon you may not know. In such cases, you may have to use context clues and logic to draw conclusions about a passage.

WHAT DO THE QUESTIONS LOOK LIKE, AND HOW DIFFICULT ARE THEY?

The difficulty of the passages and questions vary considerably as well. The most basic questions will simply require you to spot information in a relatively simple passage. The most advanced questions will require you to thoroughly understand complex passages and then use that information to draw a conclusion about a hypothetical scenario.

The passages and test questions are assigned a difficulty level between 3 and 7, according to the following criteria:

- **Level 3:** These passages are short and relatively simple; they are usually either bulleted lists or brief memorandums. The sentence structure is simple, and the vocabulary level is basic. Most of the questions are straightforward and require identifying details rather than drawing conclusions. An example of a Level 3 passage might be a note in the company kitchen explaining where to put food or dishes.
- **Level 4:** Level 4 questions also require test takers to identify details in the passages, rather than drawing complex conclusions. However, Level 4 passages are usually longer, have more information, and are written in a more complex style than Level 3 passages, making those details more difficult to spot.
- **Level 5:** These passages may feature limited jargon, or more complex sets of instructions or details. Level 5 questions are less focused on identifying details from the passage, and more focused on drawing basic conclusions from those details. Examples of Level 5 passages might include company memorandums about software or computer systems.
- **Level 6:** Level 6 passages often include legal agreements or governmental or regulatory documents. As a result, these passages are usually written in a more formal, less readable way than Level 3-5 passages. Level 6 questions may ask test takers to use context clues and logic to define terms in the passage. Other questions require drawing conclusions or explaining why a particular conclusion is correct or incorrect, based on the information in the passage.
- **Level 7:** These passages also include complex legal, regulatory, or procedural documents. However, level 7 questions tend to be a bit more difficult than level 6 questions.

WHAT STRATEGIES CAN I USE TO DO WELL ON THIS SECTION?

- **Read the questions before reading the passage.** By identifying what you need to look for ahead of time, you can more quickly read the passage to find the information you need. In addition, reading the question will give you an idea of its complexity. If the question is simply asking you to find a detail in a passage, it probably won't take nearly as long as a question that requires you to make a conclusion about a hypothetical scenario. If it looks like the question will be very time-consuming, you can skip it and come back. Although the WorkKeys assessment is not an extremely time-intensive test, many of the Level 6 and 7 passages are quite dense and difficult, and you may have to read them multiple times to understand them. Therefore, if you answer the easier questions more efficiently, you will have more time to spend on the harder ones.
- **Systematically eliminate answers that are obviously wrong.** This will make it easier to focus on the remaining choices, and more importantly, you will improve your chances of correctly answering the question if you have to randomly guess.
- **Use context clues to understand difficult words.** Many of the more difficult questions require you to understand technical or legal terms you may not have heard before. Some questions will even ask you to explicitly define those words. If you don't know what they mean, you will have to use clues in the sentence to understand their meaning.

One effective way to handle unknown words is to highlight or circle them in the passage and underline other words in the passage that provide clues to their meaning. As an example, try to use context clues figure out what the word "contraindicate" means in the sentence below:

> *Although Inventium is normally prescribed to relieve severe pain, a history of liver damage in a patient contraindicates its use.*

Even if you don't know what "contraindicates" means, you can still figure it out from the rest of the sentence. The word "although" is key because it signals contrasting ideas. In the sentence above, we know that there's a (fictional) medicine, Inventium, that's prescribed to relieve pain. The word "although" tells us that even though Inventium is **normally** prescribed to relieve severe pain, there are some situations in which that wouldn't happen, and the second part of the sentence completes the puzzle: you wouldn't prescribe Inventium if a patient has a history of liver damage. Thus, even if you don't recognize the word "contraindicate," you can deduce that it means to signal somebody to *not* do something—in this case, liver damage signals a doctor to not prescribe a particular medicine.

You might have highlighted or underlined the sentence as follows:

> *<u>Although</u> Inventium is <u>normally prescribed</u> to relieve severe pain, a <u>history of liver damage</u> in a patient* contraindicates *its use.*

Example Workplace Document Problems

LEVEL 3 SAMPLE QUESTION

MEMORANDUM

FROM: Kathy Jones

TO: All employees

RE: Disposal of waste in copy room

To reduce the company's environmental impact and ensure the security of sensitive information, please dispose of waste in the copy room as follows:

- Printed paper that is **not** marked as "Confidential" or "Restricted" should be placed in the blue recycle bin.
- Printed paper marked as "Confidential" or "Restricted" should be placed in the gray shred bin.
- All other waste should be placed in the trash bin.

Thank you for your help in this regard.

--Kathy

END PROMPT

Question: If an employee wants to dispose of a "Confidential" document, where should he or she put it?
- A. In the blue recycle bin
- B. In the gray recycle bin
- C. In the blue shred bin
- D. In the gray shred bin
- E. In the green trash bin

Explanation: There are a lot of irrelevant details in the passage, so you can approach the problem more efficiently by reading the question first. The question simply asks where an employee should get rid of a "Confidential" document, so that's all you really need to find. The second bullet point states that documents marked as "Confidential" should be placed in the gray shred bin, **so the answer is D**.

LEVEL 5 SAMPLE QUESTION

The following passage comes from a government-run web site explaining health coverage and benefits:

How Much Will You Pay Out-Of-Pocket?

Deductible: This is the initial dollar amount you must pay before your insurance company begins paying for health services. Usually, the higher the deductible, the lower your premium. However, do not choose a deductible so high that you cannot afford to pay it. The contract will dictate the specific amount you pay per year for your family. You must pay a deductible each year, which will vary depending on the number of people covered by the policy.

Coinsurance: Coinsurance is the share or percentage of covered expenses you must pay in addition to the deductible. For example, your policy may pay 80 percent of covered charges after you pay the deductible. You would then pay the remaining 20 percent as coinsurance.

Copayment: A copayment is a specified dollar amount you pay, as a subscriber to a managed care plan, for covered health care services. It is paid to the medical provider at the time the services are rendered.

Premium: The monthly or annual amount you will pay for your insurance policy.

Coordination of Benefits Provision: Even if you have more than one group policy, you cannot receive more benefits than your actual hospital and medical expenses.

Even if a husband and wife each have family coverage under separate group policies, they cannot collect on the same claim twice, even if they have paid two premiums.

Renewal and Premium Increase Provisions: These provisions determine the conditions under which you lose your eligibility, without a medical exam to prove you are in good health.

END PROMPT

Question: A young girl undergoes surgery and a subsequent hospital stay costing a total of $30,000. Her mother and father *each* have a family policy that fully covers the cost of both the surgery and hospital stay. Neither policy stipulates a copayment or coinsurance, and each policy has a coordination of benefits provision. How much in total insurance benefits is the family eligible to collect?

    A. $30,000, because the coordination of benefits provisions prevents collecting on the same claim twice.
    B. $24,000, because the insurance company will pay 80% of the expenses, and the parents will pay the remaining 20%, or $6,000.
    C. $60,000, because each of the parents has a separate policy covering the surgery, they can collect double on the same claim.
    D. $20,000, because each of the parents will pay a maximum of $10,000.
    E. $10,000, because each claim benefit is limited to $10,000.

Explanation: Again, you should start by carefully reading the question. From the question, you know the following: 1) the *total* amount of medical expenses is $30,000, and there is no copayment or coinsurance; 2) each parent has a policy that fully covers the cost, but they have a coordination of benefits provision.

Now, you can begin eliminating the answer choices. B is incorrect because there is no copayment or coinsurance, so the parents will not have to pay a partial amount of the bill. C is incorrect because according to the "Coordination of Benefits Provision," the parents can't collect twice on the same claim. D is incorrect because the document says nothing about a payment maximum. E is incorrect because the claim is only limited by the cost. **This leaves A as the only possible answer.**

LEVEL 7 SAMPLE QUESTION

The following passage is from the Manual of Patent Examining Procedures (MPEP), which explains intellectual property-related rules and regulations in the United States. The passage below concerns rules for filing an international patent application.

Confidential Nature of the International Application.

(1)

> (a)Subject to the provisions of subparagraph (b), the International Bureau and the International Searching Authorities shall not allow access by any person or authority to the international application before the international publication of that application, unless requested or authorized by the applicant.

> (b)The provisions of subparagraph (a) shall not apply to any transmittal to the competent International Searching Authority, to transmittals provided for under Article 13, and to communications provided for under Article 20.

(2)

> (a)No national Office shall allow access to the international application by third parties unless requested or authorized by the applicant, before the earliest of the following dates:

>> (i) date of the international publication of the international application

>> (ii) date of receipt of the communication of the international application under Article 20

>> (iii) date of receipt of a copy of the international application under Article 22

> (b)The provisions of subparagraph (a) shall not prevent any national Office from informing third parties that it has been designated, or from publishing that fact. Such information or publication may, however, contain only the following data: identification of the receiving Office, name of the applicant, international filing date, international application number, and title of the invention.

END PROMPT

Question: Suppose Thompson, Inc. files an international patent application. Prior to the application being published, an employee from Johnson, Inc., a rival firm, asks the patent office in the receiving country about Thompson's application. An employee of the office provides the employee from Johnson with the filing date, title, and a brief summary of the invention. Is this proper, and why?

    A. Yes, because the national office has the authority to inform third parties that the application has been designated.

    B. Yes, because the office employee only released a brief summary of the invention, instead of a detailed description.

    C. No, because the office cannot release any information about an international application to a third party, in accordance with paragraph (2)(a).

    D. No, the office could have released the filing date and title, but not a description of the invention.

    E. No, the office could have released a description of the invention, but not the filing date and title.

Explanation: Begin by reading the question, and the possible answer choices. From the question, you know that the patent office provided the third party with three pieces of information: the filing date, title, and a summary of the invention.

Now read the text. Questions at the higher levels are usually quite complex, so you will probably have to read the whole text to make sure you don't miss anything. From paragraphs (1)(a) and (2)(a), you know that the patent office generally can't allow a third party to access an unpublished international application. However, paragraph (2)(b) says that the office *can* provide a third party with basic information, limited only to the international filing date, application number, and title. This information does not, however, include any description or summaries of the invention. **Thus, the only acceptable answer is D.**

WorkKeys Practice Test #1

Want to take this practice test in an online interactive format?
Check out the bonus page, which includes interactive practice questions and
much more: **mometrix.com/bonus948/workkeys**

Applied Math

1. Matt was picking plums to fill baskets. His first basket held 27 plums, his second basket held 24 plums, and his third basket held 31 plums. How many plums did Matt pick?

    A. 51
    B. 58
    C. 70
    D. 82
    E. 84

2. Each of the 18 students brought 6 cans to the food drive. How many cans of food were collected?

    A. 24
    B. 40
    C. 62
    D. 89
    E. 108

3. Sharon was multiplying a recipe by ½ to get a smaller batch. What decimal should she multiply by each measurement?

    A. 0.5
    B. 0.33
    C. 1.5
    D. 0.25
    E. 0.75

4. It took Morgan 90 minutes to mow and edge the lawn. How many hours is this?

    A. 0.75
    B. 1.25
    C. 1.5
    D. 2.25
    E. 3.5

5. Lucy opened a roll of dimes and counted seven dollars. How many dimes is this?

    A. 70
    B. 55
    C. 35
    D. 140
    E. 85

6. Lexi studied for three quarters of an hour. How many minutes is this?

    A. 15
    B. 45
    C. 60
    D. 30
    E. 75

7. Apples cost 65 cents, muffins cost $1.50, and bottles of water cost $1 each. How much would it cost to get an apple, a muffin, and a bottle of water?

    A. $2.15
    B. $3.15
    C. $5.45
    D. $4.15
    E. $6.45

8. Including tax, Jon's total cost at the theater came to $17.83. If he paid with a $20 bill, how much change should he receive?

    A. $2.17
    B. $4.49
    C. $3.17
    D. $2.86
    E. $3.02

9. According to the pie chart, what percent of Zach's day is spent on eating, chores, and recreation?

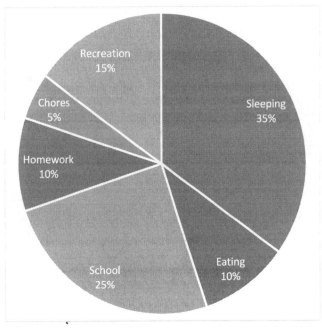

- A. 25%
- B. 30%
- C. 15%
- D. 20%
- E. 35%

10. Last Saturday Jen dug 42 dandelions out of the lawn and was paid 5 cents per plant. The previous Saturday she dug 60 plants, and the Saturday before that she dug 33 dandelions. On average, how many plants did she dig each week?

- A. 51
- B. 46.5
- C. 37.5
- D. 42
- E. 45

11. Add: ¼ + 0. 5 = _____ (decimal answer).

- A. 0.75
- B. 1.25
- C. 0.25
- D. 0.55
- E. 0.625

12. The four siblings each spent ¼ of an hour cleaning their rooms. How much time did they spend altogether?

- A. ¾ of an hour
- B. 1 hour
- C. ½ an hour
- D. 7/8 of an hour
- E. 3/12 of an hour

13. Keisha wants to make a batch of cookies but doesn't have enough chocolate chips, so she decides to multiply each ingredient by 0.75. If the original recipe called for 1 2/3 cups of chocolate chips, how many does she need now?

- A. 1¼ cups
- B. 2 cups
- C. 2 2/9 cups
- D. ¾ cup
- E. 7/9 cup

14. Jacob divided the sum of 6 and -2 into the difference of 22 and 10. What was his answer?

- A. 3
- B. 1.5
- C. 4
- D. 3.4
- E. 5

15. Between the years 2000 and 2010, the number of births in the town of Danville increased from 1432 to 2219. Which of the following is the approximate percent of increase in the number of births during those ten years?

- A. 55%
- B. 36%
- C. 64%
- D. 42%
- E. 48%

16. Suppose Eva has 12 3/4 pounds of flour. The day's baking will require triple that amount. How much flour will Eva need?

- A. 37 lb
- B. 38 1/2 lb
- C. 37 3/4 lb
- D. 38 1/4 lb
- E. 38 1/3 lb

17. If Sara can read 15 pages in 10 minutes, how long will it take her to read 45 pages?

- A. 20 minutes
- B. 30 minutes
- C. 40 minutes
- D. 50 minutes
- E. 55 minutes

18. Ben gave 7/8 of a pear to Gwen and 5/6 of another pear to Mikayla. How much more did Gwen get than Mikayla?

    A. 1/8
    B. 1/12
    C. 1/24
    D. 1/16
    E. 1/32

19. David has a board that is 10 and a half feet long. He needs a piece that is 8 feet and 10 inches for a project. How much should he cut off his board?

    A. 2 ft
    B. 1 ft, 10 in
    C. 2 ft, 6 in
    D. 3 ft
    E. 1 ft, 8 in

20. Almonds were $16.50 for a 3-lb bag. Peanuts were $38.00 for a 10-lb bag. Which is the best deal?

    A. almonds
    B. peanuts
    C. they are an equally good deal
    D. a mix of peanuts and almonds
    E. neither peanuts nor almonds

21. Lucy was given the following problem: $2.135 + 15.6$. She lined up the numbers by their final digit as shown below and obtained an answer of 2.291. What was her mistake?

```
  2.13 5
+   15.6
  2.29 1
```

    A. She did not carry the 1.
    B. She subtracted instead of adding.
    C. She did not position the larger number on top.
    D. She did not borrow from the 3.
    E. She did not align the decimal points.

22. Work is being done on a rectangular section of a street measuring 13 feet by 8 feet. Safety barricade material costing $9.75 per foot must be put around this area. What is the minimum cost to barricade this part of the street?

    A. $204.75
    B. $409.50
    C. $624
    D. $1,014
    E. $1,262

23. On a floor plan drawn at a scale of 1:100, the area of a rectangular room is 30 cm^2. What is the actual area of the room?

    A. 30,000 cm^2
    B. 3,000 cm^2
    C. 3,000 m^2
    D. 30 m^2
    E. 30 cm^2

24. Chan receives a bonus from his job. He pays 30% in taxes, gives 30% to charity, and uses another 25% to pay off an old debt. He has $600 remaining from his bonus. What was the total amount of Chan's bonus?

    A. $3000
    B. $3200
    C. $3600
    D. $4000
    E. $4600

25. A charity organization is preparing a fundraising dinner. The goal is to raise $27,000. They must pay costs of $1,000 to rent the hall for the evening, plus $2,500 in wages for staff and $25.00 per plate of food served. If tickets to the dinner cost $150, how many tickets must the organization sell in order to reach their goal?

    A. 180
    B. 216
    C. 238
    D. 281
    E. 244

26. A five-pound bag of tangerines is $6.95 and a three-pound bag of navel oranges is $4.50. Alyssa needs 15 pounds of the cheaper fruit. How much will she pay?

    A. $20.85
    B. $1.50
    C. $6.95
    D. $1.39
    E. $22.50

27. An Olympic sprinter can run a mile in approximately 4 minutes. On average, how fast must he run to achieve this time? Give your answer in kilometers per hour

    A. 6.8 kph
    B. 9.3 kph
    C. 10.8 kph
    D. 15 kph
    E. 24.2 kph

28. Curtis measured the temperature of water in a flask in Science class. The temperature of the water was 35°C. He carefully heated the flask so that the temperature of the water increased about 2°C every 3 minutes. Approximately how much had the temperature of the water increased after 20 minutes?

    A. 10 °C
    B. 13 °C
    C. 15 °C
    D. 35 °C
    E. 48 °C

29. A certain exam has 30 questions. A student gets 1 point for each question he gets right and loses half a point for a question he answers incorrectly; he neither gains nor loses any points for a question left blank. If C is the number of questions a student gets right and B is the number of questions he leaves blank, which of the following represents his score on the exam?

    A. $C - 1/2\,B$
    B. $C - 1/2\,(30 - B)$
    C. $C + B - 30$
    D. $(30 - C) - 1/2(30 - B)$
    E. $C - 1/2(30 - B - C)$

30. A hexagonal plot of land measures 280 feet long on a side. If you use grass seed at a rate of 50 pounds per acre, how many pounds of grass seed will be needed to seed the entire plot? The area of a hexagon can be found using the formula $A = \frac{3\sqrt{3}}{2} \times a^2$, where a is the length of a side.

    A. 244 lb
    B. 280 lb
    C. 262 lb
    D. 234 lb
    E. 268 lb

31. Carina consigns her children's outgrown clothing at a local consignment shop that awards her 40% of the total sales price. She uses $28 from the proceeds to purchase new clothing for her children and goes home with $64 in cash. How much did her children's old clothing sell for?

    A. $36.80
    B. $55.20
    C. $92
    D. $153.33
    E. $230

32. A bullseye with a 3-inch diameter covers 10 percent of a square target. What is the area, in square inches, of the target?

    A. $.15\pi$
    B. 22.5π
    C. 10.5π
    D. 20π
    E. 28π

33. In the 1600's, Galileo Galilei studied the motion of pendulums and discovered that the period of a pendulum, the time it takes to complete one full swing, is a function of the square root of the length of its string: $2\pi\sqrt{L/g}$, where L is the length of the string and g is the acceleration due to gravity. Consider two pendulums released from the same pivot point and at the same angle, $\theta = 30°$. Pendulum 1 has a mass of 100 g, while Pendulum 2 has a mass of 200 g. If Pendulum 1 has a period four times the period of Pendulum 2, what is true of the lengths of the pendulums' strings?

A. The length of Pendulum 1's string is four times the length of Pendulum 2's string.
B. The length of Pendulum 1's string is eight times the length of Pendulum 2's string.
C. The length of Pendulum 1's string is three times the length of Pendulum 2's string.
D. The length of Pendulum 1's string is less than the length of Pendulum 2's string.
E. The length of Pendulum 1's string is sixteen times the length of Pendulum 2's string.

34. A can has a radius of 1.5 inches and a height of 3 inches. Which of the following best represents the volume of the can?

A. 17.2 in^3
B. 19.4 in^3
C. 21.2 in^3
D. 23.4 in^3
E. 24.3 in^3

Graphic Literacy

Please refer to the following table for the following 2 questions.

On-the-Job Accidents, 2005		
Cause of Accident	Number of Accidents per 100,000 Employees	Average Worker's Compensation Payout
Falls	51	$78,927.00
Electrical	19	$91,324.00
Mechanical	30	$50,704.00
Poisoning or Chemical Exposure	11	$103,029.00
Other	35	$81,000.00
Total Accidents	146	

1. In 2005, what type of on-the-job accident was associated with the highest number of accidents per 100,000 Employees?

    A. Falls
    B. Electrical
    C. Mechanical
    D. Poisoning or Chemical Exposure

2. Which two types of accidents together contributed over half of the total accidents in 2005?

    A. Falls and Electrical
    B. Other and Falls
    C. Mechanical and Other
    D. Electrical and Poisoning or Chemical Exposure

Please refer to the following flowchart for the following 3 questions.

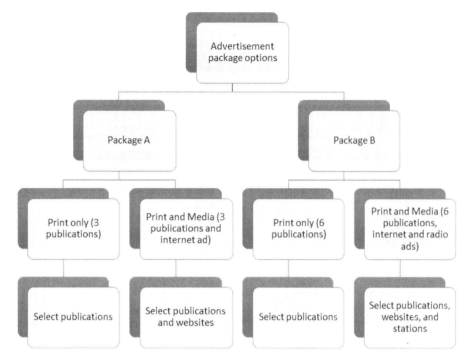

3. What is the first decision a client must make when choosing an advertisement package option?

    A. Whether to select print only ads OR print and media
    B. Whether to select publications only OR publications and websites
    C. Whether to select publications only OR publications, websites, and stations
    D. Whether to select Package A OR Package B

4. How many choices does a client have if he/she selects Package B?

    A. 1
    B. 2
    C. 3
    D. 4

5. If a client selects Package A and decides on the print only option, what is his/her next step?

    A. To choose publications and websites
    B. To choose publications
    C. To choose publications, websites, and stations
    D. To choose print and media options

Please refer to the following flowchart for the following 3 questions.

The flowchart gives the protocol to follow when a client order arrives.

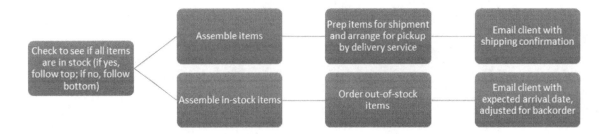

6. **What should be done first if all items are in stock?**
    A. Assemble the in-stock items
    B. Assemble items
    C. Order out-of-stock items
    D. Prep items for shipment

7. **What is the second step if all items are NOT in stock?**
    A. Assemble the in-stock items
    B. Prep items for shipment
    C. Order out-of-stock items
    D. Email client with shipping confirmation

8. **What step follows arranging for a delivery service to pick up the order?**
    A. Email client with shipping confirmation
    B. Prep items for shipment
    C. Order out-of-stock items
    D. Assemble in-stock items

Please refer to the following graph for the following 2 questions.

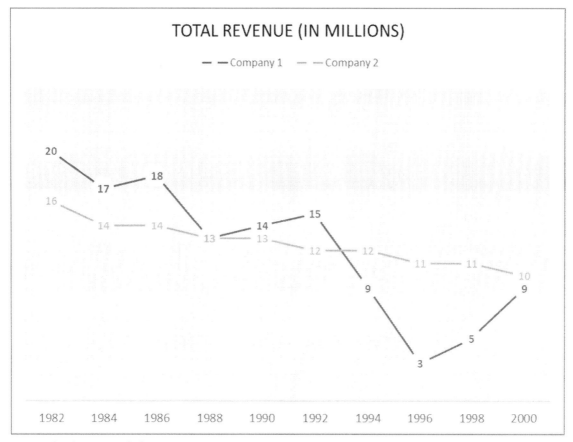

9. In which years did Company 1 not perform as well as company 2?
   A. 1982-1992
   B. 1990-1992
   C. 1992-1996
   D. 1994-2000

10. What was the difference between the revenues of the two companies in 1984?
   A. 7 Million
   B. 3 Million
   C. 8 Million
   D. 5 Million

Please refer to the following flowchart for the following 3 questions.

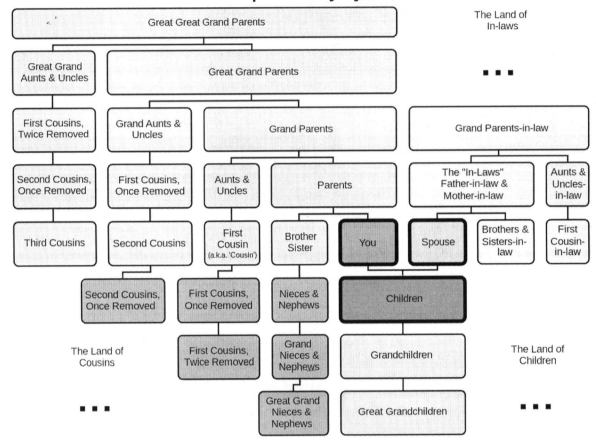

Relatives Explained by Tysen

11. What is the closest relation you can have with a person who is your great grand parents' grandchild?

- A. Second Cousin
- B. Parent
- C. First Cousin, Once Removed
- D. Aunt or Uncle

12. A First Cousin-in-law, Twice Removed is:

- A. Your Great Great Grand Parents' Great Grandchild.
- B. Your Spouse's Second Cousin
- C. Your Great Great Grand Parents-in-laws' Grandchild
- D. Your Grandparents-in-laws' Nieces and Nephews

13. What is your First Cousin, Twice Removed to your Great Grand Parents (closest possible relation)?

- A. A Niece or Nephew
- B. A Third Cousin
- C. A Second Cousin
- D. A Sibling

Please refer to the following diagram for the following 3 questions.

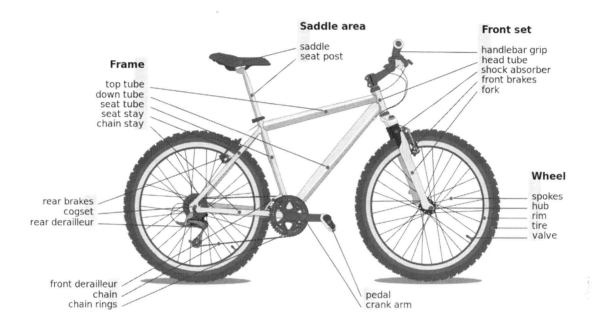

14. Which of the following is true?
    A. The saddle is at approximately the same elevation as the handlebar grip.
    B. The wheel has six listed sub-parts
    C. The seat post is located farther forward than the head tube.
    D. The crank arm is part of the steering mechanism.

15. Which of the following is true?
    A. The shock absorber is at approximately the same elevation as the valve.
    B. A bike has two cogsets, but only one down fork.
    C. A bike has two valves, but only one down tube.
    D. The fork connects the head tube with the rear wheel.

16. The seat stay performs what function?
    A. connecting the crank arm to the cogset
    B. connecting the fork to the head tube
    C. connecting the top tube to the down tube
    D. connecting the rear wheel to the seat tube

17. From the following line graph, what pattern is evident between the variables?

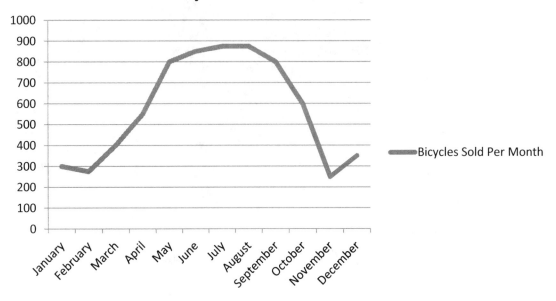

Bicycles Sold Per Month

A. Bicycle sales peak in the winter months.
B. Bicycle sales peak in the summer months.
C. Bicycle sales peak in early spring and late fall.
D. There is no discernible pattern.

18. Jake found a relationship between time of day and number of coffee sales: sales were highest in the early morning before work and school, dropped during the workday, and peaked again between 4:00 and 6:00. Which of the bar graphs below represents this?

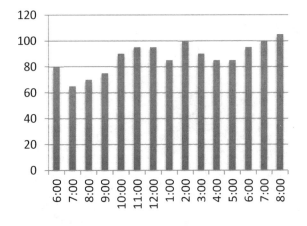

Coffee Sales (Graph 1)

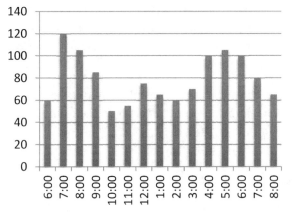

Coffee Sales (Graph 2)

A. Graph 1
B. Graph 2
C. Both graphs are accurate
D. Neither graph is accurate

Use the following charts to answer the following 2 questions.

Diego's company offers a number of paid holidays and vacation days each year.

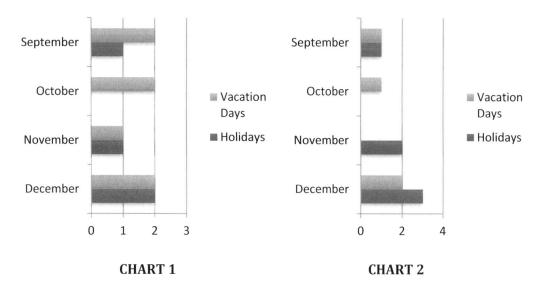

CHART 1   **CHART 2**

19. **Which of the charts shows that Diego did not take any vacation time in November?**
    A. Chart 1
    B. Chart 2
    C. Both are accurate
    D. Neither is accurate

20. **Which of the charts shows that Diego had a total of four days off in December?**
    A. Chart 1
    B. Chart 2
    C. Both are accurate
    D. Neither is accurate

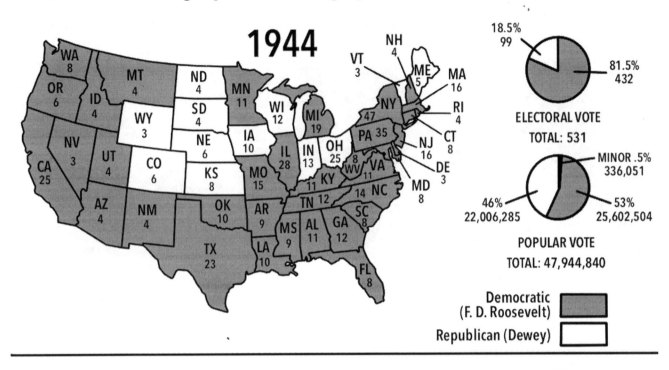

Please refer to the following maps for the following 3 questions.

21. Which of the following is true?

A. Alabama, NJ, and Washington had an increase in electoral votes from 1944 to 1952.

B. Wisconsin, Louisiana, and Idaho had no change in the number of electoral votes from 1944 to 1952.

C. Michigan, Oregon, and Kentucky had no change in the number of electoral votes from 1944 to 1952

D. Arkansas, New York, and Missouri had an increase in electoral votes from 1944 to 1952.

96

22. Which of the following is false?

A. Only nine states voted for the Democratic candidate in 1952.

B. Only eleven states voted for the Republican candidate in 1944.

C. The losing Democratic popular vote in 1952 was higher than the winning Democratic popular vote in 1944.

D. The greatest increase in electoral votes in one state from 1944 to 1952 was in California.

23. Which of the following is true?

A. The total electoral votes increased from 1944 to 1952.

B. No state decreased more than two electoral votes between 1944 and 1952

C. North Dakota, Indiana, and Georgia had no change in electoral votes between 1944 and 1952.

D. Nevada, Utah, and Colorado had an increase in electoral votes between 1944 and 1952.

24. According to the charts below, how many paper products did Megan sell in January?

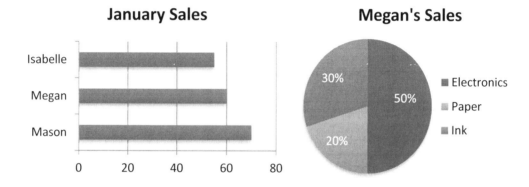

A. 60

B. 30

C. 18

D. 12

Use the chart below to answer the following 2 questions.

Ryan's company has 17 employees and is projecting the costs and benefits of hiring more.

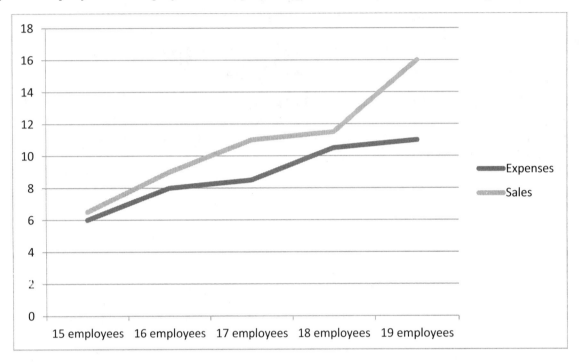

25. Ryan is deciding whether to hire one more employee (for a total of 18). Would this be profitable for the company?

    A. Profitable
    B. Unprofitable
    C. Neutral
    D. Cannot be determined

26. Now Ryan must decide whether to keep the number at 17, add on, or cut back. What is the optimal number of employees on the chart?

    A. 16
    B. 17
    C. 18
    D. 19

Use these charts to answer the following 2 questions.

Penelope created two additional charts, including survey results from a broad demographic.

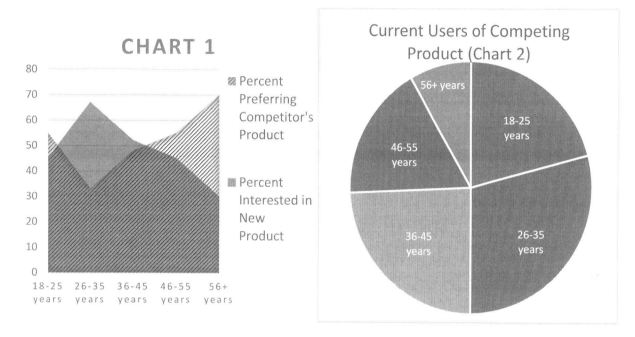

27. Which chart is most effective for showing the demographics for customers of a competitor's product?

    A. Chart 1
    B. Chart 2
    C. Both are effective
    D. Neither is effective

28. Which chart is most effective for showing the target market for the product?

    A. Chart 1
    B. Chart 2
    C. Both are effective
    D. Neither is effective

Use the charts below that detail a company's annual expenses to answer the following 2 questions:

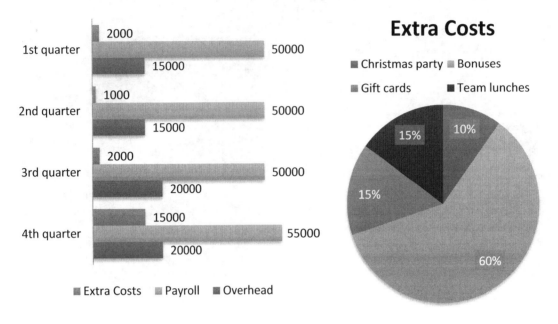

29. How much was spent on team lunches during the year?
    A. $1,500
    B. $3,000
    C. $4,250
    D. $7,500

30. Fourth quarter extra costs included the team Christmas party and $10,000 in bonuses. The rest was devoted to gift cards; how much was spent on gift cards?
    A. $3,000
    B. $5,500
    C. $6,000
    D. $7,150

31. Leigh is deciding whether to open another branch of her company. She is projecting costs and profits over the next year if she does so in the graph below. Should she open the new branch or not, based on the graph?

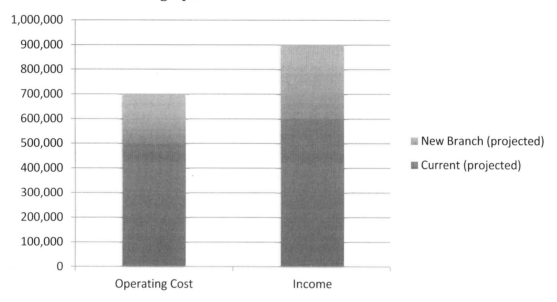

A. Open the new branch
B. Do not open the new branch
C. Wait a year
D. Inconclusive

32. Raul is making dinner plans, choosing from the recipes shown in the graph below. He gets off work at 5:15 and takes 35 minutes to get home. If a friend is coming for dinner at 6:30, can he make the chicken lazone?

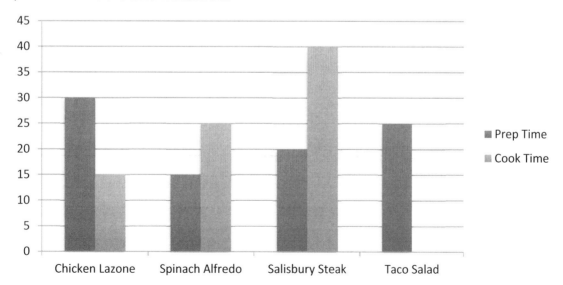

A. He can make the chicken lazone.
B. He cannot make the chicken lazone, but he can make the spinach alfredo or the taco salad.
C. He can only make the taco salad.
D. He cannot make any of the meals.

Use the graph to answer the following 2 questions:

Ramon tracked the number of projects his company received and the profit it made, as well as efficiency, each quarter in the graph below

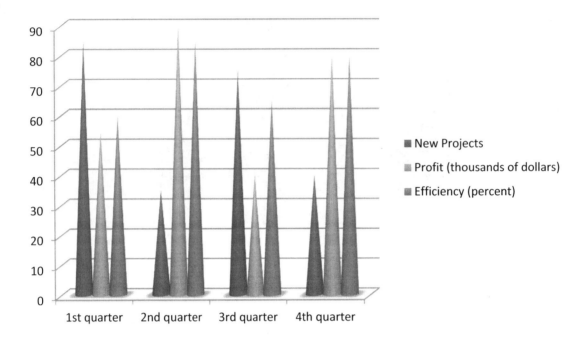

33. **What pattern do you see between new projects and profits? What could cause this?**
   A. Projects and profits rise and fall proportionately, so a greater number of projects leads to greater profit.
   B. Projects and profits rise and fall inversely, so a greater number of projects leads to lower profit.
   C. A spike in projects one quarter is followed by a spike in profit the next, so a greater number of projects leads to greater profit later on.
   D. There is no discernible pattern connecting projects and profits.

34. **What trend can be seen in regards to efficiency? What is a probable cause of this?**
   A. Efficiency rises and falls in direct proportion with new projects, so a greater number of new projects causes greater efficiency.
   B. Efficiency is inversely proportional to new projects, so a greater number of new projects causes lower efficiency.
   C. Efficiency is inversely proportional to profit, so greater profit leads to lower efficiency.
   D. There is no discernible pattern in regards to efficiency.

35. Which of the graphs shows that expenditures steadily decreased throughout the year?

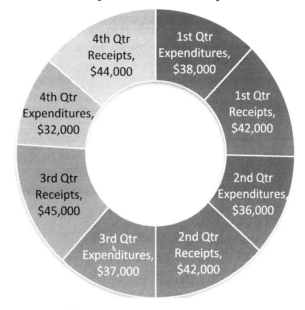

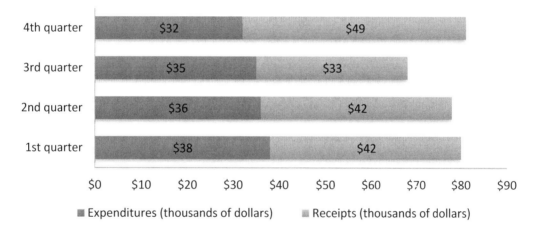

A. The pie chart
B. The bar graph
C. Both graphics
D. Neither graphic

Use the graphics below to answer the following 2 questions:

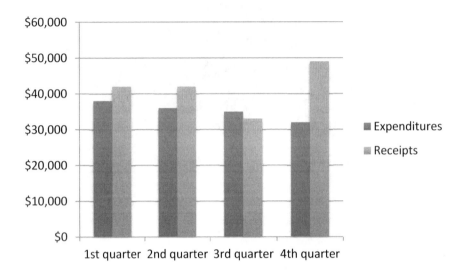

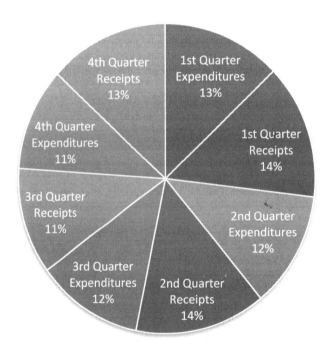

36. Which of the graphics is best for showing the profit per quarter?

    A. The bar graph
    B. The pie chart
    C. Both graphic
    D. Neither graphic

37. Which of the graphics is best for determining the total expenditures and receipts for the year?

- A. The bar graph
- B. The pie chart
- C. Both graphic
- D. Neither graphic

38. Which of the graphs below is most effective for showing that a business trip is justifiable?

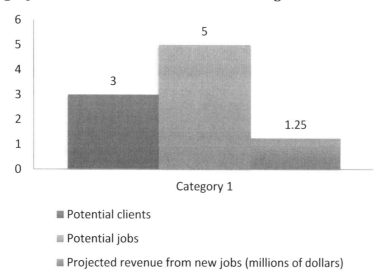

- ■ Potential clients
- ■ Potential jobs
- ■ Projected revenue from new jobs (millions of dollars)

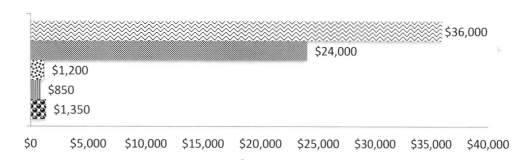

- ⋙ Expected revenue from new job ▦ Expected cost of new job
- ▦ Marketing cost ⫴ Personnel cost
- ▦ Travel cost

- A. the 1st graph
- B. the 2nd graph
- C. both graphs
- D. neither graph

Workplace Documents

1. The following excerpt is from a company memorandum on dress codes. Identify the main idea.

> We need to continue to present a professional image toward clients and the public. It is important that employees use their best judgment in dressing appropriately. Casual business wear encompasses many looks but it really means casual clothing that is appropriate for a professional office environment. It is clothing that allows you to be comfortable at work yet always look neat and professional.

A. Clothing should allow you to be comfortable at work.
B. Appropriate business clothing is casual yet appropriate for a professional environment.
C. Employees should use their best judgment to dress appropriately for the office.
D. Employees should choose business casual clothes that represent the office in a professional way.
E. Clients should see a professional image of company employees.

2. Identify the main idea from the following excerpt:

> As stated in our Supplier Code of Conduct, our employees who are involved in procurement decisions may not accept any business courtesies, with the exception of very low value promotional items. In any business relationship, our suppliers must ensure that the offering or receipt of any gift or business courtesy is permitted by law and regulation; does not violate the rules and standards of the recipient's organization; is consistent with reasonable marketplace customs; and will not adversely impact the reputation of this company.

A. Employees involved in procurement decisions may not accept anything valuable from suppliers.
B. Suppliers must check to be sure that gifts are allowed before giving to employees.
C. If employees accept gifts from suppliers, this can adversely impact the company's reputation.
D. It is important to maintain good business relationships with suppliers.
E. Gifts are not consistent with reasonable marketplace customs.

3. Elena has just been hired and received the memo below. What should she do?

> November 1–30 is open enrollment for insurance. If you have not previously enrolled, or if you wish to make any changes to your policy, please speak to HR by November 28 so that we can make any necessary adjustments. If you do not wish to make any changes, no action is necessary.

A. No action necessary
B. Fill out forms by November 28
C. Read the policy to make changes
D. Speak to HR to enroll
E. Make a list of necessary adjustments

4. What is the deadline for turning in vacation requests, according to the following excerpt?

> All employees who plan on using vacation time between December 20 and January 4: please submit your requests ASAP. Because many of you want to use PTO during this window, we need to plan ahead, so please be sure to turn in requests by December 3. Any requests received after this may not be honored.

A. December 3
B. December 14
C. December 19
D. December 20
E. January 4

5. Identify what "casual business wear" means in the following context:

> We need to continue to present a professional image toward clients and the public. It is important that employees use their best judgment in dressing appropriately. Employees who prefer to dress more formally should feel free to do so. Casual business wear encompasses many looks but it really means casual clothing that is appropriate for a professional office environment. It is clothing that allows you to be comfortable at work yet always look neat and professional. We ask that you consider each day's activities when determining what to wear (i.e., will you be meeting with a client in our office or at their office site; will you be attending a business luncheon, etc.).

A. It allows you to be comfortable at work yet neat.
B. It is casual clothing that is appropriate for a professional office environment.
C. It is appropriate for the day's activities.
D. It is appropriate for meetings or business luncheons.
E. It is determined by the employee's best judgment.

Use the company announcement below to answer the following 3 questions:

> Mark your calendars for December 12! Our annual Christmas party will be held at 6:30pm at The Homesteader. Please bring a small gift ($10 or less) for the gift exchange. RSVP to Elaine by December 3 and let her know if you'll be bringing a significant other. Festive dress is encouraged but not required. Come relax and enjoy some downtime with the team!

6. Identify the main idea.
A. Employees should come to The Homesteader at 6:30pm.
B. The company's annual Christmas party is on December 12.
C. RSVP for the Christmas party by December 3.
D. Bring a small gift to the Christmas party.
E. Bring your significant other to the Christmas party.

7. What two things might an employee bring to the Christmas party?
A. A small gift and festive clothing
B. A calendar and a small gift
C. The invitation and festive clothing
D. A small gift and the invitation
E. A small gift and a significant other

8. When and where is the party?

- A. December 12 at 6:30pm
- B. December 3 at 6:30 pm
- C. December 3 at The Homesteader, 6:30pm
- D. December 12 at the Homesteader, 6:30pm
- E. 6:30pm at the Homesteader

Use the team email below to answer the following 2 questions:

> Thanks to all for being on the call today. Per the client's request, please work on the revisions to Phase 1 of the project. We plan to meet again next Wednesday so please finalize your segment by Tuesday. If you have any questions, please contact your supervisor. Thank you for your hard work.

9. Identify the main idea.

- A. Employees should finalize their portions of the project by Tuesday.
- B. Employees should work on the client's requested project revisions.
- C. Employees should prepare for next Wednesday's meeting.
- D. Phase 1 of the project must be finished by Wednesday.
- E. Employees should work with their supervisors to finish their projects.

10. From the excerpt below, why does each segment of the project need to be finalized by Tuesday?

- A. Because today's call required it
- B. Because the client requested it
- C. So that Phase 1 can be completed
- D. In preparation for the meeting on Wednesday
- E. So that Phase 2 can begin

11. Based on the excerpt below, what is the meaning of "quickcode"?

> Remember to enter your 4-digit quickcode every morning when you arrive at the office. This number is unique to you. Since we don't use a traditional timeclock system, this will verify your time records.

- A. A passcode that allows employees in the building
- B. A method of tracking employee time on the job
- C. A code to log in to company computers
- D. A password to check email
- E. A method of identifying where in the building an employee is

12. Based on the excerpt below, deduce the meaning of "ABCpack."

> When you are assigned a workstation on your first day, log in to the computer using the username and passcode found on page 1 of your ABCpack. You will also need to set up your email account; please see the instructions on page 4 of your ABCpack.

- A. An orientation packet for new employees
- B. A bag containing necessary employee supplies
- C. A computer manual for the company computers
- D. A list of company email addresses
- E. A notepad for company use

13. Based on the excerpt below, infer the meaning of "brown bag class."

This Thursday, May 7, we will be having a brown bag class at 12:00pm. The subject this month is marketing. Please bring your lunch and notebook and meet in the conference room. Drinks and desserts will be provided.

A. A class that is a surprise, with visuals hidden in a brown bag
B. A class on wise shopping
C. A session on healthy lunch ideas to bring to work
D. A learning event that takes place during lunchtime
E. A potluck-style team lunch

14. Based on the excerpt below, what is the meaning of "focus period"?

Please keep a notebook at your desk to use during the focus period each morning. That way you can track any ideas that come to mind, and it is preferable to have the notes close at hand rather than in an electronic document that clutters up your screen. Please take no more than 15 minutes to look through your calendar and email as you create your game plan for the day, taking notes as needed, and then jump into your first task.

A. A mental health exercise time, helping an employee to de-stress
B. A daily team meeting to check in with each other before starting the day's tasks
C. A time to plan out the day, checking to see what events and tasks are coming up
D. A time for employees to organize their desks so they will be more efficient
E. A time to work on solo projects rather than team projects

Use the excerpt below to answer the following 2 questions:

> When filling out your timesheet, be sure to allocate your time to the correct project, with an appropriate description of your activities. Click on the drop-down menu under "Project" and then select the project you worked on (projects are sorted by number). If you worked on multiple projects in a day, you may have several entries. If you were working on a task that spans more than one project, select "908_Multi-Project" and record the applicable project numbers in your work description. Accounting will then allocate the hours as needed for billing. If your work was not related to any particular projects, select "912_Internal/Miscellaneous" and write a thorough description. We seek to keep a minimum of 90% of time on paid projects, so if you have a question about whether your work is project-related, please check with your supervisor.

15. Miguel was told to divide his day between two projects and bill time to both. He spent the first 3 hours of the day on the King Parking Garage project (project number 027-8). Then he spent 2.5 hours working on the Lantana Bridge project (project number 192-6). The final 2.5 hours of the day were spent running software updates that would be used primarily for Project 027-8 but also for a small part of Project 192-6. How should he bill his time for the day?

    A. Divide the final 2.5 hours between the two projects: 4.25 hours to Project 027-8 and 3.75 hours to Project 192-6

    B. All 8 hours to 908_Multi-Project with a description of how his time was spent

    C. 3 hours to Project 027-8, 2.5 hours to Project 192-6, and 2.5 hours to 912_Internal/Miscellaneous with a thorough description

    D. 3 hours to Project 027-8, 2.5 hours to Project 192-6, and 2.5 hours to 908_Multi-Project with a description of how the software will be used

    E. All 8 hours to 912_Internal/Miscellaneous with a thorough description

16. During the morning as Miguel was working on the King Parking Garage project, his supervisor asked him to troubleshoot a fellow employee's computer. Miguel worked on it for 30 minutes and was able to fix it. How should he adjust his time sheet?

    A. He should bill 30 minutes to 908_Multi-Project.

    B. He should bill 30 minutes to 912_Internal-Miscellaneous.

    C. He should continue to bill the King Parking Garage Project.

    D. He should bill 30 minutes to his coworker's project.

    E. He should use his own time since the troubleshooting was not a company project.

Use the excerpt below to answer the following 3 questions:

> When filling out your timesheet, be sure to allocate your time to the correct project, with an appropriate description of your activities. Click on the drop-down menu under "Project" and then select the project you worked on (projects are sorted by number). If you worked on multiple projects in a day, you may have several entries. If you were working on a task that spans more than one project, select "908_Multi-Project" and record the applicable project numbers in your work description. Accounting will then allocate the hours as needed for billing. If your work was not related to any particular projects, select "912_Internal/Miscellaneous" and write a thorough description. We seek to keep a minimum of 90% of time on paid projects, so if you have a question about whether your work is project-related, please check with your supervisor.

17. Katrina is filling out her timesheet. What information does she need for selecting the correct project?

    A. The project number

    B. A description of activities

    C. The login for the project site

    D. Information from her supervisor

    E. The drop-down menu

18. If Katrina's afternoon was spent in a company meeting that addressed three different projects, where should she bill her time?

    A. Divide the time among the three projects.

    B. Bill to 908_Multi-Project and record the three project numbers in the description.

    C. Bill to 912_Internal/Miscellaneous and write a thorough description.

    D. Bill to the biggest of the three projects and write a note so Accounting can allocate the hours.

    E. Refrain from billing and leave a note for Accounting so they can allocate the hours.

19. How much time should the average employee spend on paid projects from clients?

    A. 85%

    B. 100% for the production team, 70% for supervisors

    C. A maximum of 90%

    D. A minimum of 90%

    E. At least 60%

Use the excerpt below to answer the following 2 questions:

> Attention all employees: the office will be open all week (December 19–23, 8:00–5:00). However, due to the forecast for heavy snow toward the end of the week, plans may change. So keep an eye on your email: if the weather makes driving prohibitive, work may be cancelled and we will use the extra holiday time for the year. You will receive an ABCalert no later than 6:30am if work is cancelled. If the office is open but you feel unsafe driving, you may use vacation time for however much of the day you miss. To date we have two unused variable holidays, and as you know, any unassigned holiday time at the end of the year will be paid out as a bonus.

20. What is an ABCalert?

    A. A mass text in case of bad weather

    B. A call directing employees to stay home

    C. A notification if an employee has sufficient vacation time to miss work

    D. An email sent out to let employees know if work is cancelled

    E. A call or text directly employees to come in to the office

21. What is a variable holiday?

    A. A holiday that an employee worked earlier in the year, so it can now be used

    B. Vacation time that functions as a holiday

    C. Extra holiday time that can be used at different times of the year as needed

    D. Holiday time rolled over from last year

    E. Vacation time rolled over from last year

Use the excerpt below to answer the following 3 questions:

> Refer to the project schedule below to track your progress. Note that any internal revisions will add at least one day to the schedule and any client revisions will add at least two days.

Setup	2 days (complete Tuesday, January 24)
Phase 1	5 days (complete Tuesday, January 31)
Phase 2	5 days (complete Tuesday, February 7)
Phase 3	4 days (complete Monday, February 13)
Closeout	1 day (complete Tuesday, February 14)

22. Kierstin received an email from the client, requesting a revision to Phase 2 that will add 1 day of production work and ½ day of QA/QC. What is the new final completion date?

- A. February 7
- B. February 16
- C. February 13
- D. February 17
- E. February 15

23. Kierstin ordered the software for the project on January 20, but the shipment was delayed and did not arrive until January 25. The team began setup on the following day. How many days of work will they need to make up to stay on schedule?

- A. 1½ days
- B. 2 days
- C. ½ day
- D. 1 day
- E. 3 days

24. Kierstin's team discovered that part of Phase 3 would take an extra four hours to complete. What day will they complete Phase 3?

- A. February 7
- B. February 8
- C. February 12
- D. February 13
- E. February 14

Use the excerpt below to answer the following 3 questions:

> On February 23, our shareholders will vote concerning the proposed merger. There is no current plan for downsizing or terminating any positions as the two companies join. Locations of various positions are yet to be determined. Many of you have elected to receive company stock in place of bonuses in the past and may be wondering how you will be affected. If the merger is approved and consummated, each existing Common Share will be converted into the right to receive $187.00 net cash per share, should you desire to cash out your shares.

25. If the merger takes place, will employees have to sell their shares?
  A. Yes, because they will no longer have rights to them.
  B. Yes, because the company is being bought out.
  C. Yes, because the new company will be issuing new stock.
  D. No, because company employees cannot sell company stock.
  E. No, because they can choose not to sell.

26. Can employees expect to remain at the current office?
  A. Yes, because jobs will not be eliminated.
  B. No, because downsizing is expected.
  C. No, because locations for various jobs are not yet certain.
  D. Yes, because the companies are merging rather than being bought.
  E. No, because employees are selling their stock.

27. Can employees trust that their jobs will remain if the merger takes place?
  A. Yes, because there will be no downsizing or terminating.
  B. No, because locations have yet to be determined.
  C. No, because there is no assurance against downsizing and terminating.
  D. Yes, because the excerpt would let them know if jobs were being cut.
  E. No, because the company was bought out.

Use the excerpt below to answer the following 2 questions:

> We are testing a number of potential methods of website optimization, including customizing pop-ups and improving site navigation. Our goal is to increase our client base by 10% through this, so we will be holding weekly progress meetings to discuss findings. Your team will be implementing A/B testing. Please submit your two proposed website versions by Friday. Then you will upload both and track the responses to each in several areas: number of hits, length of visit, and successful client gain. This will be a two-week trial period to find the best fit.

28. What is website optimization?
  A. A way of adjusting the website to improve sales
  B. A way of improving site navigation
  C. A way of implementing A/B testing
  D. A series of weekly progress meetings
  E. Two different website version to optimize client response

29. What is A/B testing?

    A. A customization of a website so that each client sees a unique version
    B. A comparison of two potential websites to see which is optimal for client gain
    C. A dual website, in which clients see one version and potential clients see another
    D. A test of which products are most appealing to clients
    E. A test of how many of various types of products are purchased each month

Use the excerpt below to answer the following 2 questions:

> As the holiday season approaches, we would like to remind you of our Supplier Code of Conduct. Our employees who are involved in procurement decisions may not accept any gifts, with the exception of very low value promotional items. As in any business relationship, our suppliers must ensure that the offering or receipt of any gift or business courtesy does not violate the rules and standards of the recipient's organization. We look forward to continuing a long and mutually beneficial business relationship and appreciate your cooperation on this.

30. Kelli works in accounts receivable and a client gave her a $50 gift card to her favorite restaurant as a Christmas gift. Can she accept it?

    A. Yes, because she is not involved in procurement decisions.
    B. No, because it is a valuable gift and she may be tempted to show preferential treatment.
    C. Yes, because it is not a personal gift or cash.
    D. No, because employees may not accept any gift or business courtesy.
    E. Yes, because it will help preserve good relationships with the client.

31. Kelli's client asks to take her to an expensive restaurant as thanks for her help with a project. The client assures her that this will not break the rule since it is not a tangible gift that she can redeem for real value. Is this reasonable?

    A. Yes, because she is not involved in procurement decisions.
    B. No, because employees may not accept any gift or business courtesy.
    C. Yes, because it has no cash value.
    D. No, because it is still a valuable business courtesy.
    E. Yes, because it will help preserve good relationship with the client.

Use the excerpt below to answer the following 3 questions:

> When you receive a client email, respond within two hours, if at all possible, to confirm that you have received the email and will be responding fully as soon as possible. Of course, if the client is asking a simple question, you can answer in full immediately. Always CC your supervisor and archive all emails in the appropriate project folder. If a client is sending files, open each one and save in the appropriate folder on the M-drive with our naming convention and the proper project number. NOTE FOR THIS WEEK: the library project is on a very tight schedule and is our top priority. If necessary, we will push back deadlines on other projects, though we will continue to progress as much as possible on them.

32. Lindsay is working on Project 299-01 (Springtown Library) and receives an email from a different client about a new project that is scheduled to start in two weeks. The client wants to know if Lindsay can start working on it this week. How should she respond?

    A. She should accept, because it is important to meet the client's expectations.
    B. She should decline, because the schedule is already set.
    C. She should accept, because starting sooner means it can be finished (and paid) sooner.
    D. She should decline, because she doesn't yet have all the files.
    E. She should decline, because the library project is the top priority.

33. As a follow-up to a project, Lindsay receives a client email that does not contain any pertinent project information but instead is just a note touching base and inquiring about her family. Should she archive it with the other emails?

    A. Yes, because it might become pertinent later.
    B. Yes, so there will be a record of all communication with the client.
    C. Yes, because it was done on company time.
    D. No, because it is not pertinent to the project.
    E. No, because the client would not want it saved.

34. Lindsay's client sends a new batch of files in a zipped folder. All files have already been named according to the company's naming convention, with the correct project number. Since she doesn't need to rename them, can she simply save all the files to the correct folder in the M-drive? Why or why not?

    A. No, because she needs to verify that the files are all correctly labeled and are all present.
    B. Yes, because the client has already done the necessary work.
    C. No, because the client expects her to read each file.
    D. Yes, because this will give her more time to spend on actual production.
    E. No, because she needs to send the proper files to each team member.

Answer Key and Explanations for Test #1

Applied Math

1. D: The word problem asks for the total number of plums in the three baskets, so we convert the word problem to an addition equation. So $27 + 24 + 31 = n$, where n is the sum total of plums. Since $27 + 24 + 31 = 82$, Matt picked 82 plums.

2. E: To find the total number of cans, we need to multiply the number of cans each student brought by the number of students. So $18 \times 6 = n$, where $n =$ the total number of cans. Since $18 \times 6 = 108$, a total of 108 cans were collected.

3. A: The fraction ½ can be converted to the decimal 0.5 by dividing the denominator (2) into the numerator (1).

4. C: There are 60 minutes in an hour, so we convert minutes to hours by dividing by 60. Since $\frac{90}{60} = \frac{3}{2}$, which can be written as the mixed number 1½, we know that 90 minutes is 1½ hours, or 1.5 hours.

5. A: A dollar has 10 dimes, so we find the number of dimes by multiplying the number of dollars by 10. Since $7 \times 10 = 70$, Lucy has 70 dimes.

6. B: Three quarters is the fraction ¾. Since an hour is 60 minutes, we multiply 60 by ¾: $60 \times 3 \div 4 = 45$. So, three quarters of an hour is 45 minutes.

7. B: To add the three costs, we need to write them all in the same format. We rewrite 65 cents as 0.65 and $1 as 1.00. Then we can add 0.65, 1.50, and 1.00 by lining up the decimal points. The sum of these numbers is 3.15, so the total cost is $3.15.

8. A: To find the change, we subtract the total cost from $20. Since $20.00 - 17.83 = 2.17$, Jon should receive $2.17 in change.

9. B: Zach spends 10% of the day on eating, 5% on chores, and 15% on recreation. Adding $(10 + 5 + 15)$ yields 30, so Zach spends 30% of his day on these pursuits.

10. E: We calculate the average number of plants by finding the total and dividing by the number of weeks. Since $\frac{42+60+33}{3} = 45$, Jen dug an average of 45 dandelions per week.

11. A: First we need to convert the fraction to a decimal so we can add them together. The decimal equivalent of ¼ is 0.25 (this is a commonly recognized decimal, but it can be calculated by dividing 1 by 4). Then we line up the decimal points and add: $0.25 + 0.5 = 0.75$.

12. B: We find the total by adding the fractions. Since there were four people and each spent ¼ of an hour, we add ¼ + ¼ + ¼ + ¼. The fractions have a common denominator so we add the numerators and place the sum over the denominator. Since $1 + 1 + 1 + 1 = 4$, we obtain 4/4, which reduces to 1/1 or simply 1. So, the siblings spent a total of 1-hour cleaning.

13. A: To find the required amount of chocolate chips, we multiply the original amount by 0.75. Before we can multiply, we need both numbers to be in the same format. We can convert 0.75 to a fraction by placing 75 over 100 and reducing. Both 75 and 100 are divisible by 25, so the fraction is

116

¾. Then we change $1\frac{2}{3}$ to an improper fraction by multiplying the denominator by the whole number, adding the numerator, and placing this new number over the original denominator: $3 \times 1 + 2 = 5$, so our improper fraction is $\frac{5}{3}$. Then we can multiply $\frac{3}{4} \times \frac{5}{3}$ by multiplying the numerators ($3 \times 5 = 15$) and denominators ($4 \times 3 = 12$). Placing the new numerator and denominator together yields $\frac{15}{12}$, which we can convert back into a mixed number by dividing the denominator into the numerator. Dividing 15 by 12 yields 1 with a remainder of 3, so our mixed number is $1\frac{3}{12}$. We can reduce the fraction by dividing both numerator and denominator by 3 to obtain ¼, so Keisha needs $1\frac{1}{4}$ cups of chocolate chips.

14. A: The order of operations is PEMDAS: parentheses, exponents, multiplication/division, addition/subtraction. We first write the equation in order so we can see where these operations are. We can write the sum of 6 and -2 as $6 + -2$ or simply $6 - 2$. We can write the difference of 22 and 10 as $22 - 10$. Then we write these two operations as a division problem: $\frac{22-10}{6-2}$. We compute the numerator ($22 - 10 = 12$) and denominator ($6 - 2 = 4$) and rewrite the division: $\frac{12}{4}$. Since $\frac{12}{4} = 3$, Jacob's answer is 3.

15. A: Begin by subtracting 1432 from 2219. The result is 787. Then, divide 787 by 1432 to find the percent of increase: 0.549, or 54.9%. Rounded up, this is approximately a 55% increase in births between 2000 and 2010.

16. D: Multiplying $12\frac{3}{4}$ by 3 equals $36\frac{9}{4}$, or $38\frac{1}{4}$ pounds of flour.

17. B: Establishing the proportion and solving for x:

$$\frac{15}{10} = \frac{45}{x}$$
$$15x = 450$$
$$x = 30$$

18. C: To find the difference in the two portions, we subtract the fractions. Before we can subtract them, they must share a common denominator. We find the common denominator by calculating the least common multiple of 8 and 6. The smallest number that both can divide into is 24, so now we rewrite each fraction with a denominator of 24. Since $\frac{24}{8} = 3$, we multiply $\frac{7}{8}$ by $\frac{3}{3}$ to obtain $\frac{21}{24}$. Since $\frac{24}{6} = 4$, we multiply $\frac{5}{6}$ by $\frac{4}{4}$ to obtain $\frac{20}{24}$. Then we can subtract $\frac{21}{24} - \frac{20}{24}$ to obtain $\frac{1}{24}$. So, Gwen had $\frac{1}{24}$ of a pear more than Mikayla.

19. E: To find the amount to cut off, we need to subtract. We know that half of a foot is 6 inches, so we are subtracting (10 ft, 6 in) − (8 ft, 10 in). We first need to borrow to subtract the inches, since 10 is greater than 6. We borrow one foot (12 inches), rewriting the problem as (9 ft, 18 in) − (8 ft, 10 in). Then we can subtract feet and inches to obtain 1 ft, 8 in. So, David should cut 1 ft, 8 in off his board.

20. B: To compare the prices, we need to find the unit price of each (in this case, the price per pound). We find the price of almonds by dividing 16.50 by 3 to obtain $5.50 per pound. We find the price of peanuts by dividing 38.00 by 10 to obtain $3.80 per pound. Since $3.80 is less than $5.50, peanuts are the best deal.

21. E: When adding decimals, we line up the decimal points rather than the final digits. Aligning the decimal places would yield 17.735.

22. B: Use the formula for finding the perimeter of a rectangle:

$$perimeter = 2(length + width)$$
$$= 2(13 + 8)$$
$$= 2(21)$$
$$= 42 \text{ ft}$$

Then multiply by the cost of the safety barricade material per foot: $42 \times \$9.75 = \$409.50$

23. D: Since there are 100 cm in a meter, on a 1:100 scale drawing, each centimeter represents one meter. Therefore, an area of one square centimeter on the drawing represents one square meter in actuality. Since the area of the room in the scale drawing is 30 cm², the room's actual area is 30 m².

Another way to determine the area of the room is to write and solve an equation, such as this one: $\frac{l}{100} \times \frac{w}{100} = 30 \text{ cm}^2$, where l and w are the dimensions of the actual room

$$\frac{lw}{10,000} = 30 \text{ cm}^2$$

$$\text{Area} = 300,000 \text{ cm}^2$$

Since this is not one of the answer choices, convert cm² to m²:

$$300,000 \text{ cm}^2 \times \frac{1 \text{ m}}{100 \text{ cm}} \times \frac{1 \text{ m}}{100 \text{ cm}} = 30 \text{ m}^2.$$

24. D: The correct answer is $4000. Chan has paid out a total of 85% (30% + 30% + 25%) of his bonus for the items in the question. So, the $600 is the remaining 15%. To find out his total bonus, solve: $\frac{100}{15} \times 600 = \$4000$.

25. E: Translate the problem into an algebraic equation, and let x equal the number of tickets sold and therefore the number of plates of food that must be purchased. Then the desired profit will equal $27,000 = \$150(x) - \$25(x) - \$1000 - \$2500$. That is, the profit will equal the revenues per plate, minus the cost per plate and the fixed costs of the hall and staff. Simplifying this equation, $27,000 = (\$150 - \$25)x - \$3500$. Solving for x yields: $x = \frac{\$30,500}{\$125} = 244$.

26. A: To find which fruit is cheaper, we find the unit price (cost per pound) of each. We divide $6.95 by 5 to find that one pound of tangerines costs $1.39. We divide $4.50 by 3 to find that one pound of navel oranges costs $1.50. Since tangerines have a lower unit price, we multiply $1.39 by 15 to find that Alyssa will pay $20.85.

27. E: Convert miles per minute to kilometers per hour using the conversion rates given:

$$\frac{1 \text{ mile}}{4 \text{ minutes}} \times \frac{1 \text{ km}}{0.62 \text{ miles}} = \frac{1 \text{ km}}{2.48 \text{ minutes}} \times \frac{60 \text{ minutes}}{1 \text{ hour}} = \frac{60 \text{ km}}{2.48 \text{ hours}} = 24.2 \text{ kph}$$

28. B: The water temperature increased by about 2° every 3 minutes, or $\frac{2}{3}$ of a degree every minute. Multiplying the increase in degrees per minute by the total number of minutes yields

$$\frac{2°}{3 \text{ min}} \times 20 \text{ min} = \frac{40°}{3}, \text{ or } 13.33°$$

Since the problem asks for the increase in temperature and not the total temperature that results after the increases, 13 is the closest to our answer.

29. E: If the exam has 30 questions, and the student answered C questions correctly and left B questions blank, then the number of questions the student answered incorrectly must be $30 - B - C$. He gets one point for each correct question, or $1 \times C = C$ points, and loses $\frac{1}{2}$ point for each incorrect question, or $\frac{1}{2}(30 - B - C)$ points. Therefore, one way to express his total score is $C - \frac{1}{2}(30 - B - C)$.

30. D: Using the given formula, the area of the plot of land is:

$$A = \frac{3\sqrt{3}}{2} \times a^2 = 2.598 \times (280 \text{ ft})^2 = 203,689 \text{ ft}^2$$

Converting this to acres, we get $203,689 \times \frac{1 \text{ acre}}{43,560 \text{ ft}} = 4.676$ acres. At 50 pounds of seed per acre, the land will require $50 \times 4.676 = 234$ pounds of seed.

31. E: Carina's proceeds from the sale was $28 + 64 = 92$. This was 40% of the total sales price. The total sales price can be calculated by dividing \$92 by 0.40, or multiplying \$92 by 2.5, resulting in \$230.

32. B: First calculate the area of the bullseye:

$$A = \pi r^2$$
$$= \pi \left(\frac{3 \text{ in}}{2}\right)^2$$
$$= \pi (1.5 \text{ in})^2$$
$$= 2.25\pi \text{ in}^2$$

Then, let x = the area of the target, and since 10 percent of $x = 2.25\pi$:

$$0.1x = 2.25\pi \text{ in}^2$$
$$x = 22.5\pi \text{ in}^2$$

33. E: The period of the pendulum is a function of the square root of the length of its string and is independent of the mass of the pendulum or the angle from which it is released. If the period of Pendulum 1's swing is four times the period of Pendulum 2's swing, then the length of Pendulum 1's string must be 16 times the length of Pendulum 2's swing since all other values besides L in the expression $2\pi\sqrt{\frac{L}{g}}$ remain the same.

34. C: The volume of a cylinder may be calculated using the formula $V = \pi r^2 h$, where r represents the radius and h represents the height. Substituting 1.5 for r and 3 for h gives $V = \pi(1.5)^2(3)$, which simplifies to $V \approx 21.2$.

Graphic Literacy

1. A: Falls being the cause of accident constituted 51 of the 146 accidents. This is more than any other category.

2. B: The number of 'Falls' and 'Other' accidents combined is $51 + 35 = 86$. Half the total accidents is $\frac{146}{2} = 73$. 86 is greater than 73.

3. D: The first set of options under "Advertisement package options" includes Package A and Package B. So, the client must first decide between these two options.

4. B: Under "Package B" we can see two options: print only or print and media.

5. B: The step below "Print only" in Package A is "Select publications."

6. B: The top row gives the protocol to be followed if all items are in stock. The first step is to assemble the items from the client order.

7. C: The bottom row gives the protocol to be followed if all items are not in stock. The second step is to order the out-of-stock items.

8. A: Arranging for delivery service is the second step in the top row. The third step is emailing the client with shipping confirmation.

9. D: Company 1 had a revenue of 9, 3, 5, and 9 million in 1994, 1996, 1998, and 2000 respectively. These are lower than Company 2, which never had a revenue less than 10 million during that time period.

10. B: Revenue for Company 1 was 17 million and revenue for Company 2 was 14 million. $17 - 14 = 3$ million.

11. B: Your great grand parents' grandchild could be your first cousin (once removed), aunt or uncle, or parent. The closest is parent.

12. C: Your relationship to any one on your spouse's side is the same as it is on your side with the added '-in-law'. Finding the equivalent relation on your side then adding the '-in-law' gives the answer of your great-great-grandparents-in-laws' grandchild.

13. A: First cousins, twice removed shows up twice in the diagram. Relating them to the great-grandparents makes them either niece or nephew or great-great-great-grandchildren. The closest of these would be niece or nephew.

14. A: The wheel has five listed subparts, the seat post is behind the head tube, and the crank arm is part of the pedal. The only true statement is that the saddle is at approximately the same elevation as the handlebar grip.

15. C: The shock absorber is above the valve, a bike has only one cogset, and the fork connects the head tube to the front wheel. The only true statement is that a bike has two valves (one on each wheel), but only one down tube.

16. D: The seat stay has no connection to the crank arm, fork, or down tube. It connects the rear wheel to the seat tube.

17. B: From the line graph, we can see that the number of bicycles sold rises sharply in March-May, peaks in July and August, and declines sharply in September-November. A pattern we can deduce is that more bicycles are sold during the summer months than the winter.

18. B: We are looking for a graph with high points in the morning before 8:00 and between 4:00 and 6:00, with a dip between these points. The second graph has a high point at 7:00am and a second peak at 5:00, with lower values in between, so this graph is a more accurate representation of the data.

19. B: The first chart shows that Diego had one vacation day and one paid holiday in November. The second chart shows that he had two paid holidays but no vacation days in November. So, the second chart is the accurate representation.

20. A: The first chart shows that Diego had two vacation days and two holidays, for a total of four days off. The second chart shows that he had two vacation days and three holidays, for a total of five days off. So, the first chart is the accurate representation.

21. B: Alabama and NJ had the same number of votes both years. The number of votes for Michigan and Kentucky changed between 1944 and 1952. Arkansas, New York and Kentucky all had a decrease in votes. The only true statement is that Wisconsin, Louisiana, and Idaho had no change in the number of electoral votes from 1944 to 1952.

22. B: There were 12 states that voted for the Republican candidate in 1944. The other statements are all accurate.

23. C: The total number of electoral votes was the same for both years, PA decreased by 3 votes, and Nevada, Utah, and Colorado all had the same number of votes each year. The only true statement is that North Dakota, Indiana, and Georgia had no change in votes.

24. D: From the first chart, we see that Megan sold a total of 60 products in January. From the second graph, we find that 20% of Megan's sales were paper products. So, we calculate 20% of 60 to determine that Megan sold 12 paper products.

25. B: The profit is determined by how far sales exceed expenses. The current gap between sales and profits (at 17 employees) is greater than it would be at 18 employees, so it would not be profitable to hire one more employee.

26. D: Profit is determined by how far sales exceed expenses. The largest gap between sales and expenses occurs with 19 employees, so 19 is the optimal number on this chart.

27. B: Both charts include users of a competitor's product. The first chart specifically addresses which of these users would be interested in switching to the new product, while the second chart focuses on the demographics of the users of the competitor's product. So, the second chart is most effective for this purpose.

28. A: Both charts make use of demographics. The first chart specifically addresses which of these users would be interested in switching to the new product, while the second chart focuses on the demographics of the users of the competitor's product. So, the first chart is most effective for this purpose.

29. B: From the second chart, we know that team lunches make up 15% of the extra costs. We can add up the extra costs from the first chart: 2,000 + 1,000 + 2,000 + 15,000 = 20,000. Then we can calculate 15% of 20,000. Since 0.15(20,000) = 3,000, the company spent $3,000 on team lunches during the year.

30. A: We see in the second chart that the Christmas party makes up 10% of the extra costs. From the first chart we can add up the extra costs from the first chart:

$$\$2,000 + \$1,000 + \$2,000 + \$15,000 = \$20,000$$

Then we can calculate 10% of 20,000. Since 0.10($20,000) = $2,000, the company spent $2,000 on the Christmas party. We see in the first chart that $15,000 was spent on extra costs in the 4th quarter, so we can subtract $2,000 for the Christmas party and $10,000 for bonuses to find that $3,000 was spent on gift cards.

31. A: To decide whether to open the new branch, we need to determine whether the profit would increase or decrease with the new business. Profit is the difference between the income and the operating cost. The current income is $600,000 and the current operating cost is $500,000, so the current profit is $100,000. With the new branch, the projected income is $900,000 and the projected operating cost is $700,000, so the projected profit is $200,000. This means that opening a new branch would bring an additional projected $100,000 profit, so based on these numbers it would be a good idea to open the new branch.

32. B: If Raul leaves work at 5:15 and takes 35 minutes to get home, he will arrive at 5:50. This leaves him 40 minutes until 6:30. The chicken lazone takes 30 minutes to prepare and 15 to cook, for a total of 45 minutes. So Raul will not have time to make the chicken lazone. The spinach alfredo takes 40 minutes (15 minutes to prepare and 25 to cook) and the taco salad takes 25 minutes, so Raul can make either of these dishes.

33. C: The number of new projects and profit seems to be inversely proportional: when one is high, the other is low, and vice versa. A possible explanation is that projects are often paid weeks or months after they are received, so the profit associated with the new projects does not appear in the same quarter. So a large number of new projects in one quarter leads to a raise in the amount of profit the next quarter and a small number of new projects in a quarter is followed by small profit in the next quarter.

34. B: The company's efficiency is highest in the 2nd and 4th quarters and lowest in the 1st and 3rd. This inversely relates to the number of new projects, so a likely explanation is that efficiency is lower when a larger number of new projects are taken on.

35. B: In the first graph, we can see that the expenditures in the 3rd quarter are higher than in the 2nd quarter, so this is not consistent with a steady decrease. In the second graph, we see that each quarter's expenditures are less than the previous quarter, so the second graph accurately represents the data.

36. A: The profit is the difference between receipts and expenditures. In the first graph, it can be seen more easily because it is the difference in height of the two bars for each quarter. The second chart is more challenging for this purpose because it is difficult to see the difference in receipts and expenditures each quarter, as well as being listed in percentages rather than dollar amounts. So, the first graph is the most effective for this purpose.

37. A: The first graph is better because the amount of each quarter's expenditures and receipts can be added to find the total. The second chart only measures percentages rather than actual figures so the totals cannot be determined.

38. B: The first graph does a good job of projecting possible benefits of the trip, but doesn't fully justify it because it does not address the expense and project whether it will actually be profitable (for instance, even with large revenue a job can still lose money). The second graph projects specific costs and revenues so that a projected profit can be calculated. Subtracting all of the costs from the expected revenue leaves an expected profit of $8,600, so this graph justifies the business trip.

Workplace Documents

1. D: The main point of a paragraph can often be found in the opening sentence so that is a good place to look first. The first sentence tells the reader that it is important that employees are able to present a professional image toward those who may see them. We can read through the rest of the paragraph to see that this image is created by the way a person dresses. The fourth sentence restates the idea of a professional image, explaining what it means in this setting: "Casual business wear encompasses many looks but it really means casual clothing that is appropriate for a professional office environment." So, the main point of the paragraph is that employees should choose business casual clothes that will represent the office in a professional way.

2. A: The opening sentence clearly states the main idea: employees involved in procurement may not accept anything except "very low value promotional items" from suppliers.

3. D: Elena falls into the category of "not previously enrolled," so she should speak to HR by November 28 to enroll.

4. A: The second sentence explains that requests must be turned in by December 3.

5. B: We can find the phrase "casual business wear" in the 4th sentence, defined as "casual clothing that is appropriate for a professional office environment."

6. B: From the first sentence we can gather that a significant event will be taking place on December 12. The second sentence tells us that this event is the annual Christmas party. So, the main idea is that the company's annual Christmas party is coming up on December 12.

7. E: The third sentence suggests bringing a gift for the gift exchange, and the fourth sentence mentions bringing a significant other.

8. D: We can find the details in the first two sentences: the party is at 6:30pm on December 12 at The Homesteader.

9. B: The first sentence tells us that there was a call today that concerned all the recipients of the email. We can gather from the next sentence that the call was with a client, who requested revisions to a project. So, the main idea is that the team is to work on the client's requested revisions. The remainder of the paragraph gives more details on the work to be done.

10. D: We see in the third sentence that segments must be finalized by Tuesday. The reason is in the first part of the sentence: there will be a meeting on Wednesday, so the work must be completed first.

11. B: We see from the first sentence that a quickcode is something to use every morning at work, and from the third sentence we can infer that it is used as a substitute for a timeclock system. So we deduce that a quickcode is used to track employee time on the job.

12. A: The ABCpack contains both a new employee's login information and instructions on setting up an email account. We can deduce that the ABCpack is an orientation packet for new employees.

13. D: From the first sentence, we see that a brown bag class is a company event taking place at noon on Thursday, so we can guess that it is a learning event during lunchtime. This is confirmed by the second and third sentences, which give the subject of the class and direct employees to bring lunches.

14. C: We can see from the first sentence that a focus period is something that occurs each morning, and the third sentence gives more details: a time (up to 15 minutes) to plan out the day and see what events and tasks are coming up.

15. D: Miguel spent 3 hours on Project 027-8 and 2.5 hours on project 192-6, so he should bill those hours accordingly. The final 2.5 hours should be billed to 908_Multi-Project with a description of how the software will be used, and the accounting department will add the hours to the appropriate invoices.

16. B: The 30 minutes cannot to billed to the project since Miguel was not working on it (or any other project). He will need to bill half an hour to 912_Internal/Miscellaneous.

17. A: We see in the second sentence that projects are sorted by number, so Katrina will need to know the project number to find it in the drop-down menu.

18. B: She should bill her time to 908_Multi-Project and record the three project numbers in the description.

19. D: The final sentence states that a minimum of 90% of company time should be spent on paid projects.

20. D: We see in the 4th sentence that employees will receive an ABCalert if work is cancelled. The previous sentence instructs employees to watch their email, so we can infer that the ABCalert is an email sent out to let employees know if work is cancelled.

21. C: The last sentence mentions variable holidays and later refers to them as "unassigned" days that will be paid out if unused. We can deduce that these days are extra holiday time that can be used at different times of the year as needed.

22. B: The client's revisions should take a day and a half, but according to the project instructions, client revisions should add a minimum of two days. Adding two days to the final completion date means the project will be finished on Thursday, February 16.

23. E: From the second sentence we can deduce that setup began on January 26. This is three days behind schedule, so they will have to make up three days of work to finish on time.

24. E: Four hours make up less than a day, but the instructions state that any internal revisions will add a minimum of one day to the schedule, so Phase 3 will be completed on Tuesday, February 14.

25. E: The final sentence states that employees can expect to receive $187 per share, if they choose to cash out their shares. So, we can infer that they can also choose not to sell.

Mometrix

26. C: The third sentence states that locations for different jobs are not yet certain, implying that some positions may be moved to new locations.

27. C: The second sentence states that downsizing and terminating are not in the "current plan." However, there is no guarantee that jobs will be protected, so employees can infer that there is a possibility that downsizing and layoffs could occur.

28. A: Website optimization and its methods (customizing pop-ups and improving site navigation) are mentioned in the first sentence. The second sentence tells us that the intent is to increase the company's client base. So, we can infer that website optimization is a way of adjusting the website to improve sales.

29. B: A/B testing is mentioned in the third sentence. The next three sentences describe how it works: uploading two different versions of the website and tracking the visits and their results for two weeks to find the best fit. So, we can deduce that A/B testing is a comparison of two possible website layouts to see which is optimal for gaining clients.

30. B: The excerpt specifically mentions employees who are involved in procurement decisions, and Kelli is in accounts receivable. So, we must look at the principles behind the directive. Any employee who is involved financially with a client, whether through making procurement decisions or helping with billing, may be tempted to show preferential treatment if a client offers a valuable gift. So, Kelli should not accept the gift card.

31. D: Although the dinner is not a tangible gift and cannot be redeemed for tangible value, it is still a valuable business courtesy, which goes against the company rules as it could be used to seek Kelli's favor toward the client. So, she should not accept.

32. E: The instructions state that the library project is the top priority and other projects will have to be pushed back as needed. So, it would not be feasible for Lindsay to start a new project while she is busy with the library.

33. B: The instructions do not mention personal emails, but employees are instructed to archive all emails in project folders. Even if Lindsay does not see any pertinent information in the email, she should archive it so there is a record of all communication with the client.

34. A: The instructions state that each file must be opened before Lindsay saves it to the M-drive. This way any files that are incorrectly labeled, or corrupted in some way, can be caught early on. So even though Lindsay does not need to rename the files, she should still open each one.

WorkKeys Practice Test #2

Applied Math

1. Allison purchased 32 apples to share with her class. If there were 8 people in the class, including her, how many apples did each person get?

    A. 6
    B. 4
    C. 3
    D. 8
    E. 16

2. Shoes were on sale for 25% off. Write this percent as a decimal.

    A. 1.5
    B. 0.25
    C. 0.75
    D. 1.25
    E. 0.5

3. It took Everett three and a half hours to drive from his home to the college he was visiting. How many minutes is this?

    A. 120
    B. 180
    C. 200
    D. 210
    E. 240

4. Sylvia has 14 quarters. How many dollars does she have?

    A. $3.50
    B. $5.25
    C. $7.00
    D. $2.75
    E. $4.50

5. Chris buys a book for $7.99 and two DVDs for $12.99 each, including tax. If he pays with a $50 bill, how much change should he receive?

    A. $16.03
    B. $29.02
    C. $8.04
    D. $24.02
    E. $11.04

6. Lenna bought 6 cents worth of gummy bears, 14 cents worth of peppermints, and a chocolate bar for 69 cents. If tax cost $0.07, how much change should she receive if she pays with a $1 bill?

- A. 93 cents
- B. 11 cents
- C. 4 cents
- D. 16 cents
- E. 22 cents

7. Orlando the cross-country bicyclist can ride 90 miles per day. How many days will it take him to bike from Los Angeles to El Paso, assuming the distance is 802 miles? Round to the nearest day.

- A. 9 days
- B. 10 days
- C. 8 days
- D. 12 days
- E. 11 days

8. Ms. Arnold's algebra class took a pop quiz to test their knowledge of the quadratic formula. The quiz had five questions, with the third question worth twice the other questions. If the quiz grades were 97, 76, 85, and 82, what was the average grade?

- A. 79
- B. 86.2
- C. 91
- D. 85
- E. 83.5

9. Daniel's truck averages 18 miles per gallon. If it took him 3 hours to go 195 miles, what was his speed?

- A. 55 mph
- B. 70 mph
- C. 68 mph
- D. 65 mph
- E. 62 mph

10. Abby read 25% of a book on Monday and an additional 50% on Tuesday. On Wednesday, she read 25% of a second book. What fraction of the first book has she read?

- A. 1
- B. 1/2
- C. 1/4
- D. 2/3
- E. 3/4

11. June bought ¼ pound of kidney beans, ½ pound of navy beans, ¼ pound of oats, 2 pounds of rice, and ¾ pound of pinto beans. How many pounds of beans did she purchase altogether?

- A. 7/8
- B. 1 ½
- C. 1
- D. 2 ¼
- E. 9/10

12. Emma completed 1/6 of the job and then Evan completed another 1/6. How much of the job is left?

- A. 1/3
- B. 2/9
- C. 1/6
- D. 5/6
- E. 2/3

13. Jules has 1 2/5 times as many books as Jesse. If Jesse has 75 books, how many books does Jules have?

- A. 30
- B. 105
- C. 85
- D. 115
- E. 90

14. Zane subtracted 4^2 from the sum of 3 times 6 and 12 divided by 3. What was his answer?

- A. 2
- B. 8
- C. 6
- D. 9
- E. 7

15. Travis added the square of $(6 + 3)$ to the product of 7 and 2. What was his answer?

- A. 81
- B. 126
- C. 76
- D. 18
- E. 95

16. Miguel buys a loaf of bread at the grocery store for $4.25. He also buys two bottles of soda at $2.15 each, a chocolate bar for $1.90, a bottle of shampoo for $5.25, and three magazines at $1.50 each. How much did he spend in all?

- A. $16.05
- B. $19.05
- C. $20.20
- D. $20.45
- E. $21.15

17. There are 32 blue marbles, 45 red marbles, 36 green marbles, and 23 yellow marbles in a bag. What is the average number of marbles of a given color in the bag?

    A. 30
    B. 31
    C. 32
    D. 33
    E. 34

18. Jess wants to buy a bag of mixed nuts (peanuts, almonds, and cashews in equal quantities). She noticed that a 1-lb bag is $6.49, but she could separately buy peanuts for $2.97 per pound, almonds for $7.95 per pound, and cashews for $6.96 per pound. Would it be a better deal to buy the store mix or make her own mix?

    A. buy the store mix
    B. make her own mix
    C. the store mix and her own are the same price
    D. buy a different mix that costs $6.58 per pound
    E. make a different mix that costs $6.29 per pound

19. Max worked the following problem: $6 + 8 \div 2$. He added 6 and 8 to obtain 14, then divided by 2 to obtain 7. What was his mistake?

    A. He did not divide 8 by 2 first.
    B. He did not divide both the 6 and the 8 by 2.
    C. He did not write the 2 as a fraction.
    D. He mistakenly calculated the sum of 6 and 8 as 14 instead of 16.
    E. He mistakenly calculated $14 \div 2$ as 7 instead of 6.

20. You plan to build a circular wooden platform with a diameter of 28 feet. You will apply stain to the platform using a product that can cover 225 square feet per gallon. How many gallons will you need to cover the entire platform?

    A. 2
    B. 3
    C. 10
    D. 11
    E. 12

21. A patient was taking 310 mg of antidepressant each day. However, the doctor determined that this dosage was too high and reduced the dosage by a fifth. Further observation revealed the dose was still too high, so he reduced it again by 20 mg. What is the final dosage of the patient's antidepressant?

    A. 20 mg
    B. 42 mg
    C. 228 mg
    D. 248 mg
    E. 310 mg

22. Curtis is taking a road trip through Germany, where all distance signs are in metric. He passes a sign that states the city of Dusseldorf is 45 kilometers away. Approximately how far is this in miles?

    A. 42 miles
    B. 37 miles
    C. 28 miles
    D. 16 miles
    E. 12 miles

23. University Q has an extremely competitive nursing program. Historically, 3/4 of the students in each incoming class major in nursing but only 1/5 of those who major in nursing actually complete the program. If this year's incoming class has 100 students, how many students will complete the nursing program?

    A. 75
    B. 20
    C. 15
    D. 5
    E. 4

24. If 1 inch on a map represents 60 feet, how many yards apart are two points if the distance between the points on the map is 10 inches?

    A. 1,800 yards
    B. 600 yards
    C. 400 yards
    D. 200 yards
    E. 2 yards

25. The graph below shows the weekly church attendance among residents in the town of Ellsford, with the town having five different denominations: Episcopal, Methodist, Baptist, Catholic, and Orthodox. Approximately what percentage of church-goers in Ellsford attends Catholic churches?

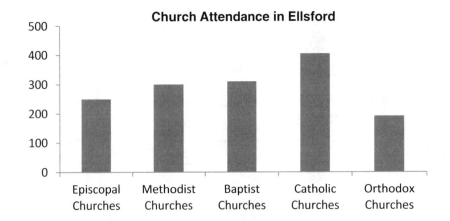

    A. 23%
    B. 28%
    C. 36%
    D. 42%
    E. 48%

26. Cheri was solving the following problem: 60 is what percent of 150? She converted the word problem into an equation, writing it as $60 = x(150)$. She then divided both sides by 150 to obtain $60/150 = x$. She reduced the fraction to obtain 2/5. Why is this answer wrong?

A. She should have multiplied both sides by 150 instead of dividing.
B. She should have moved the decimal to the left to make it a percent.
C. She should have divided both sides by 60 instead of 150.
D. She should have multiplied both sides by 60.
E. She should have converted the fraction into a percent.

27. The 5-lb bag of dog food costs $7.45 and the 8-lb bag costs $11.68. How much will it cost James to buy 80 pounds of the less expensive food?

A. $7.45
B. $11.68
C. $116.80
D. $74.50
E. $119.20

28. A portable concrete mixer can mix 275 pounds of concrete in 30 minutes. Taking the density of concrete as 150 pounds per cubic foot, how long will it take to mix enough concrete to fill wall forms that measure 30' × 8' × 8"?

A. 43.64 hours
B. 523.64 hours
C. 87.27 hours
D. 32.27 hours
E. 12.85 hours

29. The volume of a rectangular box is found by multiplying its length, width, and height. If the dimensions of a box are $\sqrt{3}$, $2\sqrt{5}$, and 4, what is its volume?

A. $2\sqrt{60}$
B. $2\sqrt{15}$
C. $4\sqrt{15}$
D. $8\sqrt{15}$
E. $24\sqrt{5}$

30. A bullseye with a 4-inch diameter covers 20 percent of a circular target. What is the area, in square inches, of the target?

A. 0.8π
B. 32π
C. 10π
D. 20π
E. 80π

31. Sally wants to buy a used truck for her delivery business. Truck A is priced at $3100 and gets 20 miles per gallon. Truck B costs $4100 and gets 36 miles per gallon. If gasoline costs $2.4 per gallon, how many miles must Sally drive to make truck B the better buy?

- A. 3000
- B. 5400
- C. 12600
- D. 15650
- E. 18750

32. A ski club charges a $48 membership fee, plus $18 to rent ski equipment per day. Which of the following equations can be used to find the total cost of membership at the club, when renting equipment for x days?

- A. $y = 66x$
- B. $y = 18x - 48$
- C. $y = 48x + 18$
- D. $y = 54x$
- E. $y = 18x + 48$

33. Pump Alpha can pump at rate of 76 gallons per minute. Pump Bravo can pump at a rate of 212 liters per minute. How many minutes would the fastest pump take to drain a spherical water tank that has an interior diameter of 9 feet?

- A. 10.16 min.
- B. 28.24 min.
- C. 37.55 min.
- D. 51.00 min.
- E. 76.12 min

34. At today's visit to her doctor, Josephine was prescribed a liquid medication with instructions to take 25 cc's every four hours. She filled the prescription on her way to work, but when it came time to take the medicine, she realized that the pharmacist did not include a measuring cup. Josephine estimated that the plastic spoon in her desk drawer was about the same size as a teaspoon and decided to use it to measure the approximate dosage. She recalled that one cubic centimeter (cc) is equal to one milliliter (mL) but was not sure how many milliliters were in a teaspoon. So, she noted that a two-liter bottle of soda contains about the same amount as a half-gallon container of milk and applied her knowledge of the customary system of measurement to determine how many teaspoons of medicine to take. Which of these calculations might she have used to approximate her dosage?

- A. $25 \times \frac{1}{1000} \times \frac{2}{0.5} \times 16 \times 48$
- B. $25 \times \frac{1}{100} \times \frac{0.5}{2} \times 16 \times 4 \times 12$
- C. $\frac{1000}{25} \times \frac{0.5}{2} \times 16 \times 4 \times 12$
- D. $\frac{25}{1000} \times \frac{1}{4} \times 16 \times 48$
- E. $\frac{25}{1000} \times \frac{4}{16} \times 48$

Graphic Literacy

Use the speedometer to answer the following 3 questions.

The speedometer below displays the speed of a car in Miles Per Hour (MPH) and Kilometers Per Hour (KPH).

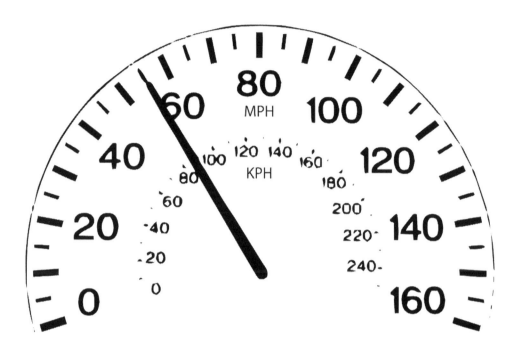

1. Approximately what speed does the speedometer read, in MPH?

    A. 98 MPH
    B. 88 MPH
    C. 72 MPH
    D. 55 MPH

2. The speed limit on a road is 75 MPH. This most closely corresponds to what speed in KPH?

    A. 42 KPH
    B. 120 KPH
    C. 140 KPH
    D. 60 KPH

3. A decrease from 120 KPH to 40 KPH is a decrease of ___ MPH?

    A. 30
    B. 40
    C. 50
    D. 60

Use the following graphic for the following 2 questions.

Trey is placing an order for supplies for his employer.

ABC Technology Solutions			Order number: 2689
ITEM	PRICE	QUANTITY	TOTAL
Wireless Mouse	$12.99	18	$233.82
Wireless Keyboard	$29.97	6	$179.82
LaserJet Printer	$149.95	1	$149.95
Solid State Hard Drive	$109.99	2	$219.98
Subtotal			$783.57
Tax			$64.64
Shipping and Handling			$24.99
First-Time Customer Discount			-$78.36
GRAND TOTAL			$794.84

4. How many wireless keyboards did Trey order?

    A. 18
    B. $29.97
    C. 6
    D. $12.99

5. What was Trey's discount for being a first-time customer?

    A. $783.57
    B. $64.64
    C. $24.99
    D. $78.36

Use the following chart to answer the following 3 questions.

> *Office Protocol for Internal Memoranda*
> 1. Proofread memo and make any necessary changes.
> 2. Save document in appropriate folder.
> 3. Send document to printer.
> 4. Deliver to workstations of all applicable personnel.
> 5. Send email to all of the above personnel, stating that the memo was delivered and attaching an electronic copy.

6. After saving the document, what is the next step?

    A. Proofread the memo
    B. Send the document to the printer
    C. Deliver the document
    D. Attach the document to an email

7. After printing the document, what is the next step?

- A. Save the document
- B. Proofread the memo
- C. Deliver the document
- D. Attach the document to an email

8. Once the document has been delivered, what is the next step?

- A. Proofread memo
- B. Save the document
- C. Print the document
- D. Attach the document to an email

9. The following data were collected over a period of:

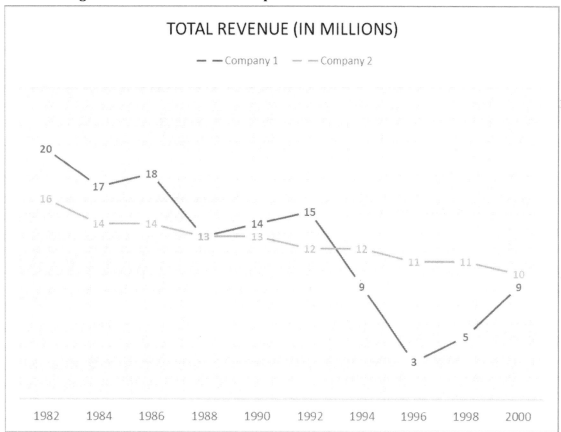

- A. 6 years
- B. 18 years
- C. 16 years
- D. 20 years

Use the following schematic to answer the following 3 questions.

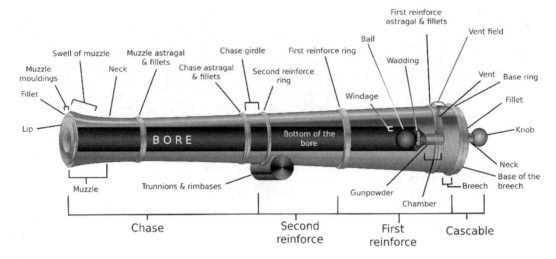

10. **According to the schematic, how many astragals are included in a cannon?**
    A. 2
    B. 3
    C. 1
    D. 4

11. **According to the schematic, which part is located farthest from the muzzle?**
    A. First reinforce ring
    B. Second reinforce ring
    C. Breech
    D. Trunnions and rimbases

12. **According to the schematic, which of the following parts are closest together?**
    A. Knob and ball
    B. Second reinforce ring and chase astragal and fillets
    C. Breech and the first reinforce ring
    D. Trunnions and muzzle

Use the following graph to answer the following 3 questions.

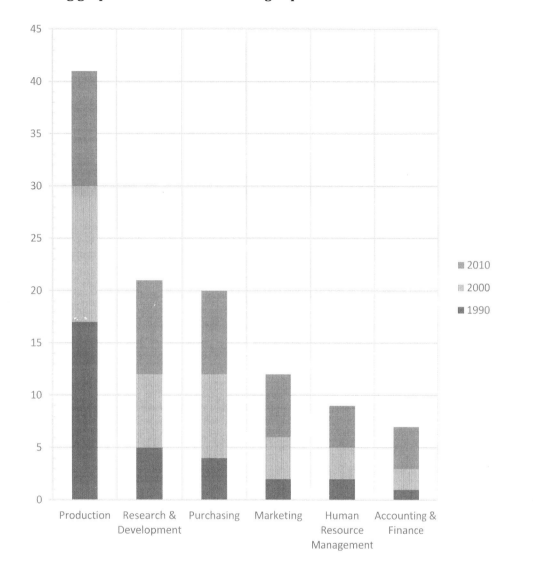

13. In which department and decade did the company expend the least?

    A. Production, 1990s

    B. Human Resource Management, 2000s

    C. Marketing, 2010s

    D. Accounting and Finance, 1990s

14. Which of the following is true?

    A. Production expenditures decreased over time.

    B. Research and Development had the highest expenditures in the 2010s.

    C. Accounting and Finance had lower expenditures than any other department every decade.

    D. Total production expenditures were greater than any other two departments' expenditures put together.

15. **In which period did the company have the least amount of expenditures?**
    - A. 1990s
    - B. 2000s
    - C. 2010s
    - D. 1990s and 2010s are tied for the least

Use the following charts to answer the following 3 questions:

Page	Item	Office Supplies	Electronics	Software	Advertising
1	Office Supplies	Pens/pencils	Monitors	Design	Business cards
2	Electronics	Paper	Keyboards	Project Management	Brochures
3	Software	Printer ink	Routers	Accounting	Web ads
4	Advertising	Staplers			CDs

16. **What page can business cards be found on?**
    - A. 1
    - B. 2
    - C. 3
    - D. 4

17. **What three items can be found on page 3?**
    - A. Pens, paper, and ink
    - B. monitors, keyboards, and routers
    - C. design, project management, and accounting software
    - D. business cards, brochures, and web ads

18. **What page should Leo look at if he needs to order replacement ink for his printer?**
    - A. 1
    - B. 2
    - C. 3
    - D. 4

Use the line graph below to answer the following 2 questions:

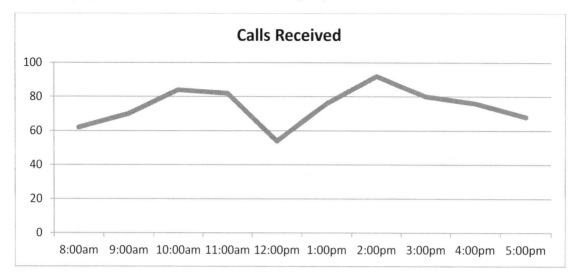

19. When is the busiest time of day?
    A. Early morning
    B. Noon
    C. Mid-afternoon
    D. End of day

20. When could a caller expect to have the shortest wait time on a call?
    A. 8:00am
    B. 9:30am
    C. 11:00am
    D. 12:00pm

21. Which of the charts shows that Diego took 2 days off in October?

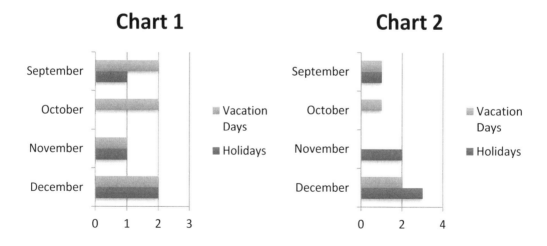

A. Chart 1
B. Chart 2
C. Both are accurate
D. Neither is accurate

Use the following table to answer the following 3 questions:

Number and percentage distribution of Title IV institutions, by control of institution, level of institution, and region: United States and other U.S. jurisdictions, academic year 2015–16

| | Number of Institutions | | | | Percent of Institutions | | | |
| | | | Private | | | | Private | |
	Total	Public	Nonprofit	For-profit	Total	Public	Nonprofit	For-profit
Total institutions	**7,177**	**1,992**	**1,913**	**3,272**	**100.0**	**100.0**	**100.0**	**100.0**
Total U.S. institutions	7,021	1,965	1,859	3,197	97.8	98.6	97.2	97.7
Level of institution								
4-year	3,089	728	1,647	714	43.0	36.5	86.1	21.8
U.S.	3,012	710	1,602	700	42.0	35.6	83.7	21.4
Other U.S. jurisdictions	77	18	45	14	1.1	0.9	2.4	0.4
2-year	2,085	1,016	178	891	29.1	51.0	9.3	27.2
U.S.	2,059	1,007	171	881	28.7	50.6	8.9	26.9
Other U.S. jurisdictions	26	9	7	10	0.4	0.5	0.4	0.3
Less-than-2-year	2,003	248	88	1,667	27.9	12.4	4.6	50.9
U.S.	1,950	248	86	1,616	27.2	12.4	4.5	49.4
Other U.S. jurisdictions	53	0	2	51	0.7	0.0	0.1	1.6
Region								
New England	405	110	161	134	5.6	5.5	8.4	4.1
Mid East	1,129	278	417	434	15.7	14.0	21.8	13.3
Great Lakes	1,062	266	293	503	14.8	13.4	15.3	15.4
Plains	619	187	190	242	8.6	9.4	9.9	7.4
Southeast	1,758	541	398	819	24.5	27.2	20.8	25.0
Southwest	774	245	113	416	10.8	12.3	5.9	12.7
Rocky Mountains	283	80	44	159	3.9	4.0	2.3	4.9
Far West	986	253	243	490	13.7	12.7	12.7	15.0
U.S. service academies	5	5	0	0	0.1	0.3	0.0	0.0
Other U.S. jurisdictions	156	27	54	75	2.2	1.4	2.8	2.3

22. In the academic year of 2015-2016, which region had the highest percentage of Title IV institutions?

    A. New England
    B. Southeast
    C. Other U.S. Service academies
    D. Great Lakes

23. In the academic year of 2015-2016, how many Private Nonprofit 2-year Title IV institutions were in the U.S.?

    A. 1859
    B. 881
    C. 178
    D. 171

24. In the academic year of 2015-2016, which set of institutions represented the lowest number of Title IV institutions?

    A. Public Title IV institutions in the Rocky Mountains region
    B. Public 4-year Title IV institutions
    C. Private For-profit Title IV institutions
    D. Far West Title IV institutions

Use the charts to answer the following 3 questions.

The charts below show the breakdown of employee time off at a company.

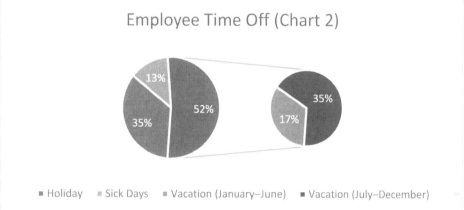

25. Which of the charts shows that the majority of vacation days are taken in the last half of the year?

    A. Chart 1
    B. Chart 2
    C. Both are accurate
    D. Neither is accurate

26. Which of the charts shows that vacation days make up more than half of the days employees take off?

    A. Chart 1
    B. Chart 2
    C. Both are accurate
    D. Neither is accurate

27. Which of the charts shows that employees take fewer holidays than any other kind of time off?

    A. Chart 1
    B. Chart 2
    C. Both are accurate
    D. Neither is accurate

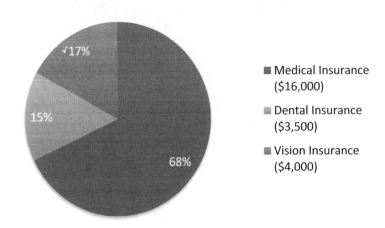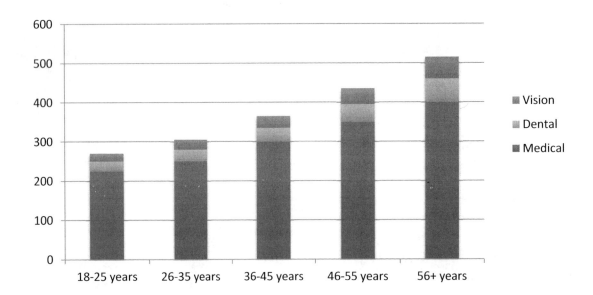

28. Which of the following charts is most effective in showing the cost of insuring a new employee?

Insurance Cost Per Month (Total)

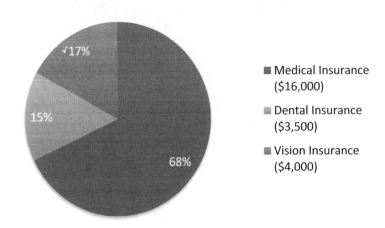

■ Medical Insurance ($16,000)

■ Dental Insurance ($3,500)

■ Vision Insurance ($4,000)

Insurance Cost Per Month (Individual)

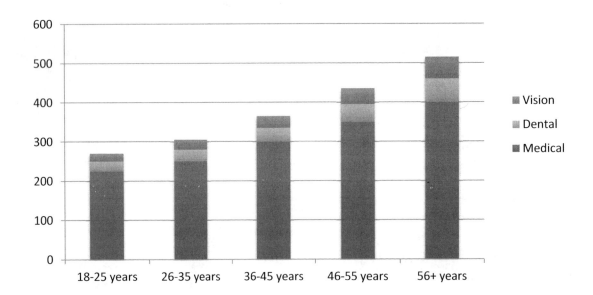

A. The pie chart
B. The bar graph
C. Both are effective
D. Neither is effective

Use the two graphs to answer the following 3 questions:

Paige is planning a 2-day, 1-night business trip. She has a daily allowance based on the federal per diem rates as shown in the table below. She is checking travel costs and recording them in another chart below.

Lodging	$136 per day
Meals	$62 per day
Mileage	$0.545 per mile

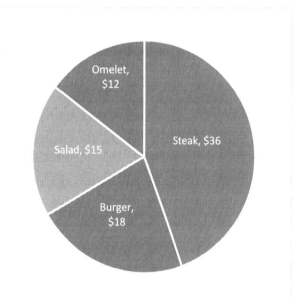

29. Paige will receive a lump sum, based on the per diem rates, to cover lodging and meals. She chose the least expensive hotel and spent $67 on meals her first day. The second day she had an omelet for breakfast and a burger for lunch. Which is the priciest meal she can afford for dinner?

    A. She cannot afford any of the meals ($11 available).
    B. She can afford the salad ($17 available).
    C. She can afford the burger ($24 available).
    D. She can afford the steak ($38 available).

30. If Paige wants to stay at the City Suites, can she afford to buy all six meals with her per diem allowance or will she need to pay for any herself? Omelets are available only at breakfast.

    A. She can buy all six meals with her allowance.
    B. She will need to buy at least one meal herself.
    C. She will need to buy at least two meals herself.
    D. She will need to buy at least three meals herself.

31. **Paige buys breakfast both days (omelets), gets salads for lunch, and attends an expenses-paid company dinner both evenings. She wants to reserve $60 for room service at the hotel. Which hotels can she afford?**
   A. Any of the hotels
   B. American Best or Rest EZ
   C. Rest EZ only
   D. none of the hotels

Use the graphics below to answer the following 2 questions:

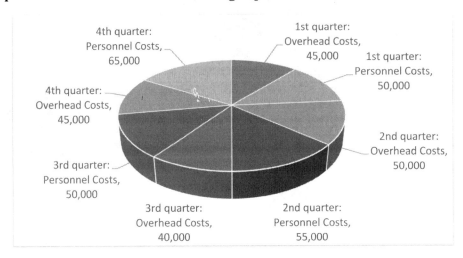

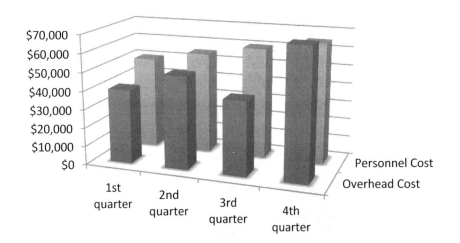

32. **Which chart shows that personnel costs are consistently higher than overhead costs?**
   A. The pie chart
   B. The bar graph
   C. Both are effective
   D. Neither is effective

33. Which chart shows that personnel costs steadily increased over the year?
   A. The pie chart
   B. The bar graph
   C. Both are effective
   D. Neither is effective

Use the graphics below to answer the following 2 questions:

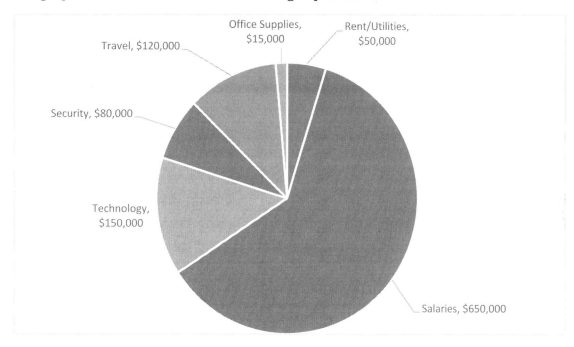

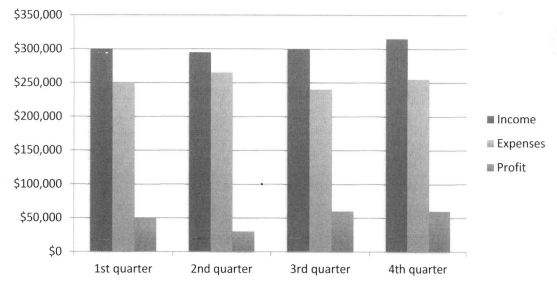

34. Which of the charts is most effective to propose an increase in employee salaries?
   A. The pie chart
   B. The bar graph
   C. Both are effective
   D. Neither is effective

35. Which of the charts is most effective for discussing areas of the budget to cut?

- A. The pie chart
- B. The bar graph
- C. Both are effective
- D. Neither is effective

Use the graphics below to answer the following 2 questions:

Consultant Agreement	
The following rates apply to the project	
Project Manager:	$105/hr
Senior Technician:	$90/hr
Junior Technician:	$55/hr
Accounting:	$60/hr
Software purchase:	$8,750

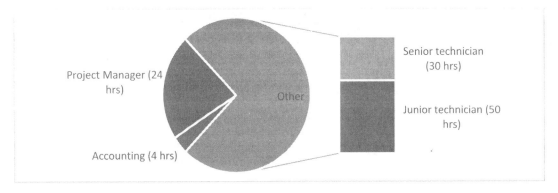

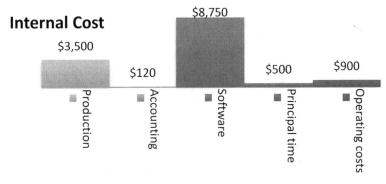

36. Emil decided to take a new project after reviewing the projected costs and profits in the charts above. Was this a justified decision?

- A. Yes, because the software is a valuable investment.
- B. Yes, because the new project is expected to be profitable.
- C. No, because the operating cost is too high.
- D. No, because the new project is expected to lose money.

37. Emil's client agrees to pay only part of the costs for the necessary software for the project (see the following counteroffer). Emil found that he could absorb $4,500 of the cost by using the software on another project. If he needs to make a profit of at least $2,000 on the project, can he accept the client's counteroffer?

Consultant Agreement			
The following rates apply to the project			
Project Manager:	$105/hr	24 hrs	$2,520
Senior Technician:	$90/hr	30 hrs	$2,700
Junior Technician:	$55/hr	50 hrs	$2,750
Accounting:	$60/hr	4 hrs	$240
Software purchase:			~~$8,750~~ $3,000
TOTAL			**~~$16,960~~** $11,210

A. Yes, because the project has an expected profit of more than $2,000 with the new rates.
B. Yes, because the software is a valuable long-term investment.
C. No, because the software can only be used on one other project.
D. No, because the project has an expected profit of less than $2,000 with the new rates.

Use the graphics below to answer the following question:

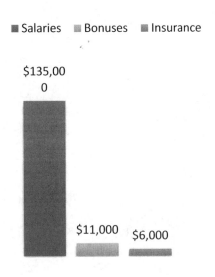

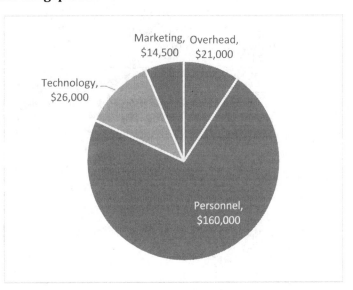

38. **Ellie was checking her company's financials to find whether she could give a $1,000 bonus to each of her 10 employees. The first chart shows the 1st quarter personnel costs, while the second chart shows the budgeted 1st-quarter spending. Can she decide to give this bonus?**

    A. Yes, because she has an extra $12,500 in the budget.

    B. Yes, because $10,000 is less than the amount Ellie spent on bonuses in the 1st quarter.

    C. No, because she only has an extra $8,000 in the budget.

    D. No, because she has already given bonuses this year.

Mometrix

Workplace Documents

1. Identify the main idea from the following excerpt:

> November 1–30 is open enrollment for insurance. If you have not previously enrolled, or if you wish to make any changes to your policy, please speak to HR by November 28 so that we can make any necessary adjustments. If you do not wish to make any changes, no action is necessary.

- A. Open enrollment for insurance is during the month of November.
- B. Employees need to speak to HR by November 28 if they want to enroll or make changes.
- C. Employees should not speak to HR if they do not need to change their policies.
- D. Changes to one's insurance policy must be handled through HR.
- E. HR will make any necessary adjustments to employee insurance policies.

2. What two things are employees requested to do while the client is in the office, based on the following excerpt?

> Please be aware that we are hosting a client, ABC Technology, on Thursday from 1:00–4:00. While all of our clients are important, ABC Technology is one of our biggest customers and it is important to maintain a professional atmosphere. To this end, please be sure that your dress is appropriate and please keep noise to a minimum so that the meeting will not be disturbed. Thank you!

- A. Be aware of the client and maintain a professional atmosphere
- B. Maintain a professional atmosphere and dress appropriately
- C. Keep noise to a minimum and avoid disturbing the meeting
- D. Dress appropriately and keep noise to a minimum
- E. Keep noise to a minimum and maintain a professional atmosphere

3. Identify the main idea from the following excerpt:

> All employees who plan on using vacation time between December 20 and January 4: please submit your requests ASAP. Because many of you want to use PTO during this window, we need to plan ahead, so please be sure to turn in requests by December 3. Any requests received after this may not be honored.

- A. All PTO requests need to be turned in by December 3.
- B. It is important to turn in PTO requests immediately because of high demand.
- C. Many employees want to take time off during the holiday season.
- D. Time off requests for days between December 20 and January 4 need to be turned in.
- E. Any requests turned in after December 3 may not be honored.

Read the following excerpt from a company handbook to answer the following 2 questions:

> When requesting vacation time, first download the Vacation Request Form off of the website. Then fill out the form, print it, and sign/date it. Scan and email to Liz with HR and copy your manager.

4. What is the final step in requesting vacation time?
   A. Downloading the Vacation Request Form
   B. Filling out the form
   C. Emailing the form
   D. Printing the form
   E. Signing the form

5. When should the form be signed?
   A. After downloading the Vacation Request Form
   B. After filling out the form
   C. After dating the form
   D. After printing the form
   E. After scanning the form

Read the following excerpt from a company handbook to answer the following 2 questions:

> All employees are to clock in by 8:00am. A two-minute grace period will be given, but after that employees will be docked an hour of vacation time for every hour or partial hour past 8:00am, unless they have express permission from a manager.

6. Julio overslept and got to work at 9:25am. How much vacation time will be docked?
   A. No time
   B. 1 hour
   C. 2 hours
   D. 3 hours
   E. 4 hours

7. Reagan got stuck in traffic and clocked in at 8:02am. How much vacation time will be docked?
   A. No time
   B. 1 hour
   C. 2 hours
   D. 3 hours
   E. 4 hours

Read the following excerpt from a company handbook to answer the following 4 questions:

> Beginning next Monday, we will use a new time-tracking software. Please visit ABCtimesheets.com no later than this Friday. Your username is your email address and your password is the last 4 digits of your Social Security number. Please reset the password and familiarize yourself with the site. There is a link to a tutorial in the top right corner. If you have any questions, please reply to this email or call/text me and I'll be glad to walk you through the setup. Please come prepared to use the new site on Monday.

8. What information is necessary to log in to the new site?

    A. A password
    B. An email address and the last 4 digits of one's Social Security number
    C. A tutorial that explains how to log in
    D. the website, ABCtimesheets.com
    E. An email address and a new password

9. Where can the tutorial be found?

    A. A link in an email
    B. A pop up when an employee logs in
    C. It is available upon request
    D. It appears after logging in with email address and password
    E. In the top right corner of the webpage

10. What should be done immediately after logging in to the new site?

    A. Watch the tutorial
    B. Prepare to use the new site, starting Monday
    C. Type in the username and password
    D. Reset the password and become familiar with the site
    E. Make a list of questions to ask

11. What should be done before Monday?

    A. Watch the tutorial
    B. Make a list of questions to ask
    C. Log in to the new website
    D. Reset the password and watch the tutorial
    E. Log in, reset passwords, and become familiar with the site

12. Identify the main idea from the following excerpt:

> All Blue team members: please note a change in your schedule (effective this week only). Report to your supervisor at 7:30am each morning for a brief meeting before beginning work. This is a crucial week on the project and we need to stay on a tight schedule while giving high-quality work. Thanks for your understanding.

    A. This week's work schedule is changing to accommodate a daily project meeting.
    B. Employees should report to their supervisors at 7:30am each morning.
    C. There will be a brief meeting before work.
    D. The project schedule is tight, so employees need to come in early each morning.
    E. This is a crucial week for the project.

13. Based on the excerpt below, what is the meaning of "matchpoint"?

> You may contribute throughout the year to your IRA, and as stated earlier, the company will match your contributions up to the matchpoint. This matchpoint is calculated as a percentage of your income as shown in your attached personnel file. Please visit with Accounting if you have any questions.

    A. The maximum an employee is allowed to contribute to his/her IRA
    B. The maximum that the company will contribute to match employee IRA contributions
    C. The minimum amount that employees are required to contribute to their IRAs to receive matching funds from the company
    D. 5% of an employee's salary
    E. The amount the company automatically contributes to employee IRAs

Use the memo below to answer the following 6 questions:

> Attention all employees: the office will be open all week (December 19–23, 8:00–5:00). However, due to the forecast for heavy snow toward the end of the week, check your email each morning. If the weather makes driving prohibitive, work may be cancelled and we will use the extra holiday time for the year. If the office is open but you feel unsafe driving, you may use vacation time for however much of the day you miss. To date we have two unused floating holidays, and as you know, any unassigned holiday time at the end of the year will be paid out as a bonus.

14. Rafael got an email Friday morning that the office would be closed for the morning, but open the remaining half day (1:00–5:00). The road was slippery so he didn't arrive until 3:00. How much holiday and vacation time did he use?

    A. 4 hrs of holiday time and 2 hrs of vacation time
    B. 6 hrs of holiday time
    C. 6 hrs of vacation time
    D. 2 hrs of holiday time and 4 hrs of vacation time
    E. 4 hrs of vacation time

15. It snowed early Thursday morning so Rafael came in at 11:00 and left at 4:00 when it started snowing again. How much vacation time did he use?

    A. 2 hrs
    B. 4 hrs
    C. 3 hrs
    D. 6 hrs
    E. 1 hr

16. On Friday it began to snow in the afternoon and the office closed at 1:00. If no more floating holidays are used for the remainder of the year, how much holiday time will be paid out to employees?

    A. ½ day
    B. 6 hrs
    C. 1 day
    D. 1½ days
    E. 2 days

17. Under what conditions will holiday time be used?

   A. If work is cancelled because of the weather
   B. If employees feel unsafe driving
   C. If there are leftover floating holidays
   D. If the forecast is for heavy snow
   E. If vacation time is used up

18. Under what conditions will vacation time be used?

   A. If there are extra floating holidays left in the year
   B. If an employee does not wish to lose his unused vacation time at the end of the year
   C. If the office is open but an employee chooses to stay home due to driving conditions
   D. If the weather makes driving prohibitive
   E. If the forecast is for heavy snow

19. If work is not cancelled and the holiday time is not used, what will happen to the unused time?

   A. It will roll over to the next year.
   B. It will be paid out as a bonus.
   C. It will be added to a vacation pool.
   D. The office will close to use the time.
   E. It will be cancelled as a new year begins.

Use the excerpt below to answer the following 2 questions:

> When attaching the project colorfiles to a client email, remember to place them in a zipped folder or they may be too large to send. Include a brief description in your email, explaining the name rules so the client can easily locate the file he or she needs.

20. What are colorfiles?

   A. Pictures of the finished project
   B. A collection of the project emails, arranged by date
   C. Color-coded charts for the client
   D. Text files requested by the client
   E. The project deliverable or a main component of it, in electronic form

21. What are name rules?

   A. The project numbers
   B. A convention for naming the files to organize them
   C. Capitalization rules for the project name
   D. A system of giving each file a coded name
   E. The Dewey Decimal System

Use the excerpt below to answer the following 2 questions:

> When you arrive at work on the first day, report immediately to your supervisor (Juan Gonzales) for your assignment. He will tell you which project you will be starting on and can give you the login to the M-drive to find project documents (projects are arranged by number chronologically). Please read over the list of necessary items before your first day and make sure that you have everything you need. It is especially important to bring the appropriate personal protective equipment, including head, eye, and foot protection. You may be going on a site visit on your first morning, so wearing PPE is necessary. If the site visit is rescheduled for another day, you can fill out your new employee paperwork and take it to HR, where you will be given a parking pass when all paperwork is completed. If you have any questions during the day, please ask Carla, whose desk is next to yours.

22. What is PPE?

- A. A company uniform
- B. A plastic suit that zips over work clothes to keep them clean on the job site
- C. Protective, wearable items such as safety goggles and steel-toed shoes
- D. Protective gear to block radiation
- E. A hazmat suit

23. What is the M-drive?

- A. A location to electronically access project documents
- B. A physical folder that can be taken to the job site
- C. A company email account
- D. A recommended store to find PPE
- E. A system to send project files to the client

Use the excerpt below to answer the following 2 questions:

> We are testing a number of potential methods of website optimization, including customizing pop-ups and improving site navigation. Our goal is to increase our client base by 10% through this, so we will be holding weekly progress meetings to discuss findings. Your team will be implementing A/B testing. Please submit your two proposed website versions by Friday. Then you will upload both and track the responses to each in several areas: number of hits, length of visit, and successful client gain.

24. Finn is working on the company website so that it is easier to find pages and move from page to page. What does he hope to accomplish through this?

- A. To increase the company's client base by 10%
- B. To customize pop-ups
- C. To implement A/B testing
- D. To determine the best website version of the two proposed
- E. To track the number of hits, length of visit, and successful client gain

25. Finn was asked to create two charts to track site visits and results of those visits for A/B testing. What will this show?

    A. Which website version is easier to navigate
    B. Which website version is easiest to customize
    C. Which website version is most effective for client gain
    D. Which website version clients prefer
    E. Which website version is easier to manage

26. Kim is not planning to make any changes to her insurance policy this year. Does she still need to fill out the form, based on the excerpt below?

> We are beginning a new insurance policy for next year, and open enrollment is during the month of November. Please turn in updated paperwork by the 25th so that we can check all documents and submit them to our agent by the end of the month. This includes your documentation as well as a form for each family member if you are including them. Check the enclosed pages carefully as several items have changed since last year and talk to Sami if you have any questions. Additionally, the insurance website (see enclosed documentation for details) has a detailed breakdown of the options and videos that explain them.

    A. Yes, because updated paperwork is needed.
    B. Yes, because prices have changed.
    C. Yes, because she is adding her family.
    D. No, because nothing is changing.
    E. No, because the forms are automatically updated.

Use the excerpt below to answer the following 3 questions:

> When you check the layout of the website text, be sure to pay specific attention to the kerning. It is important that our site looks professional, and that potential clients are not distracted by unevenness in spacing of the letters. Similarly, watch the tracking so that you don't have larger gaps between some words and smaller gaps with others. Run a check on both kerning and tracking before you upload, and check again after publishing the text. Finally, read through to make sure that the typeface is legible. If necessary, pick a different font so that clients and other visitors can easily, comfortably read the text.

27. What is kerning?

    A. The blank space around text
    B. The space between lines
    C. The spacing between words
    D. The spacing between letters
    E. The font

28. What is tracking?

    A. The blank space around text
    B. The space between lines
    C. The spacing between words
    D. The spacing between letters
    E. The font

29. What is typeface?
- A. The blank space around text
- B. The space between lines
- C. The spacing between words
- D. The spacing between letters
- E. The font

30. Jerome has an afternoon meeting that begins at 12:30, during the lunch window. Should he request a different time window for his lunch today, based on the excerpt below?

> Note that the window for lunchtime is between 11:30 and 1:00. Please check your calendar and email before leaving for lunch to verify whether you have any meetings, calls, etc., coming up in the afternoon. If your schedule requires you to be on the clock during the lunch window, ask your supervisor for an hour before or after the usual time, or choose to eat at your desk. It is unusual for our clients to call during the lunch window, but should you be expecting a call, please be sure to have your work phone on your person if you leave the office.

- A. Yes, because he needs to work during the lunch window.
- B. No, because it is important to be available to clients.
- C. Yes, because he needs to take a break to work well for the afternoon.
- D. No, because he already has an hour within the lunch window.
- E. No, because he needs to be working during business hours.

31. What is the importance of recording one's time to the correct project, based on the excerpt below?

> When filling out your timesheet, be sure to allocate your time to the correct project, with an appropriate description of your activities. Click on the drop-down menu under "Project" and then select the project you worked on (projects are sorted by number). If you worked on multiple projects in a day, you may have several entries. If you were working on a task that spans more than one project, select "908_Multi-Project" and record the applicable project numbers in your work description. Make sure the records are clear for the billing department to review. If your work was not related to any particular projects, select "912_Internal/Miscellaneous" and write a thorough description. We seek to keep a minimum of 90% of time on paid projects, so if you have a question about whether your work is project-related, please check with your supervisor.

- A. So that the employees can be paid accurately
- B. So that projects do not go over budget
- C. So that the billing department can invoice clients appropriately
- D. So that 90% of time stays on projects
- E. So that supervisors know which employees are on which projects

Use the excerpt below to answer the following 2 questions:

> We are testing a number of potential methods of website optimization, including customizing pop-ups and improving site navigation. We aim to increase our client base by 10% before the end of the year, so we will be holding weekly progress meetings for the rest of the quarter to discuss findings. Your team will be implementing A/B testing, so please submit your two proposed website versions by Friday. Be prepared to track the responses to each version in several areas: number of hits, length of visit, and successful client gain. This will be a two-week trial period to find the best fit. Use our web algorithm to calculate scores for each version.

32. What can we infer will happen to the two website versions?
   A. Customers will see either one, depending on their demographic.
   B. The version deemed the best fit will be chosen to represent the company.
   C. Versions will alternate between customer visits.
   D. The best parts of each version will be combined to create a new company website.
   E. Potential clients will see one version and clients will see another.

33. What information is used in the web algorithm?
   A. The pop-ups and site navigation
   B. The number of new clients gained each year
   C. The tracked responses to each version
   D. The demographics of new clients
   E. Number of returning clients

34. Based on the following excerpt, what is conversion?

> As part of the content marketing team, you will be in charge of selecting and uploading content of interest to potential clients. As one facet of content marketing, we are beginning a weekly podcast to share industry tips and give listeners a glimpse of what we do on a daily basis. We are looking for new podcast subjects so we welcome fresh ideas, as well as any other ideas that can help with conversion rate optimization. We have used several CRO methods in the past, from surveys and mailing lists to free offers, but are looking for new ideas on winning a greater percentage of visitors to our site. When searching for ideas, a good place to start is with data mining. Ask your supervisor for a list of the websites we prefer to use to search for behavior patterns of potential clients. As an incentive, each team member will receive a bonus for each successful conversion. Specifically, you will receive a $50 gift card for each person who becomes a client due to the content marketing efforts.

   A. Aiming marketing efforts at a specific demographic of potential clients
   B. A method of gathering data on behavior of potential clients for marketing purposes
   C. Turning a visitor into a client through content marketing
   D. Sending marketing teams to physical locations to attract potential clients
   E. Posting information or other content online to draw and engage potential clients

157

Answer Key and Explanations for Test #2

Applied Math

1. B: Since the apples are evenly divided among the class, we convert the word problem to a division equation. The total number of apples (32) must be divided by the number of people (8). So $32 \div 8 = n$, where n is the number of apples per person. Since $32 \div 8 = 4$, each person in the class will receive 4 apples.

2. B: To convert a percent to a decimal, move the decimal two places to the left. In the number 25, the decimal place is immediately following the 5, so moving it two places to the left yields 0.25.

3. D: An hour is 60 minutes, so we can convert hours to minutes by multiplying the number of hours (3.5) by 60. Since $3.5(60) = 210$, Everett's trip took 210 minutes.

4. A: A dollar has 4 quarters, so we divide the number of quarters by 4 to find the number of dollars. Since $\frac{14}{4} = 3.5$, Sylvia has 3.5 dollars, or $3.50.

5. A: First we need to calculate Chris' total cost. We add $7.99 + $12.99 + $12.99 to find a total of $33.97. Then we can subtract this total from $50.00 to find the change. Since:

$$\$50.00 - \$33.97 = \$16.03$$

Chris should receive $16.03 in change.

6. C: First we need to calculate Lenna's total cost. We convert cents to dollars and add

$$Cost = 0.06 + 0.14 + 0.69 + 0.07$$
$$= 0.96$$

We then subtract from $1.00. Since $1.00 - 0.96 = 0.04$, Lenna's change is $0.04 or 4 cents.

7. A: Plug in the known values:

$$\frac{90 \text{ miles}}{1 \text{ day}} = \frac{802 \text{ miles}}{x \text{ days}}$$
$$90x = 802$$
$$x = \frac{802}{90}$$
$$x = 8.91 \text{ days}$$

Which is rounded to the nearest day to get 9 days.

8. D: To find the average, we find the sum of the scores and divide by the number of tests. There were four quiz grades, and $\frac{97+76+85+82}{4} = 85$, so the average quiz grade is 85.

9. D: We ignore the miles per gallon since it is not used in calculating speed. To find his speed (rate), we remember that $rate \times time = distance$, so $rate = \frac{distance}{time}$. Since $\frac{195}{3} = 65$, Daniel was driving 65 mph.

10. E: First we find the percent of the book Abby has read by adding 25 and 50 to obtain 75% (ignoring the percentage of the second book, which is irrelevant). Then we need to convert the percent to a fraction. We convert a percent by writing it as a fraction with a denominator of 100 and reducing. We can reduce $\frac{75}{100}$ by dividing both numerator and denominator by 25 to obtain ¾. So, Abby has read ¾ of the book.

11. B: To find the total weight of the beans, we add ¼ + ½ + ¾ (disregarding the amounts of oats and rice). We know that ¼ and ¾ add up to 1 and adding 1 + ½ yields 1½. So, June purchased 1½ pounds of beans altogether.

12. E: First we find how much of the job has been completed by adding the two fractions. Since they share a common denominator, we add the numerators and place that sum over the denominator: $1 + 1 = 2$, so $\frac{2}{6}$ of the job is done. The whole job is $\frac{6}{6}$, so we subtract to find the remaining part: $\frac{6}{6} - \frac{2}{6} = \frac{4}{6}$, which can be reduced by dividing both the numerator and denominator by 2 to obtain $\frac{2}{3}$. So $\frac{2}{3}$ of the job is left to complete.

13. B: To find the number of Jules' books, we need to multiply $1\frac{2}{5}$ by 75. To do this, we need to convert both numbers to fractions. We change $1\frac{2}{5}$ to an improper fraction by multiplying the denominator by the whole number, adding the numerator, and placing this new number over the original denominator: $5 \times 1 + 2 = 7$, so our improper fraction is $\frac{7}{5}$. Then we convert 75 to a fraction by placing it over 1: $\frac{75}{1}$. Now we can multiply $\frac{7}{5} \times \frac{75}{1}$ by multiplying the numerators ($7 \times 75 = 525$) and denominators ($5 \times 1 = 5$). Placing the new numerator and denominator together yields $\frac{525}{5}$, which we can reduce by dividing both numerator and denominator by 5: $\frac{105}{1}$, or simply 105. Jules has 105 books.

14. C: The order of operations is PEMDAS: parentheses, exponents, multiplication/division, addition/subtraction. We first write the equation in order so we can see where these operations are. Because the 4^2 is subtracted from the rest of the equation, we move it to the end:

$$3 \times 6 + \frac{12}{3} - 4^2$$

We have no parentheses, so we perform the exponent operation first:

$$3 \times 6 + \frac{12}{3} - 16$$

Then we multiply and divide:

$$18 + 4 - 16$$

Now we can add and subtract to obtain 6.

15. E: The order of operations is PEMDAS: parentheses, exponents, multiplication/division, addition/subtraction. We first write the equation in order so we can see where these operations are:

$$(6 + 3)^2 + 7 \times 2$$

Then we perform the operations inside the parentheses: $6 + 3 = 9$, so we now have:

$$9^2 + 7 \times 2$$

Next, we calculate the exponents: $9^2 = 81$, so we now have:

$$81 + 7 \times 2$$

Then we perform the multiplication/division: $7 \times 2 = 14$, so now we have:

$$81 + 14 = 95$$

16. C: Add the numbers together, noting that there are two sodas and three magazines:

$$
\begin{aligned}
Total &= \$4.25 + 2 \times \$2.15 + \$1.90 + \$5.25 + 3 \times \$1.50 \\
&= \$4.25 + \$4.30 + \$1.90 + \$5.25 + \$4.50 \\
&= \$20.20
\end{aligned}
$$

17. E: Add up the total number of marbles in the bag, then divide by the number of different colors in the bag to get the average number of marbles of a given color:

$$32 + 45 + 36 + 23 = 136$$
$$\frac{136}{4} = 34$$

18. B: We need to find the price of one pound of the mix, which means $\frac{1}{3}$ pound of each type of nut. So, we divide each price per pound by 3 to find that $\frac{1}{3}$ pound of peanuts would cost \$0.99, $\frac{1}{3}$ pounds of almonds would cost \$2.65, and $\frac{1}{3}$ pound of cashews would cost \$2.32. We add these three prices together (\$0.99 + \$2.65 + \$2.32 = \$5.96) to find that a pound of nuts would cost \$5.96. Since this is less than \$6.49, it is a better deal if Jess makes her own mix.

19. A: The order of operations (PEMDAS) states that division must be performed before addition, unless the addition is within parentheses. So, Max should first divide 8 by 2 to obtain 4, then add it to 6 to obtain 10.

20. B: First find the surface area of the platform using the equation for area of a circle:

$$
\begin{aligned}
area &= 3.14 \times (radius)^2 \\
&= 3.14 \times (14)^2 \\
&= 615.44 \text{ ft.}^2
\end{aligned}
$$

Dividing the area to cover by the area covered by one gallon of stain, $\frac{615.44}{225} = 2.74$ gallons, rounded to 3 gallons.

21. C: To obtain the new dosage, subtract $\frac{1}{5}$ of 310 mg from the original dosage of 310 mg, then subtract 20 mg. $310 \text{ mg} - \left(310 \times \frac{1}{5}\right) \text{mg} - 20 \text{ mg} = 228 \text{ mg}$

22. C: One kilometer is about 0.62 miles, and $45(0.62)$ is 27.9, or approximately 28 miles.

23. C: If the incoming class has 100 students, then $\frac{3}{4}$ of those students will major in nursing: $(100)\left(\frac{3}{4}\right) = 75$. So, 75 students will major in nursing but only $\frac{1}{5}$ of that 75 will complete the nursing program: $(75)\left(\frac{1}{5}\right) = 15$. Therefore, 15 students will complete the program.

24. D: Start by setting up a proportion to solve by cross multiplication: $\frac{1 \text{ inch}}{60 \text{ feet}} = \frac{10 \text{ inches}}{x \text{ feet}}$. When the numbers are cross multiplied, you get $x = 600$ feet. Now we need to convert 600 feet to yards. There are 3 feet in 1 yard, so divide 600 by 3 to find the number of yards between the two points: $600 \div 3 = 200$. Therefore, the two points are 200 yards apart.

25. B: Adding up the number of church-goers in Ellsford results in about 1450 residents who attend a church in the town each week. There are approximately 400 people in Ellsford who attend a Catholic church each week. This number represents about 28% of the 1450 church-goers in the town.

26. E: The problem asked for the answer as a percent. As a final step, Cheri needs to convert the fraction to a percent by multiplying by 100. This yields 40, so the correct answer is 40%.

27. C: To find which dog food is cheaper, we find the unit price (cost per pound) of each. We divide $7.45 by 5 to find that one pound of the first dog food costs $1.49. We divide $11.68 by 8 to find that one pound of the second dog food costs $1.46. Since the 8-lb bag has a lower unit price, we multiply $1.46 by 80 to find that James will pay $116.80.

28. A: First convert pounds of concrete per minute to cubic feet of concrete per hour:

$$\frac{275 \text{ lb}}{30 \text{ min}} \times \frac{1 \text{ ft}^3}{150 \text{ lb}} \times \frac{60 \text{ min}}{1 \text{ hour}} = 3.66 \text{ ft}^3/\text{hr}$$

Calculate the volume of the forms to be filled:

$$volume = 30 \times 8 \times \frac{8}{12} = 160 \text{ ft}^3$$

Therefore:

$$\frac{1 \text{ hour}}{3.66 \text{ ft}^3} \times 160 \text{ ft}^3 = 43.64 \text{ hours}$$

29. D: The volume of the box is the product of $\sqrt{3}$, $2\sqrt{5}$, and 4. To multiply two or more square root radicals, multiply the coefficients and then multiply the radicands.

$$\sqrt{3} \times 2\sqrt{5} \times 4 = 8\sqrt{3}\sqrt{5} = 8\sqrt{15}$$

Then, simplify the radicand if possible by factoring out any squares. Since 15 cannot be factored into any square factors, it cannot be simplified further.

30. D: First calculate the area of the bullseye:

$$A = \pi r^2$$
$$= \pi \left(\frac{4 \text{ in}}{2}\right)^2$$
$$= \pi (2 \text{ in})^2$$
$$= 4\pi \text{ in}^2$$

Then, let x = the area of the target. Since 20 percent of $x = 4\pi$

$$0.2x = 4\pi \text{ in}^2$$
$$x = 20\pi \text{ in}^2$$

31. E: Let P_A represent the price of truck A and P_B that of truck B. Similarly let M_A and M_B represent the gas mileage obtained by each truck, respectively. The total cost of driving a truck n miles is

$$C = P + n \times \frac{\$2.4}{M}$$

To determine the break-even mileage, set the two cost equations equal to one another and solve for n:

$$P_A + n \times \frac{\$2.4}{M_A} = P_B + n \times \frac{\$2.4}{M_B}$$

$$n \times \left(\frac{\$2.4}{M_A} - \frac{\$2.4}{M_B}\right) = P_B - P_A$$

$$n = \frac{P_B - P_A}{\frac{\$2.4}{M_A} - \frac{\$2.4}{M_B}} = \frac{P_B - P_A}{\frac{\$2.4M_B - \$2.4M_A}{M_A M_B}} = \frac{M_A M_B (P_B - P_A)}{\$2.4(M_B - M_A)}$$

Plugging in the given values:

$$n = \frac{(20)(36)(4100 - 3100)}{2.4(36 - 20)} = 18750 \text{ miles}$$

32. E: The situation can be represented by the slope of 18, since the cost of renting equipment is $18 per day, for x days. The y-intercept is 48 because a member must pay a $48 membership fee, regardless of whether or not ski equipment is rented. Thus, the situation can be represented by the linear equation, $y = 18x + 48$.

33. C: The volume of the water tank is calculated using the formula:

$$volume = \frac{4}{3} \times 3.14 \times (radius)^3$$
$$= 4.186 \times (4.5)^3$$
$$= 381.51 \text{ ft.}^3$$

To determine which pump is faster, we need to convert both of their pumping rates into cubic feet per minute. For pump Alpha,

$$\frac{76 \text{ gallons}}{\min} \times \frac{231 \text{ in}^3}{1 \text{ gallon}} \times \frac{1 \text{ ft}^3}{1728 \text{ in}^3} = \frac{10.16 \text{ ft}^3}{\min}$$

For pump Bravo,

$$\frac{212 \text{ liters}}{\min} \times \frac{0.264 \text{ gal}}{1 \text{ liter}} \times \frac{231 \text{ in}^3}{1 \text{ gallon}} \times \frac{1 \text{ ft}^3}{1728 \text{ in}^3} = \frac{7.48 \text{ ft}^3}{\min}$$

Pump Alpha is faster, and it would take $381.51 \text{ ft}^3 \times \frac{1 \min}{10.16 \text{ ft}^3} = 37.55$ minutes to drain the tank.

34. D: There are many ways Josephine may have applied her knowledge to determine how to approximately measure her medicine using her plastic spoon. The only choice which correctly uses dimensional analysis is choice D: the dosage

$$\approx 25 \text{ cc} \times \frac{1 \text{ ml}}{1 \text{ cc}} \times \frac{1\text{L}}{1000\text{ml}} \times \frac{0.5 \text{ gal}}{2\text{L}} \times \frac{16\text{c}}{1 \text{ gal}} \times \frac{48\text{t}}{1\text{c}} \times \frac{1 \text{ spoonful}}{1\text{t}} \approx \frac{25 \times 16 \times 48}{1000 \times 4} \approx 5$$

Graphic Literacy

1. D: The mark halfway between 40 and 60 is 50, since $(40 + 60)/2 = 50$. The mark indicated by the needle is halfway between 50 and 60, which means $(50 + 60)/2 = 55$. Thus, the speedometer reads 55 MPH.

2. B: The mark for 70 MPH is halfway between 60 and 80, since $(60 + 80)/2 = 70$, and the mark for 75 is halfway between 70 and 80, since $(70 + 80)/2 = 75$. Drawing a line from the 75 MPH mark to the base of the needle would pass right through 120 KPH.

3. C: Extending a line from the base of the needle to the 120 KPH mark would pass right through 75 MPH, and extending a line from the base of the needle to the 40 KPH mark would pass near 25 MPH. The decrease in speed would be the difference between the speeds or $75 - 25 = 50$. Thus, the decrease is 50 MPH

4. C: We find the line item for "Wireless Keyboard" in the first column and trace it to the QUANTITY column to find that Trey ordered 6 wireless keyboards.

5. D: We find "First-Time Customer Discount" just above the grand total and see that the amount is -$78.36. It is negative because it is being subtracted from the amount owed, so Trey's discount is $78.36.

6. B: Step 2 is saving the document. Step 3 involves sending the document to the printer.

7. C: Step 3 is printing the memo. Step 4 states to deliver it to the workstations of all applicable personnel.

8. D: Step 4 is delivering the document. Step 5 is to email all involved, stating that the memo has been delivered and attaching an electronic copy.

9. B: The data was collected from the beginning of 1982 to the end of 2000, which is a period of approximately eighteen years.

10. B: There are three (3) total astragals: the muzzle astragal, the chase astragal, and the first reinforce astragal.

11. C: Of the parts listed, the breech is at the back of the canon and is the farthest from the muzzle at the front.

12. B: The closeness of each pair can be estimated visually. By this measure it is clear that the closest pairing is that of the second reinforce ring and the chase astragal & fillets.

13. D: The shortest partition of the columns is in Accounting and Finance in the 1990s with a height around 1 unit.

14. A: The production department had the greatest expenditure of the 2010s, accounting and finance had the same expenditure as human resource management in the 2010s, and total production (41 units) is equal to research and development and purchasing combined (41 units). The only true statement is that production expenditures decreased each decade, from 17 to 13 to 11 units.

15. A: A way to estimate the answer is to note that the section for the 1990s in all but one department is the smallest. You can quantify the estimate by using the scale on the left and adding all the department expenditures to find the year with the least. For each department in the 1990s, the sum is $17 + 5 + 4 + 2 + 2 + 1 = 31$. Similarly, for the 2000s and 2010s the sums are $13 + 7 + 8 + 4 + 3 + 2 = 37$ and $11 + 9 + 8 + 6 + 4 + 4 = 42$, respectively.

16. D: We see in the second chart that business cards are under the "Advertising" heading. From the first chart we can determine that advertising is on page 4, so business cards can be found on page 4.

17. C: From the first chart we know that page 3 contains software options. So, we look under the "Software" heading in the second graphic to find that page three includes design, project management, and accounting software.

18. A: We find "Printer ink" under "Office Supplies" in the second chart, so we look for "Office Supplies" in the first chart. Leo should turn to page 1 to find printer ink.

19. C: According to the chart, the number of calls peaks at 2:00pm, so mid-afternoon appears to be the busiest time of day.

20. D: From the chart we see that the lowest number of calls occurs at 12:00pm, so we can infer that this time would have the shortest waiting period.

21. A: We can see in the first chart that Diego had two vacation days in October, while the second chart shows only one. So, the first chart is the accurate representation.

22. B: The percentages are listed as follows: New England - 5.6%, Southeast - 24.5%, Other U.S. service academies - 0.1%, and Great Lakes - 14.8%. The greatest of these is Southeast with 24.5%.

23. D: 171 is the correct answer as this number excludes other U.S. jurisdictions. 1859 is the total number of U.S. institutions, 881 is the number of private for-profit 2-year institutions in the U.S., and 178 is the number of private nonprofit 2-year institutions in both the U.S. and U.S. jurisdictions.

24. A: The number of institutions for each choice is as follows: Public Title IV institutions in the Rocky Mountains region - 80, Public 4-year Title IV institutions - 728, Private For-profit Title IV institutions - 3272, and Far West Title IV institutions - 986. The least of these is Public Title IV institutions in the Rocky Mountains region - 80.

25. B: The smaller pie shows the breakdown of vacation days. In the first chart, an equal number of days are taken January–June (24%) as are taken July–December (24%). In the second chart, the number of July–December vacation days is higher. So, the second chart gives the accurate portrayal.

26. B: In the first chart, vacation days total 48% of the time off, while in the second chart they total 52%. Since 52% is more than ½, the second chart gives the accurate portrayal.

27. A: In the first chart, holidays make up 19% of the total time off. This number is smaller than any of the other sectors. In the second chart, holidays make up 35% of the total time off. This percentage is not smaller than any of the other sectors. So, the first chart gives the accurate portrayal.

28. B: The first chart shows the total cost of insurance to the company per month. The second chart shows the cost for an individual, based on age. So, the second chart is more useful for finding the cost for a new employee.

29. D: We can see in the original prompt that Paige will be staying for two days and one night. So, she will receive two days of meals at $62 per day and one night of lodging at $136 per night. Her total lump sum for expenses can be calculated as follows: $62(2) + $136(1) = $260. The least expensive hotel is the Rest EZ Hotel at $125 per night, so we can subtract this amount from her total: $260 − $125 = $135. Then we find the cost of the meals Paige has already purchased: $67 for the first day, $12 for the omelet, and $18 for the burger. These add up to $97, so we subtract $97 from $135 to find that Paige has $38 to spend on her last meal. Since the steak is $36, she can afford it.

30. A: We can see in the original prompt that Paige will be staying for two days and one night. So, she will receive two days of meals at $62 per day and one night of lodging at $136 per night. Her total allowances for expenses can be calculated as follows: $62(2) + $136(1) = $260. The City Suites costs $150, so subtracting this from $260 leaves Paige with $110 for her six meals. Omelets are the cheapest menu items but available only at breakfast, so Paige can order two omelets for a total of $24, leaving her with $86 for her other four meals. We can divide 86 by 4 to find that Paige needs to average $21.50 or less per meal. Since the salad and burger are both less than $21.50, her allowance can cover all of her meals.

31. B: First we add up Paige's expenses. She orders two omelets at $12 each, two salads at $15 each, and sets aside $50 for room service. So $12(2) + $15(2) + $60 = $114. She will receive two days of meal allowance at $62 per day and one night of lodging allowance at $136 per night. Her total allowance for expenses can be calculated as follows: $62(2) + $136(1) = $260. So, we subtract $114 from $260 to find that Paige has $146 to spend on lodging. So, she can choose either American Best or the Rest EZ Hotel.

32. A: In the first chart, we can compare the overhead and personnel costs for each quarter by numbers. Each quarter has a higher personnel cost than overhead cost. In the second chart, we can see that the bar for personnel costs is higher than the bar for overhead costs except for in the 4th quarter. So, the first chart is accurate.

33. B: In the first chart we can see that personnel costs for the 1st–4th quarters are $50,000, $55,000, $50,000, and $65,000, respectively. So, the cost is generally increasing, but drops in the

3rd quarter. In the second chart we can see that the bar for personnel costs increases for each subsequent quarter, so the second chart is accurate.

34. B: While the pie chart can be helpful in viewing the breakdown of company spending, it does not give a justification for increasing salaries. The bar graph shows the amount of profit for each quarter, which explains how much extra money may be available for raising salaries. So, the second graphic is more effective for this purpose.

35. A: The first chart shows a breakdown of the entire budget and the spending in each sector. The second chart shows the total amount spent and earned per quarter but does not address specific areas of the budget. So, the first chart will be most effective.

36. B: To know if the decision is justified, we must know whether the new project is expected to be profitable. So, we need to know the expected cost and the expected income. We can use the top two graphics to project the income by adding all the charges. For instance, a project manager is billed at $105/hr and is expected to put 24 hours into the project, so the charge is $105(24) = \$2,520$. The total charges to the client can be calculated as follows:

$$105(24) + 90(30) + 55(50) + 60(4) + 8750 = \$16,960$$

The total internal cost can then be calculated by adding the projected costs from the third graphic: $\$3500 + \$120 + \$8750 + \$500 + \$900 = \$13,770$. Since the total income is projected to be greater than the total cost, this project is expected to be profitable and the decision is justified.

37. D: The total projected cost of the project is $13,770, as seen in the previous question. If the client will only pay $11,210, the income is lower than the cost. But if Emil can share $4,500 of the software cost with another project, then the total projected cost drops to $9,270. We calculate profit by subtracting the total projected cost from the total projected income:

$$\$11,210 - \$9,270 = \$1,940$$

Since this is less than $2,000, Emil cannot accept the counteroffer.

38. C: Ellie wants to give $1,000 to each of the 10 employees, so we multiply $1000(10) = \$10,000$ in bonuses. Next, we calculate how much was spent on personnel in the first quarter by adding the costs from the first chart: $\$135,000 + \$11,000 + \$6,000 = \$152,000$. Since she had budgeted $160,000 for personnel and only spent $152,000, this gives her an additional $8,000 she can spend on personnel. This is not sufficient for the $10,000 in proposed bonuses, so Ellie cannot give this bonus.

Workplace Documents

1. B: We can gather the subject from the first sentence: open enrollment for insurance. We read the rest of the paragraph to get a better idea of the main idea, which can be found in the second sentence: that if employees want to enroll or change their insurance policies, they need to speak to HR before the end of open enrollment (by the 28th so that changes can be made before the end of the month).

2. D: The third sentence requests employees to do two things: dress appropriately and keep noise to a minimum during the client's visit.

3. D: The main idea is clearly stated in the first sentence: time off requests for days between December 20 and January 4 need to be submitted. We find the specific deadline (December 3) in the second sentence.

4. C: The last step is for an employee to email the form to HR and his/her manager.

5. D: Signing the form is mentioned in the second sentence: it comes directly after filling out the form and printing it.

6. C: Julio clocked in an hour and 25 minutes past 8:00am. This is an hour plus a partial hour, so two hours of vacation time will be docked.

7. A: According to the second sentence, there is a two-minute grace period. So Reagan will not lose any vacation time.

8. B: We see in the third sentence that the username is the employee's email address and the password is the last 4 digits of his/her Social Security number.

9. E: In the fifth sentence, we see that the link for the tutorial is in the top right corner of the page.

10. D: We see in the fourth sentence that each person is to reset the password and become familiar with the site (by watching a tutorial if needed).

11. E: The new time-tracking system begins on Monday. Before then, employees are asked to log in, reset passwords, and become familiar with the site.

12. A: We see in the first sentence that the work schedule is changing this week. The second sentence explains the change: work will begin at 7:30am so the team can meet to discuss the project. So, the main idea is that this week's work schedule is changing to accommodate a daily project meeting.

13. B: The matchpoint, we can see from the first sentence, is an upper limit on the amount the company will contribute to an employee's IRA. So, any contributions the employee makes to his/her IRA will be matched by the company, up to a certain point (a percentage of the employee's income).

14. A: Since work was cancelled for a half-day, holiday time is used to cover it. But Rafael arrived two hours after the office opened, so his vacation time is used to cover that. So, he used a half-day (four hours) of holiday time and two hours of vacation time.

15. B: We find in the first sentence that business hours are 8:00-5:00. So, Rafael came in three hours late and left an hour early. He used a total of four hours of vacation time.

16. D: The office closes at 1:00 instead of 5:00, so four hours (or half a day) of holiday time is used. The memo states that there were two unused floating holidays prior to this, so 1½ days remain and will be paid out to employees.

17. A: The extra holiday time will be used if work is cancelled due to the weather making driving prohibitive.

18. C: If work is not cancelled but an employee chooses to stay home due to driving conditions, he/she may use vacation time.

19. B: According to the final sentence, any holiday time left at the end of the year will be paid out as a bonus.

20. E: From the first sentence we find that colorfiles are electronic files, related to the project, that can be sent to the client. Additionally, we find that they are large, so we can infer that they contain large amounts of data and likely some type of pictures, charts, or other items that take up more storage space. We can infer that colorfiles are either the main deliverable of the project, or at least an important component of the project.

21. B: Name rules are mentioned in the second sentence. Employees are to explain these to the client when sending the colorfiles. Since explaining these rules will help the client locate files from the zipped folder, we can infer that the name rules are a convention for naming the files to organize them.

22. C: PPE is mentioned in the fifth sentence as something worn for a site visit. The previous sentence defines the acronym as "personal protective equipment" designed to protect the head, eyes, and feet, among other body parts. We can deduce that PPE refers to items such as protective clothing and shoes, headwear, and safety goggles.

23. A: The M-drive is discussed in the second sentence. From context we can see that it is a location to electronically access project documents.

24. A: Finn is working on improving website navigation, a method of website optimization. The goal for this is to increase the company's client base by 10%.

25. C: A/B testing involves publishing two versions of a website to see which has a better response from potential customers. So, Finn's charts will compare the results of site visits (for example, which visits resulted in new or repeat clients) to find which website version is most effective for client gain.

26. A: The second sentence refers to updated paperwork, and the fourth sentence mentions that several items have changed since last year. So, Kim can infer that she needs to fill out new forms even if she doesn't wish to change anything.

27. D: Kerning is mentioned in the first sentence. The second sentence mentions that it is important for the company website to look professional—specifically, that the spacing of the letters in the website text is even. So, we can infer that kerning refers to the spacing of letters in the text.

28. C: Tracking is mentioned in the third sentence. The employee is directed to pay attention to tracking to avoid uneven gaps between words, so we can infer that tracking refers to the distance between words.

29. E: The fifth sentence instructs the reader to check that the typeface is legible. The employee is directed to change fonts if it is not legible, so we can infer that typeface refers to the font.

30. D: The passage states that if an employee needs to work during the lunch window, he may ask for one hour outside of that window. Since the lunch window begins at 11:30 and Jerome's meeting is at 12:30, he already has an hour within the window, so there is no need to ask for an hour at a different time.

31. C: The excerpt gives detailed instructions on filling out timesheets. The fifth sentence mentions that the billing department will be reviewing the entries. We can deduce that it is important to record time correctly so that the billing department can invoice clients appropriately.

32. B: The notice instructs the reader to create two website versions for A/B testing. The following sentences discuss tracking the response each site receives for two weeks and finding the best fit. This implies that at the end of the two-week period, one of the versions will be chosen to represent the company.

33. C: The instructions are to track several categories of response to each website, and to use the algorithm to calculate scores, so we can infer that the tracked responses are the data that is put into the algorithm to compare the two versions.

34. C: The seventh sentence mentions conversion. It is not defined, but we understand that it is a business success because it is rewarded with a bonus. The following sentence explains it as a "person who becomes a client due to the content marketing efforts." So, conversion is turning a visitor into a client through content marketing.

WorkKeys Practice Test #3

Applied Math

1. Luke counted the gumballs in a machine and found that there were 1.37 times as many gumballs as he had estimated. What is this number as a percent?

    A. 1.37%
    B. 0.137%
    C. 13.7%
    D. 0.0137%
    E. 137%

2. Samantha found that 42% of her socks were missing their mates. What decimal is this?

    A. 4.2
    B. 1.42
    C. 0.42
    D. 0.042
    E. 0.58

3. The 24 students in class each dropped a quarter in the box. How much money did they collect?

    A. $4.00
    B. $4.50
    C. $12.00
    D. $6.00
    E. $8.00

4. Elsa bought 3 lbs of pecans for $5.89 per pound. What was her total cost, assuming no tax?

    A. $11.78
    B. $17.67
    C. $13.59
    D. $19.91
    E. $15.16

5. Brent purchases 2 movie tickets for $6.50 each, a large popcorn for $7, and two drinks for $3.50 each. Tax is $2.25. How much change should Brent receive if he pays with $30?

    A. $3.27
    B. $5.25
    C. $1.18
    D. $2.02
    E. $0.75

6. Kent has \$643.82 in a checking account. He spends \$312.45 on new tires for his car. How much money does he have left?

    A. \$408.72

    B. \$328.68

    C. \$956.27

    D. \$331.37

    E. \$289.15

7. If a package of 12 cans of cola costs \$7.12, how much does each can cost? Round to the nearest cent.

    A. 63¢

    B. 62¢

    C. 61¢

    D. 60¢

    E. 59¢

8. If Louis travels on his bike at an average rate of 20 mph, how long will it take him to travel 240 miles?

    A. 48 hours

    B. 12 hours

    C. 20 hours

    D. 8 hours

    E. 6 hours

9. Find the mean temperature for the week shown in the graph below:

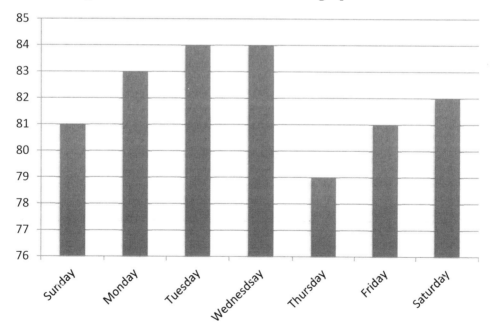

    A. 80

    B. 79.5

    C. 82

    D. 81.25

    E. 83

10. Annie, David, Mark, and Liz each had several coins as shown in the graph below. What was the average number of dimes per person?

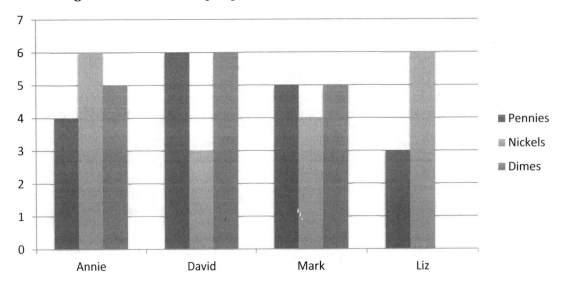

A. 4
B. 4.5
C. 4.75
D. 5
E. 5.5

11. According to the graph below, how many hours this week did Levi spend practicing his saxophone?

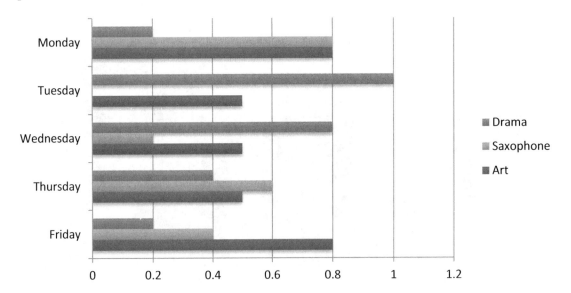

A. 1.6 hours
B. 2.4 hours
C. 1.8 hours
D. 2 hours
E. 3 hours

12. Amy, Lee, and Dani were collecting coins as shown in the chart below. How many more dimes than nickels did they have?

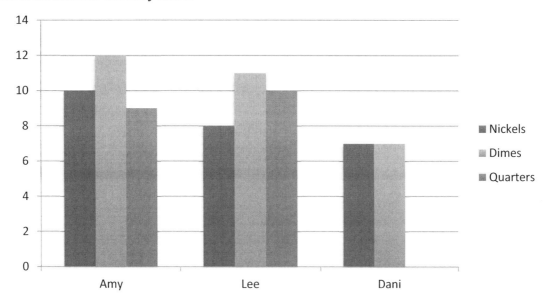

A. 55
B. 17
C. 38
D. 5
E. 1

13. Zoe had 7/8 of a pizza. She gave 1/8 to Marie and 3/8 to Kenna. What fraction of the pizza does she still have?

A. $1\frac{3}{8}$
B. $\frac{1}{2}$
C. $\frac{3}{8}$
D. $\frac{1}{4}$
E. $\frac{5}{16}$

14. Jared thought it would take 4 2/5 hours to finish his project, but it actually took 2.1 times as long. How long did the project take?

A. $6\frac{1}{2}$ hours
B. $8\frac{1}{2}$ hours
C. $7\frac{9}{10}$ hours
D. $9\frac{6}{25}$ hours
E. 9 hours

15. Marie purchased highlighters for 30 cents each, notebooks for $1.79 each, and pens for $2.49 per dozen. She bought 3 notebooks, 2 dozen pens, and 6 highlighters. What was her cost before tax?

    A. $4.58
    B. $12.15
    C. $66.93
    D. $17.88
    E. $53.12

16. A rancher has 40 adult cows, half of which are female. If all the female cows give birth to calves, how many cattle will the rancher have in total?

    A. 20
    B. 40
    C. 60
    D. 80
    E. 100

17. A Ford dealership has 137 vehicles on the lot. 38 of them are sedans, 27 are SUVs, and 64 are trucks. What is the ratio of trucks to sedans?

    A. 137:38
    B. 64:27
    C. 38:64
    D. 32:19
    E. 27:38

18. Austin needs to cut a piece of lumber to an exact size. His first cut takes off 16/64ths of an inch. The lumber is still too long, so he removes 2/64ths of an inch. Then, to get it just right, he sands off the last 64th of an inch. What length of lumber has Austin removed in total?

    A. 1 in.
    B. 19/64 in.
    C. 9/32 in.
    D. 16/64 in.
    E. 1/64 in.

19. Emily ate 1/6 of a box of chocolates. The next day she ate an additional 2/9, and the third day she ate ¼ of the box. What fraction of the box did she eat in all?

    A. 23/36
    B. 3/4
    C. 15/16
    D. 7/8
    E. 11/12

20. Grant's car holds 10 gallons of gas and can go 275 miles on a tank. Ana's car holds 12 gallons of gas and can go 324 miles on a tank. Which vehicle has better gas mileage?

    A. Grant's car
    B. Ana's car
    C. they get equally good gas mileage
    D. neither car
    E. another car that gets 28mpg

21. Miles added ½ + ½ by adding numerators and denominators to get 2/4. What mistake did he make?

    A. He multiplied instead of adding.
    B. He added only the numerators.
    C. He added only the denominators.
    D. He added both the numerators and the denominators.
    E. He added the numerators and multiplied the denominators.

22. If a space heater draws 10 amps from a 120-volt household circuit, and electricity costs 10¢ per kilowatt-hour, how much has it cost to run the space heater for 3 hours? Note that a watt-hour is equal to 1 watt of power used for one hour.

    A. $0.12
    B. $0.36
    C. $1.20
    D. $3.60
    E. $4.28

23. A dress is marked down by 20% and placed on a clearance rack, on which is posted a sign reading, "Take an extra 25% off already reduced merchandise." What fraction of the original price is the final sale price of the dress?

    A. $\frac{1}{4}$
    B. $\frac{2}{5}$
    C. $\frac{3}{5}$
    D. $\frac{9}{20}$
    E. $\frac{11}{20}$

24. Martin's bed is 7 feet in length. Which of the following represents the length of the bed, in centimeters?

    A. 221.25 cm
    B. 217.94 cm
    C. 215.52 cm
    D. 214.68 cm
    E. 213.36 cm

25. Rufus is a plumber working for ACME Plumbing Co. For a given job, he bills the customer $50 plus a rate of $85 per hour. 22% of the money goes to ACME Plumbing, the rest belongs to Rufus. How much does Rufus receive for a job that takes him 2.5 hours to complete?

    A. $204.75
    B. $165.75
    C. $57.75
    D. $262.50
    E. $252.50

26. You are constructing a semi-circular wall around some property. The wall will be a 300° arc with a radius of 38 feet. What is the total length of the wall?

    A. 99.43 ft.
    B. 198.87 ft.
    C. 238.64 ft.
    D. 97.58 ft.
    E. 256.08 ft.

27. Zane ate 5/12 of a pizza for lunch, and an additional 3/8 for dinner. What percent of the pizza is left?

    A. $79\frac{1}{6}\%$
    B. $\frac{19}{24}\%$
    C. $31\frac{5}{6}\%$
    D. $20\frac{5}{6}\%$
    E. $\frac{5}{24}\%$

28. Jordan was solving the following equation for x: $3x + 24 = 51 - 6x$. He moved the variables to the left by subtracting $3x - 6x$. Then he moved the constants to the other side by subtracting 51 – 24. His new equation was $-3x = 27$, and he divided 27 by –3 to find that $x = -9$. Why is this solution wrong?

    A. He should have added 24 to each side instead of subtracting.
    B. He should have added $6x$ to each side instead of subtracting.
    C. He should have divided 3 by 27 instead of dividing 27 by 3.
    D. He should have divided $3x$ by $-6x$ instead of subtracting.
    E. He should have canceled the negative sign.

29. A cargo container has interior dimensions of 52'5" by 7'8.5" by 7'10" and is half full of barley. Taking the density of barley at 37 pounds per cubic foot, what is the weight of the cargo?

    A. 58,553 lb
    B. 11,7106 lb
    C. 31,650 lb
    D. 83,422 lb
    E. 8,435 lb

30. Margery is planning a vacation, and she has added up the cost. Her round-trip airfare will cost $572. Her hotel cost is $89 per night, and she will be staying at the hotel for five nights. She has allotted a total of $150 for sightseeing during her trip, and she expects to spend about $250 on meals. As she books the hotel, she is told that she will receive a discount of 10% off the price of $89 for each additional night after the first night she stays there. Taking this discount into consideration, what is the amount that Margery expects to spend on her vacation?

    A. $1328.35
    B. $1373.50
    C. $1381.40
    D. $1417.60
    E. $1428.65

31. A gift box has a length of 14 inches, a height of 8 inches, and a width of 6 inches. How many square inches of wrapping paper are needed to wrap the box?

    A. 56
    B. 244
    C. 672
    D. 582
    E. 488

32. Identical rugs are offered for sale at two local shops and one online retailer, designated Stores A, B, and C, respectively. The rug's regular sales price is $296 at Store A, $220 at Store B, and $198.00 at Store C. Stores A and B collect 8% in sales tax on any after-discount price, while Store C collects no tax but charges a $35 shipping fee. A buyer has a 30% off coupon for Store A and a $10 off coupon for Store B. Which of these lists the stores in order of lowest to highest final sales price after all discounts, taxes, and fees are applied?

    A. Store A, Store B, Store C
    B. Store B, Store A, Store C
    C. Store B, Store C, Store A
    D. Store C, Store A, Store B
    E. Store C, Store B, Store A

33. An ice cream cone is 6 inches tall, and the opening at the top has a diameter of 2 inches. What percentage of a gallon of ice cream can the cone hold?

    A. 2.7%
    B. 5.8%
    C. 6.3%
    D. 10.9%
    E. 14.4%

34. In a town of 35,638 people, about a quarter of the population is under the age of 35. Of those, just over a third attend local K-12 schools. If the number of students in each grade is about the same, how many fourth graders likely reside in the town?

    A. Fewer than 100
    B. Between 200 and 300
    C. Between 300 and 400
    D. Between 400 and 500
    E. More than 500

Graphic Literacy

1. The following is a diagram of the office suite leased by a law firm. Which room is the farthest, by walking distance, from the entrance of the suite?

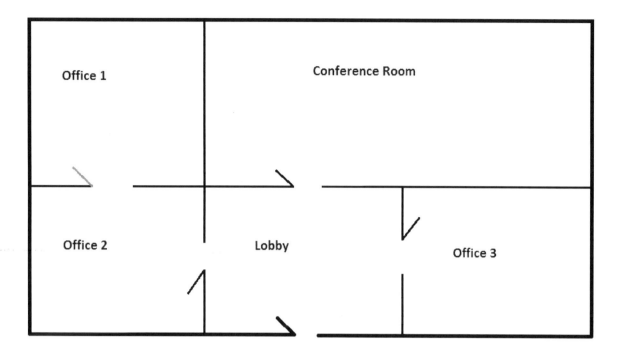

A. The lobby
B. The Conference room
C. Office 2
D. Office 1

Use the following graphic for the following 3 questions.

Shara is tracking some of her business costs for the first quarter of the year.

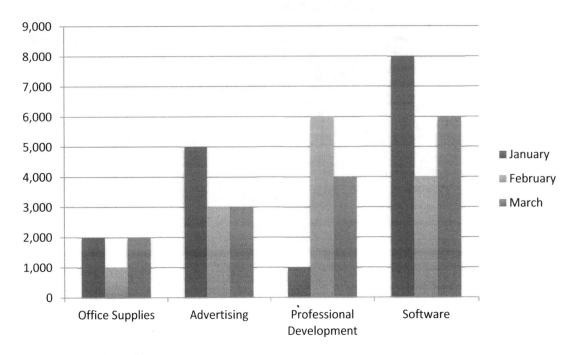

2. How much was spent on professional development in February?

    A. $4,000

    B. $6,000

    C. $1,000

    D. $8,000

3. In what month did Shara's company spend the most on advertising?

    A. January

    B. February

    C. March

    D. both February and March

4. In which two months did Shara's company spend the same amount on office supplies?

    A. January and February

    B. February and March

    C. January and March

    D. all three months were the same

Use the chart below to answer the following 3 questions.

7:45	Arrive and clock in
7:50	Check daily calendar for meetings, upcoming deadlines, etc.
7:55	Check email for any updates on schedules, client requests, etc.
8:00	Begin morning meeting if applicable, or begin daily checklist

5. What is the first thing to do after clocking in?

    A. Check email
    B. Check calendar
    C. Begin morning meeting
    D. Begin daily checklist

6. What is the last thing to do before the workday officially begins at 8:00?

    A. Check email
    B. Check calendar
    C. Begin morning meeting
    D. Begin daily checklist

7. What should be done after checking email if there is no morning meeting?

    A. Clock in
    B. Check calendar
    C. Check for updates on schedules and client requests
    D. Begin daily checklist

Use the following chart to answer the following 3 questions.

Place Order:	1. Check inventory for low supplies	2. Obtain written permission to place order	3. Order and send receipt to accounting
Receive Shipment:	1. Sign for delivery	2. Check contents against manifest	3. Enter into inventory log
Stock Supplies:	1. Check supply number on inventory sheet	2. Place on proper shelf	3. Sign stocking sheet

8. What should be done after obtaining permission to order supplies?

    A. Order and send receipt to accounting
    B. Check contents against manifest
    C. Sign for delivery
    D. Enter into inventory log

9. When all the steps in receiving a shipment have been completed, what comes next?

    A. Placing the order
    B. Signing for delivery
    C. Checking the contents against the manifest
    D. Stocking the supplies

10. What should be done after placing the received supplies on shelves?
   A. Checking the supply number
   B. Receiving the shipment
   C. Signing the stocking sheet
   D. Sending the receipt to accounting

Use the following bar graph to answer the following 3 questions:

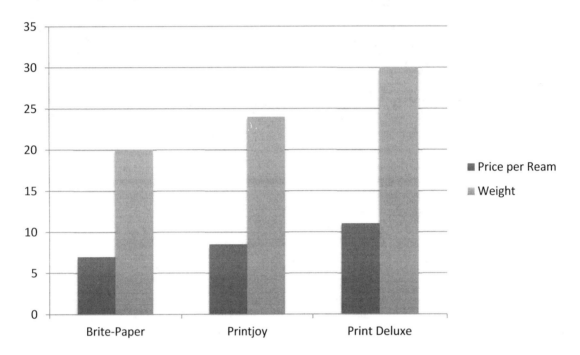

11. Noah is looking for the most inexpensive paper for his printer. Which brand should he select?
   A. Brite-Paper
   B. Printjoy
   C. Print Deluxe
   D. Either Brite-Paper or Printjoy

12. Based on the graph, what can we infer about the relationship between price per ream and weight of the paper?
   A. As weight increases, price decreases.
   B. As weight increases, price also increases.
   C. Weight and price are inversely proportional.
   D. There is no discernible relationship.

13. Olivia is printing her resume and wants the heaviest possible weight of paper to print on. Which brand should she select?
   A. Brite-Paper
   B. Printjoy
   C. Print Deluxe
   D. Either Brite-Paper or Printjoy

Use the following line graphs to answer the following 2 questions.

The company Sara and Kevin work for tracks the number of pages each employee prints.

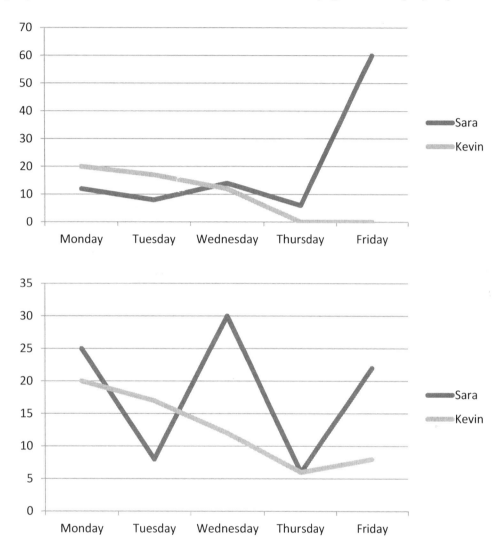

14. This week, Sara had a small amount of printing until Friday, when she printed handouts for a meeting. Which of the graphs gives an accurate representation of that information?
- A. the 1st graph
- B. the 2nd graph
- C. both are accurate
- D. neither is accurate

15. Kevin was on vacation Thursday and Friday. Which of the graphs gives an accurate representation of that information?
- A. the 1st graph
- B. the 2nd graph
- C. both are accurate
- D. neither is accurate

Use the graph below to answer the following 3 questions:

16. In which two years were exactly 11 of the shown composers concurrently alive?
    A. 1660 and 1710
    B. 1670 and 1680
    C. 1700 and 1720
    D. 1660 and 1690

17. Of the composers listed, which composer with a last name beginning with the letter, "S" died first?
    A. Samuel Scheidt
    B. Domenico Scarlatti
    C. Heinrich Schültz
    D. Johann H. Schein

18. Of the composers listed, how many died between 1650 and 1700?
    A. 5
    B. 9
    C. 7
    D. 11

Use the graph below to answer the following 3 questions:

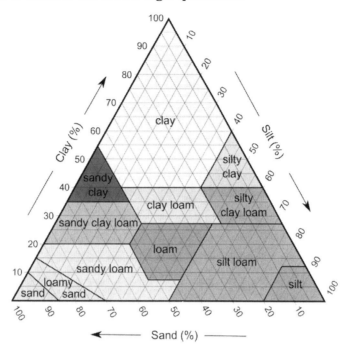

19. A soil is comprised of 30% clay, 20% silt, and 50% sand. What is the soil's classification?

  A. sandy loam
  B. clay loam
  C. loam
  D. sandy clay loam

20. A soil is comprised of 50% clay, 20% silt, and 30% sand. What is the soil's classification?

  A. silt
  B. clay
  C. silty clay
  D. loamy sand

21. A soil is comprised of 5% clay and 80% sand. What is the soil's classification?

  A. silt loam
  B. silt
  C. sandy loam
  D. loamy sand

Use the charts below to answer the following 2 questions:

Sales Schedule	
Monday	Mason
Tuesday	Megan
Wednesday	Isabelle
Thursday	Mason
Friday	Megan

Sales

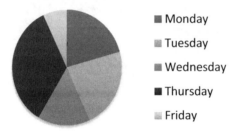

- ■ Monday
- ▦ Tuesday
- ▨ Wednesday
- ■ Thursday
- ▨ Friday

22. Which employee had the highest sales day of the week?

- A. Mason
- B. Isabelle
- C. Megan
- D. both Mason and Megan

23. Which employee had the lowest sales day of the week?

- A. Mason
- B. Isabelle
- C. Megan
- D. both Mason and Megan

24. What pattern can be seen in the line graph below?

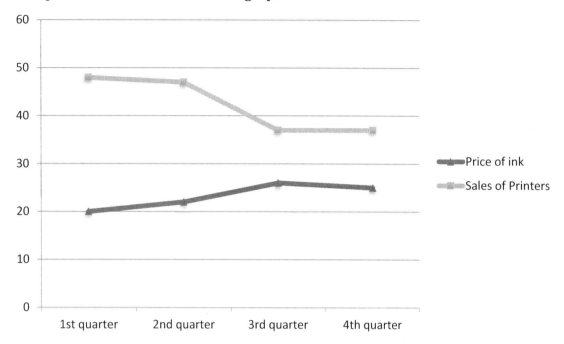

A. As the price of ink rises, printer sales also rise.
B. There is a directly proportionate relationship between ink price and printer sales.
C. As the price of ink rises, printer sales drop.
D. There is no discernible relationship.

Use the charts below to answer the following 3 questions.

The charts below show the breakdown of a company's advertising expenses per quarter.

Chart 1

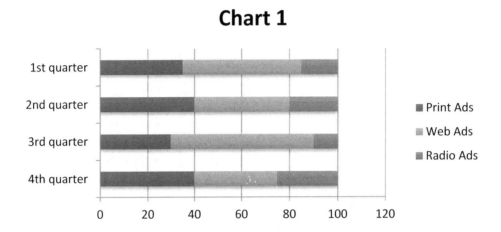

Chart 2

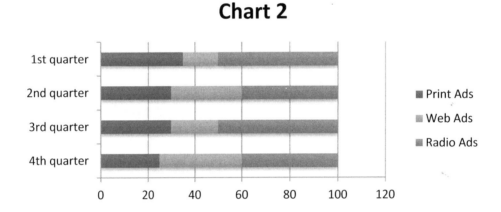

25. Which of the charts accurately portrays that web ad expenses were highest in the 3rd quarter?

    A. Chart 1
    B. Chart 2
    C. Both are accurate
    D. Neither is accurate

26. Which of the charts accurately portrays that radio ads were consistently the greatest advertising expense?

    A. Chart 1
    B. Chart 2
    C. Both are accurate
    D. Neither is accurate

27. Which of the charts accurately portrays that the cost of print ads was the same in the 2nd and 3rd quarters?

    A. Chart 1
    B. Chart 2
    C. Both are accurate
    D. Neither is accurate

28. What relationship can be seen in the graph below?

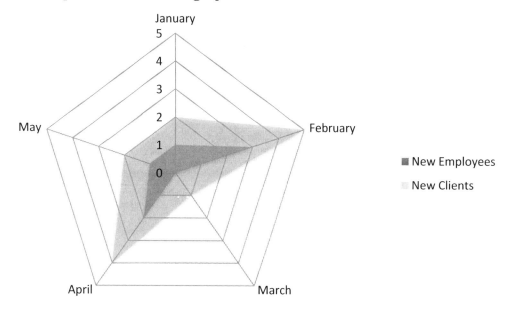

    A. There is a direct correlation between the number of new employees and new clients.
    B. There is an inverse relationship between the number of new employees and new clients.
    C. As the number of new employees rises, the number of new clients drops.
    D. There is no discernible relationship between the number of new employees and new clients.

Use the graphs below to answer the following 3 questions.

Harper tracked the days she was off work last year.

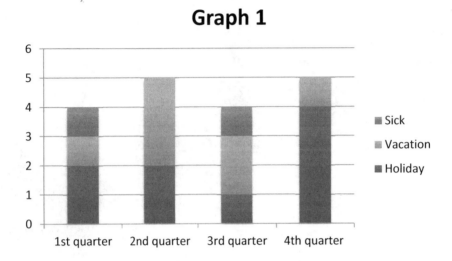

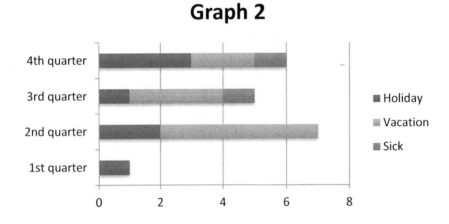

29. **Which graph shows that half of the vacation time that Harper took was in the 2nd quarter?**
    A. Graph 1
    B. Graph 2
    C. Both graphs
    D. Neither graph

30. **Which graph shows that Harper had more holiday time than vacation time last year?**
    A. Graph 1
    B. Graph 2
    C. Both graphs
    D. Neither graph

31. Which graph shows that Harper took sick days only in the latter half of the year?

    A. Graph 1
    B. Graph 2
    C. Both graphs
    D. Neither graph

Use the graphs below to answer the following 2 questions.

Alli is planning to purchase a new vehicle in July. She is charting how much she sets aside in savings each month for the car, and how much the car will cost depending on the size of down payment she makes (tax and interest are figured in).

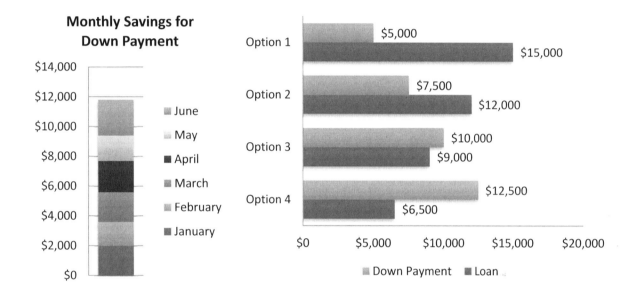

32. Which down payment should Alli choose? Take note of what she can afford and how much the car will cost with the various options.

    A. $5,000
    B. $7,500
    C. $10,000
    D. $12,500

33. The dealership runs a special in May, taking $1,000 off the price of the vehicle Alli wants. Should she buy it then or wait until she has more saved up for the down payment?

    A. Buy in April
    B. Buy in May
    C. Wait until June
    D. Wait until July

34. Ethan submitted a vacation request for 5 days in July. Will he be eligible, based on the graphs below?

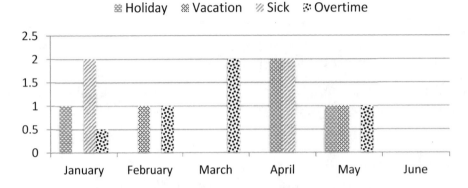

January 1	PTO Report (vacation and sick time)
Rollover from last year:	4.6 days
Days earned last year	13.6 days
Days taken last year	9.0 days
Monthly accrual:	1.25 days
New Year bonus:	1 day

A. Yes, because he has enough PTO accrued.
B. Yes, because he has only used 3 of his allotted vacation days for the year.
C. No, because he has used too many sick days.
D. No, because he does not have enough PTO.

35. Aubrey is designing a web ad for her employer and finds a service to publish it for $3,500. Will this decision be approved, according to the charts below?

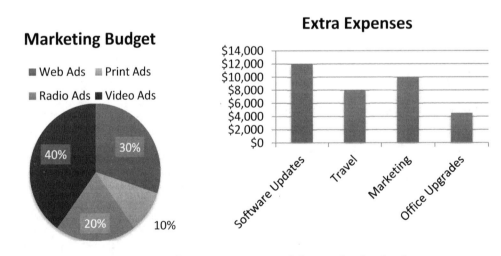

A. Yes, because web ads are a significant percentage of the marketing budget.
B. Yes, because the marketing budget is $10,000, which easily covers the $3,500.
C. No, because the web ad budget should not be spent on a single ad.
D. No, because the web ad budget is only $3,000.

Use the graphics below to answer the following 2 questions:

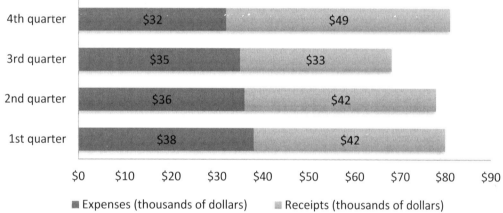

■ Expenses (thousands of dollars)   ■ Receipts (thousands of dollars)

36. Which of the graphs shows that there was a deficit in the 3rd quarter?

A. The pie chart
B. The bar graph
C. Both graphs
D. Neither graph

37. Which of the graphs portrays that the profit steadily increases throughout the year?

A. The pie chart
B. The bar graph
C. Both graphs
D. Neither graph

38. Alan decided to offer a 10% discount to a new client to secure a job. He needs to leave a buffer of at least $2,000 to address unexpected costs of production. Was his decision correct? Use the chart below to justify your answer (the chart shows the original costs before the discount).

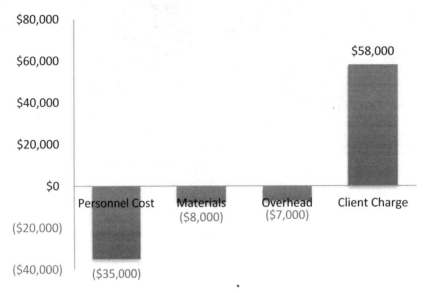

A. Yes, because the expected profit is $2,200.
B. Yes, because the client costs outweigh the internal costs.
C. No, because the expected profit is $1,750.
D. No, because the project is expected to lose money with the discount.

Workplace Documents

1. Based on the following excerpt, which task does NOT need to be completed before 8:00am?

> Please note that employees must be on the clock by 8:00am. This means that you must have clocked in, taken care of any personal responsibilities, and be seated at your desk at 8:00am. Employees are welcome to put lunches in the refrigerator, pour coffee, and greet coworkers, but please do this BEFORE 8:00am so that you are ready to start the workday promptly. We must be available to our clients during business hours, so it is important that we are at our desks when business hours begin.

A. Take care of personal responsibilities
B. Clocking in
C. Putting lunches in the refrigerator
D. Sitting at one's desk
E. Making oneself available to clients

2. Identify the main idea from the following excerpt:

> Note that lunchtime has changed: all employees will now take lunch between 11:45 and 12:45. Clocking out before 11:45 or clocking back in after 12:45 may result in disciplinary action unless you have the express permission of your manager. Please remember that traffic is unpredictable and leave yourself plenty of time to get back to the office.

A. Do not clock out before 11:45 or back in after 12:45.
B. You will need your manager's permission to take lunch at any other time than 11:45–12:45.
C. There is a new lunch window for all employees: 11:45–12:45.
D. Be mindful of traffic so you aren't late.
E. Going out of the office for lunch creates a risk of returning late.

3. Identify the main idea from the following excerpt:

> Please be aware that we are hosting a client, ABC Technology, on Thursday from 1:00–4:00. While all of our clients are important, ABC Technology is one of our biggest customers and it is important to maintain a professional atmosphere. To this end, please be sure that your dress is appropriate and please keep noise to a minimum so that the meeting will not be disturbed. Thank you!

A. ABC Technology will be in the office for 3 hours.
B. Dress appropriately and be quiet while the client is in the office.
C. ABC Technology is one of the company's most important clients.
D. Employees should make sure the meeting is not disturbed.
E. Employees should maintain a professional atmosphere while the client is visiting.

Read the following excerpt from a memo to the production team to answer the following 3 questions:

> When writing an email to a client, first introduce yourself (name, position, and company). Second, explain what project you are working on. Next give the reason you are writing (such as asking a question about the project, giving a progress report, or explaining a change in scope). The next step is to assure the client that his/her project is a priority and is receiving careful attention. Finally, close by letting the client know to contact you with any questions.

4. What is the third step in emailing a client?
   A. Introducing yourself
   B. Giving your name, position, and company
   C. Explaining what project you are working on
   D. Giving the reason for writing
   E. Assuring the client that his/her project is a priority

5. When should an employee introduce him/herself?
   A. At the beginning
   B. After identifying the project
   C. After giving the reason for writing
   D. After assuring the client that his/her project is a priority
   E. In the closing

6. When should an employee invite the client to ask questions?
   A. At the beginning
   B. After identifying the project
   C. After giving the reason for writing
   D. After giving a progress report
   E. In the closing

7. Identify the main idea from the following memorandum excerpt:

> As all of you know, our clients are the reason we stay in business. While we believe that our employees are our first clients, we sometimes need to take special measures for our outside clients. Please be aware that we are hosting ABC Technology on Thursday from 1:00–4:00. ABC Technology is one of our biggest customers and it is important to maintain a professional atmosphere. To this end, please be sure that your dress is appropriate and please keep noise to a minimum so that the meeting will not be disturbed. Thank you!

   A. Clients keep the company in business.
   B. Some clients need special treatment.
   C. ABC Technology will be visiting on Thursday from 1:00–4:00.
   D. Employees should maintain a professional atmosphere during the client's visit.
   E. Employees should avoid disturbing the meeting while the client is present.

8. Identify the main idea from the following excerpt from a company handbook:

> Please remember that our staff is a direct reflection of our business. When our clients see you, they see the company. To this end it is important to maintain a professional appearance. We welcome a business casual environment. Please select items that not only fit into the dress code outlined below but also are neat, well-maintained, and modest. We are grateful for each person on this team and hope you will help us to present the best possible image of our business!

A. Staff reflect the business.
B. Staff should make sure their clothing fits into the dress code.
C. Staff clothing should be neat, well-maintained, and modest.
D. Staff should plan their clothing based on which clients they may see.
E. Staff should maintain a professional appearance.

Use the excerpt below to answer the following 2 questions:

> All Blue team members: please note a change in your schedule (effective this week only). Report to your supervisor at 7:30am each morning for a brief meeting before beginning work. This is a crucial week on the project and we need to stay on a tight schedule while giving high-quality work. Thanks for your understanding.

9. What change is being made to the schedule?
A. The project is having a crucial week and will be on a tight schedule.
B. There will be a pre-work meeting tomorrow.
C. Employees are to arrive at 7:30am each morning this week.
D. The supervisor will be adjusting the schedule to finish a big project.
E. Supervisors will arrive at 7:30 each morning for a meeting.

10. How long will this new schedule be in place?
A. Today
B. This week
C. This month
D. Indefinitely
E. The passage does not specify

Use the following excerpt from an employee orientation packet to answer the following 2 questions:

> When you are assigned a workstation, log in to the computer with the information given (username and passcode are on your welcome letter). First open your email and make sure that notifications are turned on. Then set your email signature following the instructions on the next page. Finally, send a test email to _admin@abctechnology.com_ to make sure it is working. You should receive a reply within 15 minutes.

11. What is the first thing a new employee should do after logging in to the computer?
A. Open his/her email and turn on notifications
B. Type in username and password to log in
C. Go to his/her workstation
D. Set email signature
E. Send a test email

12. When should the employee send a test email?

A. After logging in to the computer
B. After setting the email signature
C. After opening email
D. After typing in the username and password
E. After receiving a reply

Use the excerpt below to answer the following 2 questions:

> When you arrive for your first day, get a visitor's pass at the gate. It will be good for three days, so before the third day you'll need to visit HR to get a permanent pass. You can download the form from the "New Team Members" folder on the website. When you turn it in, HR will print a permanent pass for you. Affix it to the inside of your windshield to the left of the steering wheel. Be sure to park in the area designated by the color of your pass (see map on the next page).

13. Jane's first day is Friday. When does she need to have a permanent pass (assuming a regular Monday–Friday schedule)?

A. Friday
B. Monday
C. Tuesday
D. Wednesday
E. Thursday

14. What does Jane need to do to get her permanent pass?

A. Stop at the gate
B. Affix it to her windshield
C. Park in the correct area
D. Print it from her computer
E. Fill out the form and turn it in to HR

Gillian's company drew up an agreement for a project as shown below. Use the agreement to answer the following 2 questions:

Consultant Agreement		
The Client agrees to pay The Company the following for services rendered:		
Software Package	n/a	$3,500
Setup	12 hrs	$960
Phase 1	64 hrs	$5,120
Phase 2	90 hrs	$7,200
Phase 3	56 hrs	$4,480
QA/QC	6 hrs	$480
Closeout	8 hrs	$640
TOTAL	**236 hrs**	**$22,380**
Note: for any addition to the scope, extra hours may be added at $85/hr.		

15. Gillian was invoicing a client for Phase 1 and realized that the scope changed from 64 project hours to 82 project hours. How should she adjust the invoice?

    A. Move the extra hours to Phase 2 in case it comes under budget

    B. Add on the cost of 18 extra hours at $85/hr

    C. Create an Additional Services bill for the extra hours

    D. Tell the project team to cut 18 hours out of Phase 2

    E. Leave the invoice as it stands due to contractual obligation

16. The client decided to remove Phase 3 from the scope but to add an extra segment to Phase 2. The extra segment took the team 12 hours. How should Gillian adjust the project invoice?

    A. Subtract 44 hours out of Phase 3 to leave 12 hours

    B. Add 12 hours at production rate plus principal time

    C. Delete the line item for Phase 3 and add 12 hours to Phase 2 at $85/hr

    D. Create an Additional Services bill for the extra hours and reimburse the Phase 3 bill

    E. Leave the invoice as it stands due to contractual obligation

Use the excerpt below to answer the following 3 questions:

> When you arrive at work on the first day, report immediately to your supervisor (Juan Gonzales) for your assignment. He will tell you which project you will be starting on and can give you the login to find project documents, etc., on the M-drive (projects are arranged by number chronologically). Be prepared with proper clothes and shoes as you may be going with him on a site visit. If the site visit is rescheduled for another day, you can fill out your new employee paperwork and take it to HR, where you will be given a parking pass when all paperwork is completed. If you have any questions during the day, please ask Carla, whose desk is next to yours.

17. Today is Cameron's first day on the job and he has received the notice above. When he arrives at work, Juan is not there. What should Cameron do?

    A. He should wait at his desk.

    B. He should fill out his new employee paperwork.

    C. He should ask Carla for direction.

    D. He should search for Juan.

    E. He should go home and wait for further instructions.

18. Juan is in a meeting when Cameron arrives, but when he comes out he tells Cameron that they will be leaving in an hour and to try to get his parking pass in the meantime. What should Cameron do?

    A. He should fill out his new employee paperwork and submit to HR.

    B. He should ask Carla for help.

    C. He should go to HR and ask for a parking pass.

    D. He should make sure he has the proper clothes and shoes with him.

    E. He should look up the project documents.

19. After the site visit, Juan told Cameron to print the project plan for Project 023-12. What other information does Cameron need to ask for?

    A.   The project documents
    B.   The project number
    C.   The proper clothes and shoes
    D.   The M-drive login
    E.   The printer password

Use the excerpt below to answer the following 3 questions:

> Please refer to the Sales Funnel graph on the next page to understand our marketing method. The first (widest) portion of the funnel involves attracting potential clients. As part of the IT department, you can help with this by focusing on Search Engine Optimization to make sure that our site appears in applicable online searches. SEO will be a major part of our marketing efforts this month. The second layer of the funnel, narrower than the first, encourages visitors to learn more about the company. The third layer is the narrowest and involves securing sales, turning visitors into clients. IT is also in charge of data visualization, so please track info such as number of hits for each layer of the funnel and create graphs to illustrate this info for our meetings.

20. What is a Sales Funnel graph?

    A.   A graph to aid employees in project efficiency, giving a series of steps to follow in each stage of a project
    B.   A graph of the company's marketing method, involving multiple layers that represent steps to gain new clients
    C.   A graph that shows number of new clients gained, sorted by employee responsible
    D.   A method of measuring the number of sales per employee, charted to show best performance in the company
    E.   A method of Search Engine Optimization to retain clients

21. What is SEO?

    A.   A tactic to attract new clients with a customized website
    B.   A method of attracting new clients by making the website easier to navigate
    C.   A method of making the company website more visible by appearing in online searches
    D.   A way to retain clients by tracking their web searches and tailoring the website to them
    E.   A system of categorizing new clients

22. What is data visualization?

    A.   A running list of the number of hits each layer gets
    B.   A detailed description of the sales funnel information
    C.   Converting interested visitors into paying clients
    D.   The step between the second and third layers of the sales funnel
    E.   A method of graphically showing information

Mometrix

Use the excerpt below to answer the following 2 questions:

> When you arrive at New Construction on the first day, report immediately to your supervisor (Juan Gonzales) for your assignment. He will tell you which project you will be starting on and can give you the login to the M-drive to find project documents (projects are arranged by number chronologically). Please read over the list of necessary items before your first day and make sure that you have everything you need. You may be going on a site visit on your first morning, so come prepared with the appropriate PPE for eyes, head, and feet. If the site visit is rescheduled for another day, you can fill out your new employee paperwork and take it to HR, where you will be given a parking pass when all paperwork is completed. If you have any questions during the day, please ask Carla, whose desk is next to yours.

23. Shane received the notice above before beginning a new job and is shopping for work supplies. What can he infer that he needs for a site visit?

  A. Protective shoes, hardhat, safety goggles
  B. Ear muffs, safety goggles, hardhat
  C. Hardhat, ear muffs, protective shoes
  D. Safety goggles, dust mask, hardhat
  E. Dust mask, ear muffs, protective shoes

24. When Shane arrived at work, Juan told him to arrive at 7:45am the following day with his PPE and a notepad. What can Shane infer that he will be doing tomorrow, and how should he spend his time this morning?

  A. He will be filling out his paperwork tomorrow, and going on a site visit this morning.
  B. He will be purchasing his PPE tomorrow, and filling out his paperwork this morning.
  C. He will be going on a site visit tomorrow, and purchasing his PPE this morning.
  D. He will be going on a site visit tomorrow, and filling out his paperwork this morning.
  E. He will be filling out his paperwork tomorrow, and purchasing his PPE this morning.

25. Amy's rec center team is two days ahead of schedule. What can she infer the notice means by "resources" and what should she do, based on the following excerpt?

> The parking garage and rec center projects are currently ahead of schedule. Please verify your progress, using the WBS to assess when you project the next phase will be completed. Email Julio with a progress report, including expected completion date and how much leeway you have in your time budget. Then move all available resources to Mike's team to work on the library project.

  A. "Resources" refers to the project budget, so Amy should funnel extra funds to Mike's project.
  B. "Resources" are tools and materials, so Amy should send any extra materials to Mike.
  C. "Resources" refers to outside subject experts, so Amy should direct the experts to help Mike.
  D. "Resources" refers to project space, so Amy should invite Mike to share her workspace.
  E. "Resources" are team members, so Amy should send any personnel she can spare to Mike.

201

Use the excerpt below to answer the following 2 questions:

> Please refer to the Sales Funnel graph on the next page to understand our marketing method. The first (widest) portion of the funnel involves attracting a large number of potential clients. You can help with this by focusing on Search Engine Optimization to make sure that our site appears in applicable online searches. SEO will be a major part of our marketing efforts this month. The second layer of the funnel, narrower than the first, encourages interested visitors to learn more about the company. The third layer is the narrowest and involves securing sales. Once visitors have become clients, we move to a new marketing strategy to encourage repeat business. The IT department is also in charge of data visualization, so please track info such as numbers in each layer of the funnel and create graphs to illustrate this info for our meetings.

26. **What can be inferred about the number of people in each layer of the funnel?**
    A. Each successive layer has a larger amount of people.
    B. Each successive layer has a smaller amount of people.
    C. Each layer has a different set of potential clients.
    D. Each layer has the same number of people.
    E. Each layer has five more people than the layer before it.

27. **Does the Sales Funnel strategy apply to all website visitors or only new ones?**
    A. First-time visitors only
    B. Both visitors and current clients
    C. Clients who have made a single purchase in the past
    D. Clients only
    E. All visitors, but more emphasis on first-time visitors

Use the excerpt below from an employee contract to answer the following 2 questions:

> At ABC Technology, much of your work will involve developing new systems and software solutions. While you should prioritize your given assignments, employees are encouraged to develop their own solutions. Any inventions and ideas generated on company time and with company resources are the intellectual property of the company. All software purchased and installed by the company, and every product thereof, is the sole property of the company.

28. **Reese installed his company's software on a personal laptop so he could work from home. On his own time, he created a program on his laptop, using the software, and wanted to patent it. Can he do so?**
    A. Yes, because it is his own idea.
    B. Yes, because he used his own time.
    C. Yes, because he worked on it at home.
    D. No, because he used a company computer.
    E. No, because he used company software.

29. Reese uses his lunch break to brainstorm a new idea, jotting down ideas at his desk and working on it later at home on his own computer. Whose property is his invention?

    A. The company's, because he was at the office.
    B. His own, because he used his own time and property.
    C. The company's, because he was on company time.
    D. His own, because it was handwritten.
    E. The company's, because it was during his period of employment.

30. Based on the excerpt below, infer why suppliers may only give small, promotional items as gifts.

> As the holiday season approaches, we would like to remind you of our Supplier Code of Conduct. Our employees who are involved in procurement decisions may not accept any business courtesies, with the exception of very low value promotional items. As in any business relationship, our suppliers must ensure that the offering or receipt of any gift or business courtesy does not violate the rules and standards of the recipient's organization. We look forward to continuing a long and mutually beneficial business relationship and appreciate your cooperation on this.

    A. Because employees may be tempted to show favor to the suppliers who give large gifts
    B. Because employees may be recruited by suppliers to change companies
    C. Because employees would have to report the gifts on their tax returns
    D. Because suppliers would develop a relationship with a single employee rather than the company
    E. Because it is not professional to give a gift to a single employee

Use the excerpt below to answer the following 3 questions:

> As part of the content marketing team, you will be in charge of selecting and uploading content of interest to potential clients. As one facet of content marketing, we are beginning a weekly podcast to share industry tips and give listeners a glimpse of what we do on a daily basis. We are looking for new podcast subjects so we welcome fresh ideas, as well as any other ideas that can help with conversion rate optimization. We have used several CRO methods in the past, from surveys and mailing lists to free offers, but are looking for new ideas on winning a greater percentage of visitors to our site. When searching for ideas, a good place to start is with data mining. Ask your supervisor for a list of the websites we prefer to use to search for behavior patterns of potential clients. As an incentive, each team member will receive a bonus for each successful conversion. Specifically, you will receive a $50 gift card for each person who becomes a client due to the content marketing efforts.

31. What is content marketing?

    A. Aiming marketing efforts at a specific demographic of potential clients
    B. Posting information or other content online to draw and engage potential clients
    C. A method of increasing sales by marketing to multiple demographics
    D. Sending marketing teams to physical locations to attract potential clients
    E. Offering free products to catch the interest of potential clients

32. What is data mining?

A. A method of gathering data on behavior of potential clients for marketing purposes
B. Aiming marketing efforts at a specific demographic of potential clients
C. Posting information or other content online to draw and engage potential clients
D. A method of increasing sales by marketing to multiple demographics
E. Sending marketing teams to physical locations to attract potential clients

33. What is CRO?

A. Sending marketing teams to physical locations to attract potential clients
B. Aiming marketing efforts at a specific demographic of potential clients
C. Posting information or other content online to draw and engage potential clients
D. A method of turning an increasing percentage of website visitors into clients
E. A method of gathering data on behavior of potential clients for marketing purposes

34. Why is it important for employees to be punctual, as described in the excerpt below?

> Good morning! This is just a reminder to be mindful of your use of company time. Please note that employees must be on the clock by 8:00am. This means that you must have clocked in, taken care of any personal responsibilities, and be seated at your desk at 8:00am. Employees are welcome to put lunches in the refrigerator, pour coffee, and greet coworkers, but please do this BEFORE 8:00am so that you are ready to start the workday promptly. It is important to be at our desks whenever possible during business hours. To further serve our clients, please check your calendar and email before beginning any work to make sure that you are aware of any changes to schedule or client needs, and that you are prepared for any scheduled meetings that may come up.

A. Employees should not be paid for time spent on personal responsibilities.
B. Projects may fall behind if employees are not punctual.
C. Employees need to be available to clients during business hours.
D. Visiting with coworkers should take place outside of business hours.
E. Employees should set good examples for each other.

Answer Key and Explanations for Test #3

Applied Math

1. E: A decimal can be converted to a percent by moving the decimal two places to the right. So, 1.37 becomes 137%.

2. C: To convert 42% to a decimal, we move the decimal point two places to the left. So, 42% becomes 0.42.

3. D: There are 4 quarters in a dollar, so we can divide the number of quarters by 4 to find the number of dollars. Since $\frac{24}{4} = 6$, the students collected $6.00.

4. B: To find the total, we can add the cost of each pound. Since Elsa bought 3 pounds, we add $5.89 + $5.89 + $5.89 to achieve $17.67. Alternatively, we can multiply the cost per pound by the number of pounds. Since $5.89 × 3 = $17.67, Elsa's total cost was $17.67.

5. E: First we need to calculate Brent's total cost, including tax. We add $6.50 + $6.50 + $7.00 + $3.50 + $3.50 + $2.25 to find a total of $29.25. We then subtract this total from $30. Since $30.00 − $29.25 = $0.75, Brent's change is $0.75 or 75 cents.

6. D: $643.82 minus $312.45 is $331.37

7. E: Divide the price of the 12-pack by 12 to get the price per can: $\frac{\$7.12}{12} = \$0.593$, or 59¢ after rounding to the nearest cent.

8. B: Establish the proportion and solve for x:

$$\frac{20}{1} = \frac{240}{x}$$
$$20x = 240$$
$$x = \frac{240}{20} = 12 \text{ hours}$$

9. C: We calculate the mean by finding the sum of the temperatures and dividing by the number of days.

$$\frac{81 + 83 + 84 + 84 + 79 + 81 + 82}{7} = 82$$

Therefore, the mean temperature for the week was 82 degrees.

10. A: We calculate the average number of dimes by finding the total number of dimes and dividing by the number of people. Since $\frac{5+6+5+0}{4} = 4$, the average number of dimes per person was 4. Note that even though Liz did not have any dimes, she is calculated into the number of people.

11. D: We find the number of hours spent on saxophone each day (note that he did not practice his saxophone on Tuesday, so we insert 0 for this day) and add them: $0.8 + 0 + 0.2 + 0.6 + 0.4 = 2.0$, or 2 hours total.

12. D: First we need to organize our information. From the chart we can see that Amy had 10 nickels and 12 dimes, Lee had 8 nickels and 11 dimes, and Dani had 7 nickels and 7 dimes. The number of quarters is irrelevant so we ignore that information. We need to find the total number of dimes and the total number of nickels so that we can calculate the difference. We add the number of nickels: $10 + 8 + 7 = 25$. Then we add the number of dimes: $12 + 11 + 7 = 30$. Finally, we subtract nickels from dimes: $30 - 25 = 5$. So they had 5 more dimes than nickels.

13. C: First we add the portions that Zoe gave away by adding the numerators and placing the sum over the denominator: $\frac{1}{8} + \frac{3}{8} = \frac{4}{8}$. Then we subtract this from the original amount: $\frac{7}{8} - \frac{4}{8} = \frac{3}{8}$. So Zoe still has 3/8 of the pizza.

14. D: To find the total amount of time, we need to multiply $4\frac{2}{5}$ by 2.1. To do this, we need to convert both numbers to fractions. We change $4\frac{2}{5}$ to an improper fraction by multiplying the denominator by the whole number, adding the numerator, and placing this new number over the original denominator: $5 \times 4 + 2 = 22$, so our improper fraction is $\frac{22}{5}$. Then we convert 2.1 to a mixed number by placing the 1 over 10 to obtain $2\frac{1}{10}$. We can follow the same process as above to convert this mixed number to an improper fraction: $10 \times 2 + 1 = 21$, so the fraction is $\frac{21}{10}$. We can multiply $\frac{22}{5} \times \frac{21}{10}$ by multiplying the numerators ($22 \times 21 = 462$) and denominators ($5 \times 10 = 50$). Placing the new numerator and denominator together yields $\frac{462}{50}$, which we can convert back into a mixed number by dividing the denominator into the numerator. Dividing 462 by 50 yields 9 with a remainder of 12, so our mixed number is $9\frac{12}{50}$. The fraction can be reduced by dividing both numerator and denominator by 2, so Jared spent $9\frac{6}{25}$ hours on the project.

15. B: First we need to organize our information. Marie bought 6 highlighters for 30 cents each, 3 notebooks for $1.79 each, and 2 dozen pens at $2.49 per dozen. So, we can calculate the cost of each type of item and then add the three costs together. First, we change 30 cents to $0.30 so that all units match and then we write out the whole equation: $6 \times \$0.30 + 3 \times \$1.79 + 2 \times \$2.49$. Because multiplication comes before addition in the order of operations, we perform each of the multiplication parts of the problem to obtain $\$1.80 + \$5.37 + \$4.98 = \$12.15$. So, Marie's total cost before tax was $12.15.

16. C: The rancher starts with 40 cows. If all the female cows give birth to calves, 20 calves will have been born, and the rancher will have 60 cows.

17. D: To determine the ratio of trucks to sedans on the lot, put the number or trucks on the left side of a colon, and the number of sedans on the right side. Doing this yields 64:38, but that isn't an answer choice, but we can simplify it to 32:19. Note that choice C is incorrect because it represents the ratio of sedans to trucks, not trucks to sedans.

18. B: To obtain the total, add up the fractions given: $\frac{16}{64} + \frac{2}{64} + \frac{1}{64} = \frac{19}{64}$ in.

19. A: To find the total fraction of the chocolates, we add the three fractions: $\frac{1}{6} + \frac{2}{9} + \frac{1}{4}$. Before we can add the fractions, they must share a common denominator. We find the common denominator by calculating the least common multiple of 6, 9, and 4. The smallest number that all three can divide into is 36, so now we rewrite each fraction with a denominator of 36. Since $\frac{36}{6} = 6$, we multiply $\frac{1}{6}$ by $\frac{6}{6}$ to obtain $\frac{6}{36}$. Since $\frac{36}{9} = 4$, we multiply $\frac{2}{9}$ by $\frac{4}{4}$ to obtain $\frac{8}{36}$. Since $\frac{36}{4} = 9$, we multiply ¼ by $\frac{9}{9}$ to obtain $\frac{9}{36}$. Then we can add $\frac{6}{36} + \frac{8}{36} + \frac{9}{36}$ to obtain $\frac{23}{36}$. So, Emily ate $\frac{23}{36}$ of the box of chocolates.

20. A: We need to calculate the miles per gallon of each vehicle so we can compare them. We divide miles by gallons, so Grant's mileage is $275 \div 10 = 27.5$ mpg. Ana's mileage is $324 \div 12 = 27$ mpg. Since 27.5 is greater than 27, Grant's car has better gas mileage.

21. D: When adding fractions, only the numerators are added, while the denominator remains the same. Miles should have obtained $\frac{2}{2}$, or simply 1.

22. B: Use the equation for electric power: $amps = \frac{watts}{volts}$. Rearrange the equation and solve for watts, $watts = amps \times volts = 10 \text{ A} \times 120 \text{ V} = 1200$. The heater uses 1200 watts, and it is used for 3 hours. This means that it has used $1200 \times 3 = 3600$ watt-hours of energy, or 3.6 kilowatt-hours. Multiplying by the cost of electricity, the total cost is $3.6 \times \$0.10 = \$0.36$

23. C: When the dress is marked down by 20%, the cost of the dress is 80% of its original price. Since a percentage can be written as a fraction by placing the percentage over 100, the reduced price of the dress can be written as $\frac{80}{100}x$, or $\frac{4}{5}x$, where x is the original price. When discounted an extra 25%, the dress costs 75% of the reduced price. This results in the expression $\frac{75}{100}\left(\frac{4}{5}x\right)$, which can be simplified to $\frac{3}{4}\left(\frac{4}{5}x\right)$, or $\frac{3}{5}x$. So the final price of the dress is three-fifths of the original price.

24. E: Since 7 feet equals 84 inches, and 1 inch equals 2.54 centimeters, the following proportion can be written: $\frac{84}{x} = \frac{1}{2.54}$. Solving for x gives: $x = 213.36$. Thus, the bed is 213.36 centimeters in length.

25. A: The amount Rufus makes for a given job can be modeled by the equation:

$$Income_{Rufus} = (\$50 + \$85 \times hours) \times 0.78$$

For a job that takes him 2.5 hours,

$$\begin{aligned} Income_{Rufus} &= (\$50 + \$85 \times 2.5) \times 0.78 \\ &= (50 + 212.50) \times 0.78 \\ &= \$204.75 \end{aligned}$$

26. B: Calculate the circumference of a circle with a radius of 38 feet:

$$\begin{aligned} circumference &= 3.14 \times diameter \\ &= 2 \times 3.14 \times radius \\ &= 6.28 \times 38 \\ &= 238.64 \text{ ft.} \end{aligned}$$

Multiply this number by the ratio of the degrees the wall will cover to the total degrees in a circle:

$$238.64 \times \frac{300°}{360°} = 198.87 \text{ ft}$$

27. D: First we need to find the total amount he ate by adding $\frac{5}{12}$ and $\frac{3}{8}$. We find a common denominator by finding the least common multiple of 12 and 8. The smallest number divisible by both 12 and 8 is 24, so we multiply $\frac{5}{12}$ by $\frac{2}{2}$ to obtain $\frac{10}{24}$, and we multiply $\frac{3}{8}$ by $\frac{3}{3}$ to obtain $\frac{9}{24}$. Then we add the fractions by adding the numerators and placing them over the denominator: $\frac{19}{24}$. Now we can subtract $\frac{19}{24}$ from 1 to find the amount of pizza left. We write 1 as $\frac{24}{24}$ and subtract the numerators to obtain $\frac{5}{24}$. Finally, we must convert the fraction to a percent. We can do this by setting up a proportion: $\frac{5}{24} = \frac{x}{100}$. We cross multiply and rewrite: $24x = 500$, or $x = \frac{500}{24}$. We reduce the improper fraction by dividing numerator and denominator by 4 to obtain $\frac{125}{6}$. We then convert to a mixed number by dividing 6 into 125, which yields 20 with a remainder of 5. So, the percent of pizza left is $20\frac{5}{6}\%$.

28. B: In Jordan's first step, he was subtracting a negative number. The subtraction and the negative value cancel each other out, so

$$3x - (-6x) = 51 - 24$$
$$3x + 6x = 27$$
$$9x = 27$$

So Jordan's new equation should read $9x = 27$, and therefore $x = 3$.

29. A: Find the volume of the cargo container:

$$volume = length \times width \times height$$
$$= 52\frac{5}{12}\,\text{ft} \times 7\frac{8.5}{12}\,\text{ft} \times 7\frac{10}{12}\,\text{ft}$$
$$= 3165.02\ \text{ft.}^3$$

The container is half full, so multiply half the volume by the density of barley to get the weight of the cargo:

$$\frac{3165.02}{2} \times \frac{37\ \text{lb}}{1\ \text{ft}^3} = 58,553\ \text{lb}$$

30. C: Start by adding up the costs of the trip, excluding the hotel cost: $572 + $150 + $250, or $972. Then, calculate what Margery will spend on the hotel. The first of her five nights at the hotel will cost her $89. For each of the other four nights, she will get a discount of 10% per night, or $8.90. This discount of $8.90 multiplied by the four nights is $35.60. The total she would have spent on the five nights without the discount is $445. With the discount, the amount goes down to $409.40. Add this amount to the $972 for a grand total of $1381.40.

31. E: The surface area of a rectangular prism may be calculated by substituting the given values into the formula:

$$SA = 2lw + 2wh + 2hl$$
$$SA = 2(14)(6) + 2(6)(8) + 2(8)(14)$$
$$SA = 488\ \text{in}$$

Thus, the surface area is 488 square inches.

32. A: Calculate the final sales price of the rug at each store.

$$1.08(0.7 \times \$296) = \$223.78 \text{ at Store A}$$
$$1.08(\$220 - \$10) = \$226.80 \text{ at Store B}$$
$$\$198 + \$35 = \$233 \text{ at Store C}$$

Therefore, the stores in order of lowest to highest prices are Store A, Store B, Store C.

33. A: First find the volume of the cone using the equation given:

$$volume = \frac{3.14 \times (radius)^2 \times height}{3}$$
$$= \frac{3.14 \times 1 \times 6}{3}$$
$$= 6.28 \text{ in.}^3$$

Then convert this amount to gallon using the conversion given: $1 \text{ gal} = 231 \text{ in}^3$.

$$6.28 \text{ in}^3 \times \frac{1 \text{ gal}}{231 \text{ in}^3} = 0.0272 \text{ gal}$$

$$0.0272 \text{ gal} \times \frac{100\%}{1 \text{ gal}} = 2.7\%$$

34. B: The population is approximately 36,000, so one quarter of the population consists of about 9,000 individuals under age 35. A third of 9,000 is 3,000, the approximate number of students in grades K-12. Since there are thirteen grades, there are about 230 students in each grade. So, the number of fourth graders is between 200 and 300.

Graphic Literacy

1. D: The lobby is directly connected to the outside door and all other rooms except office 1 are connected directly to the lobby. Also, each of the doors from the lobby is close to the same distance apart. Thus, the farthest room (by walking) is office 1.

2. B: We find "Professional Development" along the x-axis below the chart. The legend to the right states that February is represented by the orange bar, so we see along the y-axis that the orange bar in professional development comes to the 6,000 mark. So Shara's company spent $6,000 on professional development in February.

3. A: We find "Advertising" along the x-axis below the chart. The dark gray bar is the longest, so we see in the legend to the right that dark gray refers to January. So Shara's company spent the most on advertising in January.

4. C: We find "Office Supplies" along the x-axis below the chart. We can see that the blue and gray bars are equal, both stopping at $2,000. From the legend to the right we find that blue refers to January and gray refers to March. So, the company spent the same amount on office supplies in January and March.

5. B: The line item below "Arrive and clock in" states to check the daily calendar.

6. A: The last directive before 8:00 states to check email.

7. D: The line item after "Check email…" is "Begin morning meeting if applicable, or begin daily checklist." If there is no morning meeting, the next duty is to begin the daily checklist.

8. A: Obtaining permission is Step 2 in the first row. Step 3 is ordering the supplies and sending the receipt to accounting.

9. D: The line item after "Receive Shipment" is "Stock Supplies," so stocking the received supplies is the next phase.

10. C: Placing supplies on the proper shelf is Step 2 in the third row. Step 3 is signing the stocking sheet.

11. A: We can see that the lowest price per ream occurs with Brite-Paper, so Noah should choose Brite-Paper.

12. B: We can see that both price and weight rise as we view the graph from left to right, so we can infer that as weight increases, so does the price of the paper (or vice versa).

13. C: We can see from the graph that Print Deluxe has the highest weight of the three brands, so Olivia should select Print Deluxe.

14. A: In an accurate graph, Sara's line will peak on Friday when she prints handouts for the meeting. The first graph meets these requirements.

15. A: Kevin's line will drop to 0 Thursday and Friday when he is on vacation. The first graph meets these requirements.

16. D: The years listed have varying numbers of concurrently living composers. In sequential order, the amount is as follows: 1660 – 11,1670 – 9,1680 – 12,1690 – 11, 1700 – 10, 1710 – 9, and 1720 – 9. The only two with exactly 11 were 1660 and 1690.

17. D: The year each of these composers died is as follows: Samuel Scheidt – 1654, Domenico Scarlatti – 1757, Heinrich Schültz – 1672, and Johann H. Schein – 1630. The earliest of these dates is 1630, thus Johann H. Schein died first.

18. B: By noting the number of bars that terminate in the section between 1650 and 1700, you can determine how many composers died in that time period. Specifically, there are nine (9) bars that end in that section, so there were nine (9) composers who died.

19. D: Soil that is 30% clay and 20% silt and 50% sand can be classified by tracing the gridline across from 30% clay to where it meets the 20% silt gridline in the sandy clay loam region. Note that the angle of the numbers on the edges determine which line to follow.

20. B: Soil that is 50% clay and 20% silt and 30% sand can be classified by tracing the gridline across from 50% clay to where it meets the 20% silt gridline in the clay region. Note that the angle of the numbers on the edges determine which line to follow.

21. D: Soil that is 5% clay and 80% sand is also 15% silt. By tracing the gridline across from 5% clay, you can see that it meets the 80% sand gridline in the loamy sand area. Note that the angle of the numbers on the edges determine which line to follow.

22. A: In the pie chart we can see that the Thursday sector is the largest. From the table we can see that Mason was scheduled to work Thursday, so he had the highest sales day.

23. C: In the pie chart we can see that the Friday sector is the smallest. From the table we can see that Megan was scheduled to work Friday, so she had the lowest sales day.

24. C: From the graph we see that the price of ink rises, in general, from left to right, while the sales of printers falls. We can conclude that there is an inverse relationship between the price of ink and the sales of printers: as one goes up, the other comes down.

25. A: In the first chart we can see that the light gray section in the 3rd quarter, representing web ads, is larger than the web ad section in any other quarter. In the second chart, the web ad section in the 3rd quarter is smaller than the corresponding section in the 2nd and 4th quarters. So, the first chart gives the accurate portrayal.

26. B: In the first chart, the gray portions, representing radio ads, are typically smaller than the other portions. Conversely, in the second chart, the gray sections are the largest part of each quarter. Thus, the radio ads were the greatest advertising cost in each quarter in the second chart.

27. B: The print ads are represented by the dark gray portion of each bar, so we are looking for a chart in which the dark gray portion is equal in the 2nd and 3rd quarters. In the first chart, they are different lengths, but in the second chart they are equal, so the second chart gives the accurate portrayal.

28. A: We can see that the graphs of new employees and new clients are similar in shape. In other words, on months where new employees were added, there is a greater number of new clients. So seemingly there is a direct correlation between the number of new employees and new clients.

29. B: We can count the vacation days in each chart. In the first chart, Harper took one vacation day in the 1st quarter, three in the 2nd quarter, two in the 3rd quarter, and one in the 4th quarter, for a total of 7 days. Since 3 out of 7 vacation days were in the 2nd quarter, she spent 3/7 of her vacation time then (less than half). In the second chart, Harper took no vacation days in the 1st quarter, five in the 2nd quarter, three in the 3rd quarter, and two in the 4th quarter, for a total of 10 days. Since 5 out of 10 vacation days were in the 2nd quarter, she spent ½ of her vacation time then. So, the second graph is accurate.

30. A: We can count the holiday and vacation days in each chart. In the first chart, she had 9 holidays (2 + 2 + 1 + 4) and 7 vacation days (1 + 3 + 2 + 1). In the second chart she had 7 holidays (3 + 1 + 2 + 1) and 10 vacation days (2 + 3 + 5 + 0). Holidays exceed vacation days only in the first chart, so the first graph is the accurate one.

31. B: In the first chart, Harper took a sick day in the 1st quarter and another in the 3rd quarter. In the second chart, she took one in the 3rd quarter and another in the 4th, so only in the latter half of the year. The second graph is the accurate one.

32. C: By July, Alli will have saved up almost $12,000, according to the first chart. She cannot choose option 4, which requires a down payment of $12,500, but the other three are possible. So, we find the total cost with each to see which is the best deal, simply by adding the down payment and the loan for each option. Option 1 has a down payment of $5,000 and a loan of $15,000, so the total cost will be $20,000. Option 2 has a down payment of $7,500 and a loan of $12,000, so the total cost will be $19,500. Option 3 has a down payment of $10,000 and a loan of $9,000, so the total cost will be $19,000. Option 3 is the best deal, so Alli should make a down payment of $10,000.

33. B: If Alli waits until July, she can make a down payment of $10,000 and owe $9,000, for a total of $19,000. If she buys in May, she can only make a down payment of $7,500, owing $12,000 at the regular price for a total of $19,500. But if $1,000 is subtracted from the cost, the total cost will only be $18,500. This is less than the price Alli will pay if she waits until July, so it would be cost-effective to buy in May instead.

34. A: First we can calculate how much vacation/sick time Ethan will have earned by July. From the second graph we can add the time rolled over from last year (4.6), the time accrued in January-June (1.25×6), the New Year bonus (1), and the May holiday bonus (1). Adding these means that Ethan will have 14.1 days earned by July, assuming none is used. From the first graph we can see how much time he uses in January-June: $2 + 1 + 0 + 4 + 1 + 0 = 8$. We subtract this from 14.1 to find that Ethan will have 6.1 days of PTO he can use in July, so he will be eligible for the vacation.

35. D: We can see in the second chart that the marketing budget totals $10,000. In the first chart, we find that web ads should be 30% of the total. Since 30% of $10,000 is $3,000, Aubrey cannot spend $3,500 on a web ad, so her decision will not be approved.

36. B: A deficit occurs when the expenses are greater than the receipts. The first graph shows that 3rd quarter expenses ($37,000) are less than the receipts ($45,000), but the second graph shows that 3rd quarter expenses ($35,000) are greater than the receipts ($33,000). So, the second graph accurately represents the data.

37. A: The profit is the difference between receipts and expenses. We can calculate it for each quarter. In the first graph the profit is $4,000 in the 1st quarter, $6,000 in the 2nd quarter, $8,000 in the 3rd quarter, and $12,000 in the 4th quarter. So, the profit increases each quarter. In the second graph, we can see that there is a deficit in the 3rd quarter, which means that profit is negative, so even without calculating the profit in the other quarters we know that profit does not steadily increase. The first graph gives the accurate representation.

38. A: To find the amount of buffer, we subtract the total costs from the total charge to the client. The total cost of the project is found by adding personnel cost, materials, and overhead: $35,000 + $8,000 + $7,000 = $50,000$. We subtract this from the original charge to the client: $58,000 − $50,000 = $8,000$. So originally the project would have a projected $8,000 of profit or buffer. But the discount removes 10% of the client charges: $58,000(0.10) = $5,800$. So, we subtract the $5,800 from $8,000 to find that we have a buffer of $2,200. Since this is greater than $2,000, Alan's decision was correct.

Workplace Documents

1. E: Making oneself available to clients is the only task that is not required to be completed before 8:00am. The second sentence states that employees must clock in, take care of personal responsibilities, and be at their desks before 8:00am. The third sentence further explains the personal responsibilities: putting lunches in the refrigerator, pouring coffee, and greeting coworkers.

2. C: The main idea is clearly stated in the first sentence. There is a new lunchtime for all employees, from 11:45 to 12:45. The remainder of the paragraph gives supporting details but does not add any main ideas.

3. E: The subject is that a client (ABC Technology) will be in the office Thursday afternoon. We read further to find the significance of this announcement. In the third sentence we read that "it is important to maintain a professional atmosphere." So, the main idea of the excerpt is that employees should maintain a professional atmosphere while the client is visiting.

4. D: We don't see a step marked "third," but we can find the step after "second." This step is giving the reason for writing.

5. A: The introduction is the first step, including name, position, and company.

6. E: The final step in writing an email to a client is to let the client know to contact the employee with any questions.

7. D: The first sentence gives us a clue that the paragraph is about clients, but we cannot see the main idea until we read further. The fourth sentence explains the intent of the memo, requesting employees to "maintain a professional atmosphere" while a particular client is visiting.

8. E: The main idea is stated in the third sentence: that staff should maintain a professional appearance. From the rest of the paragraph we can see that this is in reference to clothing.

9. C: According to the second sentence, Blue team members are now to report to their supervisor at 7:30am each morning.

10. B: We can see in the first sentence that the changed schedule is only for this week.

11. A: The first sentence tells the new employee to log in to the computer. The next sentence directs the employee to open his/her email and check that notifications are turned on.

12. B: Sending a test email is the final step in the process, after turning on notifications and setting the email signature.

13. D: The visitor's pass lasts for three days, so that would be Friday, Monday, and Tuesday. So, Jane will need a permanent pass before Wednesday.

14. E: She will need to fill out a form and turn in in to HR. Then a permanent pass will be printed for her.

15. B: The consultant agreement states that extra hours will be billed at $85/hr. So, Gillian needs to add on the cost of 18 extra hours, changing the total for Phase 1 to $6,650.

16. C: Gillian should delete the line item for Phase 3 (subtracting $4,480 from the cost) and add 12 hours to Phase 2 at $85/hr. Phase 2 will now be billed for $8,220 and the project total will change to $18,920.

17. C: Cameron's instructions are to report immediately to his supervisor. Clearly, he cannot do that if his supervisor is not there. However, the final sentence of the instructions states to ask Carla if Cameron has any questions, so he can ask her for direction.

18. A: We can see in Cameron's instructions that before he can get a parking pass, he must have all of his new employee paperwork completed and turned in to HR. So, Cameron should try to complete his paperwork and submit to HR before they leave.

19. D: The second sentence of the notice tells Cameron that he can find project documents on the M-drive and that projects are arranged chronologically by number. It also directs Cameron to get the login from Juan, so Cameron needs to ask for this login.

20. B: The first sentence tells us that the graph will explain the company's marketing method. We can further read that the sales funnel involves multiple layers that represent steps to gain new clients. It is shaped like a funnel, wide at the top and increasingly narrow as it moves down.

21. C: From the third sentence we can see that SEO, or Search Engine Optimization, is a method of making the company website more visible by appearing in online searches.

22. E: Data visualization is mentioned in the last sentence. The department in charge of data visualization is directed to track information and create graphic illustrations of it, so we can extrapolate that data visualization is a method of graphically showing information.

23. A: The notice tells Shane to bring "the appropriate PPE for eyes, head, and feet." Since he is working for a construction company, he can infer that he may need to protect eyes, head, and feet on the site with safety items such as protective shoes (perhaps steel-toed), a hardhat, and safety goggles.

24. D: According to the excerpt above, PPE is associated with site visits, so Shane can infer that the site visit will be tomorrow, and therefore he should work on his paperwork and get his parking pass today.

25. E: The notice directs all available resources to be moved to Mike's team to help with the library project, so we can infer that the "resources" Mike needs refers to other team members. Amy should send any team members she can spare to Mike's team to help with his project.

26. B: The funnel begins with the widest portion and shrinks with each level, implying that each successive layer has a smaller amount of people as they move from potentially interested to actual clients.

27. A: The second sentence mentions that the marketing method is designed to attract potential clients. Later in the paragraph, there is a mention of a new marketing strategy that applies once visitors have become clients. So, we can infer that the Sales Funnel strategy is geared toward first-time customers.

28. E: Reese is using his own computer and his own time, but the company's software, so according to the contract above, every product resulting from the software belongs to the company. So, Reese cannot patent the program.

29. B: Reese used his lunch break, which is his own time, and did not use any company property or resources. Though not stated directly in the contract, we can presume that the invention is Reese's property since he did not fulfill any of the conditions that would make it company property.

30. A: The rule applies specifically to employees who are involved in procurement decisions. We can deduce that these employees are not allowed to receive large gifts since they may be tempted to show favor to those suppliers.

31. B: Content marketing is introduced in the first sentence. The same sentence mentions that the content marketing team finds and uploads content in hopes of catching the interest of potential clients. The second sentence mentions podcasts as a specific form of content marketing. So we can infer that content marketing involves posting information or other content online to draw and engage potential clients.

32. A: Data mining is mentioned in the fifth sentence as a way to find new ideas for podcasts. The following sentence instructs the reader to go through specific websites, searching for behavior patterns of potential clients. So, we can infer that data mining is a method of gathering data on behavior of potential clients, which can be used for marketing purposes.

33. D: CRO, or conversion rate optimization, is discussed in the third and fourth sentences. We can see that it involves attracting visitors with surveys, mailing lists, and free offers in the hope that they will become clients. So, we can infer that CRO is a method of turning an increasing percentage of website visitors into clients.

34. C: The excerpt clearly places great importance on employees beginning their workday by 8:00am. The reasoning can be seen in the last two sentences, which explain that employees need to be available during business hours for the sake of clients.

How to Overcome Test Anxiety

Just the thought of taking a test is enough to make most people a little nervous. A test is an important event that can have a long-term impact on your future, so it's important to take it seriously and it's natural to feel anxious about performing well. But just because anxiety is normal, that doesn't mean that it's helpful in test taking, or that you should simply accept it as part of your life. Anxiety can have a variety of effects. These effects can be mild, like making you feel slightly nervous, or severe, like blocking your ability to focus or remember even a simple detail.

If you experience test anxiety—whether severe or mild—it's important to know how to beat it. To discover this, first you need to understand what causes test anxiety.

Causes of Test Anxiety

While we often think of anxiety as an uncontrollable emotional state, it can actually be caused by simple, practical things. One of the most common causes of test anxiety is that a person does not feel adequately prepared for their test. This feeling can be the result of many different issues such as poor study habits or lack of organization, but the most common culprit is time management. Starting to study too late, failing to organize your study time to cover all of the material, or being distracted while you study will mean that you're not well prepared for the test. This may lead to cramming the night before, which will cause you to be physically and mentally exhausted for the test. Poor time management also contributes to feelings of stress, fear, and hopelessness as you realize you are not well prepared but don't know what to do about it.

Other times, test anxiety is not related to your preparation for the test but comes from unresolved fear. This may be a past failure on a test, or poor performance on tests in general. It may come from comparing yourself to others who seem to be performing better or from the stress of living up to expectations. Anxiety may be driven by fears of the future—how failure on this test would affect your educational and career goals. These fears are often completely irrational, but they can still negatively impact your test performance.

Elements of Test Anxiety

As mentioned earlier, test anxiety is considered to be an emotional state, but it has physical and mental components as well. Sometimes you may not even realize that you are suffering from test anxiety until you notice the physical symptoms. These can include trembling hands, rapid heartbeat, sweating, nausea, and tense muscles. Extreme anxiety may lead to fainting or vomiting. Obviously, any of these symptoms can have a negative impact on testing. It is important to recognize them as soon as they begin to occur so that you can address the problem before it damages your performance.

The mental components of test anxiety include trouble focusing and inability to remember learned information. During a test, your mind is on high alert, which can help you recall information and stay focused for an extended period of time. However, anxiety interferes with your mind's natural processes, causing you to blank out, even on the questions you know well. The strain of testing during anxiety makes it difficult to stay focused, especially on a test that may take several hours. Extreme anxiety can take a huge mental toll, making it difficult not only to recall test information but even to understand the test questions or pull your thoughts together.

Effects of Test Anxiety

Test anxiety is like a disease—if left untreated, it will get progressively worse. Anxiety leads to poor performance, and this reinforces the feelings of fear and failure, which in turn lead to poor performances on subsequent tests. It can grow from a mild nervousness to a crippling condition. If allowed to progress, test anxiety can have a big impact on your schooling, and consequently on your future.

Test anxiety can spread to other parts of your life. Anxiety on tests can become anxiety in any stressful situation, and blanking on a test can turn into panicking in a job situation. But fortunately, you don't have to let anxiety rule your testing and determine your grades. There are a number of relatively simple steps you can take to move past anxiety and function normally on a test and in the rest of life.

Physical Steps for Beating Test Anxiety

While test anxiety is a serious problem, the good news is that it can be overcome. It doesn't have to control your ability to think and remember information. While it may take time, you can begin taking steps today to beat anxiety.

Just as your first hint that you may be struggling with anxiety comes from the physical symptoms, the first step to treating it is also physical. Rest is crucial for having a clear, strong mind. If you are tired, it is much easier to give in to anxiety. But if you establish good sleep habits, your body and mind will be ready to perform optimally, without the strain of exhaustion. Additionally, sleeping well helps you to retain information better, so you're more likely to recall the answers when you see the test questions.

Getting good sleep means more than going to bed on time. It's important to allow your brain time to relax. Take study breaks from time to time so it doesn't get overworked, and don't study right before bed. Take time to rest your mind before trying to rest your body, or you may find it difficult to fall asleep.

Along with sleep, other aspects of physical health are important in preparing for a test. Good nutrition is vital for good brain function. Sugary foods and drinks may give a burst of energy but this burst is followed by a crash, both physically and emotionally. Instead, fuel your body with protein and vitamin-rich foods.

Also, drink plenty of water. Dehydration can lead to headaches and exhaustion, especially if your brain is already under stress from the rigors of the test. Particularly if your test is a long one, drink water during the breaks. And if possible, take an energy-boosting snack to eat between sections.

Along with sleep and diet, a third important part of physical health is exercise. Maintaining a steady workout schedule is helpful, but even taking 5-minute study breaks to walk can help get your blood pumping faster and clear your head. Exercise also releases endorphins, which contribute to a positive feeling and can help combat test anxiety.

When you nurture your physical health, you are also contributing to your mental health. If your body is healthy, your mind is much more likely to be healthy as well. So take time to rest, nourish your body with healthy food and water, and get moving as much as possible. Taking these physical steps will make you stronger and more able to take the mental steps necessary to overcome test anxiety.

Mental Steps for Beating Test Anxiety

Working on the mental side of test anxiety can be more challenging, but as with the physical side, there are clear steps you can take to overcome it. As mentioned earlier, test anxiety often stems from lack of preparation, so the obvious solution is to prepare for the test. Effective studying may be the most important weapon you have for beating test anxiety, but you can and should employ several other mental tools to combat fear.

First, boost your confidence by reminding yourself of past success—tests or projects that you aced. If you're putting as much effort into preparing for this test as you did for those, there's no reason you should expect to fail here. Work hard to prepare; then trust your preparation.

Second, surround yourself with encouraging people. It can be helpful to find a study group, but be sure that the people you're around will encourage a positive attitude. If you spend time with others who are anxious or cynical, this will only contribute to your own anxiety. Look for others who are motivated to study hard from a desire to succeed, not from a fear of failure.

Third, reward yourself. A test is physically and mentally tiring, even without anxiety, and it can be helpful to have something to look forward to. Plan an activity following the test, regardless of the outcome, such as going to a movie or getting ice cream.

When you are taking the test, if you find yourself beginning to feel anxious, remind yourself that you know the material. Visualize successfully completing the test. Then take a few deep, relaxing breaths and return to it. Work through the questions carefully but with confidence, knowing that you are capable of succeeding.

Developing a healthy mental approach to test taking will also aid in other areas of life. Test anxiety affects more than just the actual test—it can be damaging to your mental health and even contribute to depression. It's important to beat test anxiety before it becomes a problem for more than testing.

Study Strategy

Being prepared for the test is necessary to combat anxiety, but what does being prepared look like? You may study for hours on end and still not feel prepared. What you need is a strategy for test prep. The next few pages outline our recommended steps to help you plan out and conquer the challenge of preparation.

STEP 1: SCOPE OUT THE TEST

Learn everything you can about the format (multiple choice, essay, etc.) and what will be on the test. Gather any study materials, course outlines, or sample exams that may be available. Not only will this help you to prepare, but knowing what to expect can help to alleviate test anxiety.

STEP 2: MAP OUT THE MATERIAL

Look through the textbook or study guide and make note of how many chapters or sections it has. Then divide these over the time you have. For example, if a book has 15 chapters and you have five days to study, you need to cover three chapters each day. Even better, if you have the time, leave an extra day at the end for overall review after you have gone through the material in depth.

If time is limited, you may need to prioritize the material. Look through it and make note of which sections you think you already have a good grasp on, and which need review. While you are studying, skim quickly through the familiar sections and take more time on the challenging parts.

Write out your plan so you don't get lost as you go. Having a written plan also helps you feel more in control of the study, so anxiety is less likely to arise from feeling overwhelmed at the amount to cover.

STEP 3: GATHER YOUR TOOLS

Decide what study method works best for you. Do you prefer to highlight in the book as you study and then go back over the highlighted portions? Or do you type out notes of the important information? Or is it helpful to make flashcards that you can carry with you? Assemble the pens, index cards, highlighters, post-it notes, and any other materials you may need so you won't be distracted by getting up to find things while you study.

If you're having a hard time retaining the information or organizing your notes, experiment with different methods. For example, try color-coding by subject with colored pens, highlighters, or post-it notes. If you learn better by hearing, try recording yourself reading your notes so you can listen while in the car, working out, or simply sitting at your desk. Ask a friend to quiz you from your flashcards, or try teaching someone the material to solidify it in your mind.

STEP 4: CREATE YOUR ENVIRONMENT

It's important to avoid distractions while you study. This includes both the obvious distractions like visitors and the subtle distractions like an uncomfortable chair (or a too-comfortable couch that makes you want to fall asleep). Set up the best study environment possible: good lighting and a comfortable work area. If background music helps you focus, you may want to turn it on, but otherwise keep the room quiet. If you are using a computer to take notes, be sure you don't have any other windows open, especially applications like social media, games, or anything else that could distract you. Silence your phone and turn off notifications. Be sure to keep water close by so you stay hydrated while you study (but avoid unhealthy drinks and snacks).

Also, take into account the best time of day to study. Are you freshest first thing in the morning? Try to set aside some time then to work through the material. Is your mind clearer in the afternoon or evening? Schedule your study session then. Another method is to study at the same time of day that you will take the test, so that your brain gets used to working on the material at that time and will be ready to focus at test time.

STEP 5: STUDY!

Once you have done all the study preparation, it's time to settle into the actual studying. Sit down, take a few moments to settle your mind so you can focus, and begin to follow your study plan. Don't give in to distractions or let yourself procrastinate. This is your time to prepare so you'll be ready to fearlessly approach the test. Make the most of the time and stay focused.

Of course, you don't want to burn out. If you study too long you may find that you're not retaining the information very well. Take regular study breaks. For example, taking five minutes out of every hour to walk briskly, breathing deeply and swinging your arms, can help your mind stay fresh.

As you get to the end of each chapter or section, it's a good idea to do a quick review. Remind yourself of what you learned and work on any difficult parts. When you feel that you've mastered the material, move on to the next part. At the end of your study session, briefly skim through your notes again.

But while review is helpful, cramming last minute is NOT. If at all possible, work ahead so that you won't need to fit all your study into the last day. Cramming overloads your brain with more information than it can process and retain, and your tired mind may struggle to recall even previously learned information when it is overwhelmed with last-minute study. Also, the urgent nature of cramming and the stress placed on your brain contribute to anxiety. You'll be more likely to go to the test feeling unprepared and having trouble thinking clearly.

So don't cram, and don't stay up late before the test, even just to review your notes at a leisurely pace. Your brain needs rest more than it needs to go over the information again. In fact, plan to finish your studies by noon or early afternoon the day before the test. Give your brain the rest of the day to relax or focus on other things, and get a good night's sleep. Then you will be fresh for the test and better able to recall what you've studied.

STEP 6: TAKE A PRACTICE TEST

Many courses offer sample tests, either online or in the study materials. This is an excellent resource to check whether you have mastered the material, as well as to prepare for the test format and environment.

Check the test format ahead of time: the number of questions, the type (multiple choice, free response, etc.), and the time limit. Then create a plan for working through them. For example, if you have 30 minutes to take a 60-question test, your limit is 30 seconds per question. Spend less time on the questions you know well so that you can take more time on the difficult ones.

If you have time to take several practice tests, take the first one open book, with no time limit. Work through the questions at your own pace and make sure you fully understand them. Gradually work up to taking a test under test conditions: sit at a desk with all study materials put away and set a timer. Pace yourself to make sure you finish the test with time to spare and go back to check your answers if you have time.

After each test, check your answers. On the questions you missed, be sure you understand why you missed them. Did you misread the question (tests can use tricky wording)? Did you forget the information? Or was it something you hadn't learned? Go back and study any shaky areas that the practice tests reveal.

Taking these tests not only helps with your grade, but also aids in combating test anxiety. If you're already used to the test conditions, you're less likely to worry about it, and working through tests until you're scoring well gives you a confidence boost. Go through the practice tests until you feel comfortable, and then you can go into the test knowing that you're ready for it.

Test Tips

On test day, you should be confident, knowing that you've prepared well and are ready to answer the questions. But aside from preparation, there are several test day strategies you can employ to maximize your performance.

First, as stated before, get a good night's sleep the night before the test (and for several nights before that, if possible). Go into the test with a fresh, alert mind rather than staying up late to study.

Try not to change too much about your normal routine on the day of the test. It's important to eat a nutritious breakfast, but if you normally don't eat breakfast at all, consider eating just a protein bar. If you're a coffee drinker, go ahead and have your normal coffee. Just make sure you time it so that the caffeine doesn't wear off right in the middle of your test. Avoid sugary beverages, and drink enough water to stay hydrated but not so much that you need a restroom break 10 minutes into the test. If your test isn't first thing in the morning, consider going for a walk or doing a light workout before the test to get your blood flowing.

Allow yourself enough time to get ready, and leave for the test with plenty of time to spare so you won't have the anxiety of scrambling to arrive in time. Another reason to be early is to select a good seat. It's helpful to sit away from doors and windows, which can be distracting. Find a good seat, get out your supplies, and settle your mind before the test begins.

When the test begins, start by going over the instructions carefully, even if you already know what to expect. Make sure you avoid any careless mistakes by following the directions.

Then begin working through the questions, pacing yourself as you've practiced. If you're not sure on an answer, don't spend too much time on it, and don't let it shake your confidence. Either skip it and come back later, or eliminate as many wrong answers as possible and guess among the remaining ones. Don't dwell on these questions as you continue—put them out of your mind and focus on what lies ahead.

Be sure to read all of the answer choices, even if you're sure the first one is the right answer. Sometimes you'll find a better one if you keep reading. But don't second-guess yourself if you do immediately know the answer. Your gut instinct is usually right. Don't let test anxiety rob you of the information you know.

If you have time at the end of the test (and if the test format allows), go back and review your answers. Be cautious about changing any, since your first instinct tends to be correct, but make sure you didn't misread any of the questions or accidentally mark the wrong answer choice. Look over any you skipped and make an educated guess.

At the end, leave the test feeling confident. You've done your best, so don't waste time worrying about your performance or wishing you could change anything. Instead, celebrate the successful completion of this test. And finally, use this test to learn how to deal with anxiety even better next time.

> **Review Video: Test Anxiety**
> Visit mometrix.com/academy and enter code: 100340

Important Qualification

Not all anxiety is created equal. If your test anxiety is causing major issues in your life beyond the classroom or testing center, or if you are experiencing troubling physical symptoms related to your anxiety, it may be a sign of a serious physiological or psychological condition. If this sounds like your situation, we strongly encourage you to seek professional help.

Additional Bonus Material

Due to our efforts to try to keep this book to a manageable length, we've created a link that will give you access to all of your additional bonus material:

mometrix.com/bonus948/workkeys

223